Writing and Speaking for Excellence

A Guide for Physicians

Deborah St. James
Medical Editor
West Haven, Connecticut

with

Howard Spiro, M.D.
Professor of Medicine
Director, Program for Humanities in Medicine
Yale University School of Medicine
New Haven, Connecticut

Jones and Bartlett Publishers
Sudbury, Massachusetts

Boston   Toronto   London   Singapore

World Headquarters

Jones and Bartlett Publishers
40 Tall Pine Drive
Sudbury, MA 01776
978-443-5000
info@jbpub.com
www.jbpub.com

Jones and Bartlett Publishers Canada
P.O. Box 19020
Toronto, ON M55 1X1
CANADA

Jones and Bartlett Publishers International
Barb House, Barb Mews
London W6 7PA
UK

Library of Congress Cataloging-in-Publication Data

St. James, Deborah.
  Writing and speaking for excellence : a guide for physicians /
Deborah St. James, with Howard Spiro.
      p.   cm.
  Includes bibliographical references and index.
  ISBN 0-86720-935-6
  1. Medical writing. 2. Public speaking. I. Spiro, Howard M.
(Howard Marget). II. Title.
  [DNLM: 1. Writing. 2. Speech. 3. Physicians. WZ 345 S143W 1995]
  R119.S7 1995
  808'.06661—dc20
  DNLM/DLC
  for Library of Congress   95-19476
                                                                    CIP

Acquisitions Editor: Joseph E. Burns
Production Coordinator: Joan M. Flaherty
Manufacturing Buyer: Dana L. Cerrito
Design: Ann E. Flanders, UltraGraphics
Typesetting: UltraGraphics
Cover Design: Hannus Design Associates
Printing and Binding: Edwards Brothers
Cover Printing: New England Book Components, Inc.

Printed in the United States of America
99 98   10 9 8 7 6 5 4 3 2

◆

Contents

Contents

◆

Preface

Several years ago while I was teaching English at the University of Akron, a neighbor, who is a physician on the faculty of Case Western Reserve School of Medicine, mentioned to me that several of his residents were having a difficult time producing a publishable paper, a departmental requirement. "I'm baffled," my dapper, bow-tied neighbor complained. "These residents are all well-educated, bright, motivated, and excellent clinicians, but they seem unable to write, or for that matter speak, in a clear, well-organized fashion." Following several discussions, we decided to set up a writing seminar to meet one night a week for six weeks. Any resident who felt he or she might benefit from some writing instruction was invited to come.

The first night three residents showed up, looking like cliches of themselves: tired, overworked, and disheveled. It became immediately clear that, indeed, they were bright, well-educated, and motivated. They were also frustrated and bewildered. How, they asked themselves, could someone go through four years each of high school, college, medical school, an internship and residency and still not be able to put together a well-organized clear, concise piece of writing? It didn't take long to figure out; and the answer was surprisingly simple: no one had ever taught them.

Several years later, while working as a medical editor for a pharmaceutical company, I began thinking about those residents and came upon the idea that I might be able to combine my English teaching skills with my medical editing skills and develop a writing and speaking course designed specifically for physicians. Initially my plans were met with skepticism. "No doctor in his right mind," I was told, "is going to take three hours out of his or her busy schedule to go back to English 101." I persisted and in 1991 I began conducting

Writing and Speaking for Excellence seminars for physicians at various medical centers around the country.

Within three years, my colleagues and I had been invited to more than 200 medical centers, universities, medical meetings and had worked with more than 8000 physician-writers. We are consistently booked at least six months in advance.

What follows are my observations during the last three years. I have not intended this to be a textbook; for a comprehensive guide to grammar, punctuation, and word usage, you will need another book. My intention instead is to address some of the most frequently asked questions, comments, frustrations, and problems I have heard from medical writers and to offer practical solutions. Not all chapters will be of interest to all readers. Finally, because I have found "modeling" one of the best ways to improve writing, whenever possible, I have used actual examples of physicians' writing—both the good and the bad.

I have many people to thank in this effort: Bayer Pharmaceutical Division for their support; the physicians who were kind enough to write essays for the book; Howard Spiro, M.D., my neighbor, friend, and editor; Mary Collopy, Paul Casella, Cathy Coffin, Laura Hortas, my fellow trainers; Marla Benedetti, researcher and editor; all the physicians who have attended the seminars, for much of what follows is a result of their participation.

I would also like to thank Joseph E. Burns, Vice President of Jones and Bartlett, for his early encouragement and editorial advice. Special mention also goes to Joan M. Flaherty, a patient and perceptive editor, whose comments and suggestions sharpened and improved the manuscript.

Finally, I'd like to offer a particular thanks to those three residents who showed up that first night in Ohio. Wherever you may be now, you taught me two valuable lessons: (1) Most physicians don't get the training or practice in writing and speaking that they need to do their jobs, and (2) Writing and speaking effectively are skills that physicians can learn relatively quickly and painlessly.

Part I

Writing for Excellence

♦

Introduction

Writing: What Makes It So Hard?

Although the young research workers are constantly goaded to write to justify their existences, they have never been prodded to learn to write.

Robert Bjork, M.D. (1983, 112)

How many times have you finished reading a journal article or textbook chapter to realize that you have no idea what you just read? If you're like most of us, your first reaction is, "I'm tired. I can't seem to concentrate." Or "I must have a lot on my mind; I can't seem to focus on this article." At this point you usually put the article down, go to bed, watch TV, spend time with the kids, and hope tomorrow your concentration will be better. But the next day, you pick up the article again, after a good night's sleep, and it still doesn't make sense.

How come? Having read thousands of medical articles and having worked with hundreds of physicians, I've found if a piece of medical writing is hard to understand, usually it's a problem with the writing, not the reader. A journal article, textbook chapter, or abstract that is clear, concise, and well organized is easy to read. The writer uses short sentences, simple and concrete words, transition words, and has a logical sequence of ideas. In short, writing that is clear, concise, and well organized is no accident. It's deliberate and hard work.

Much is written and spoken about the low level of medical writing, often with good reason. How is it that physicians who are

3

frequently brilliant in one area are so lacking in another? The following are some of the main causes of bad medical writing I have found:

1. **Lack of training and practice.** Most teachers of scientific writing would agree that the ability to write clear, concise, well-organized prose is a skill not a talent. And like any other skill, writing can be taught. Unfortunately, in this country, we don't always properly train teachers to teach writing. Only in the last few years have universities and colleges been offering a separate writing major within the English department.

   In addition to a lack of proper training, many students get little writing practice in high school. If a student has a math- and science-oriented curriculum, he or she has few opportunities to write. Most math and science tests are multiple choice or require short answers, and the math and science teachers rarely ask students to write papers. Consequently, these students get little writing practice. And the problem continues into college. If a student is particularly bright, as many physicians are, he or she may even "test out" of English in college. In brief, when it comes to writing, many of our best and brightest are getting short-changed in the current high school and college systems: they are getting neither training nor practice in writing.

   Interestingly, many educators are aware of the problem. A survey of 101 medical schools in the United States, conducted by Robert Bjork, M.D. (1983), reported that only 15% of medical schools offer writing courses. Of the 85% that don't offer writing courses, 84% reported a course in writing to be a "great need." If the majority of medical schools are aware that medical students need training in writing, why aren't they training them?

2. **Lack of time.** As anyone who has gone through medical school knows, the one thing that a medical student doesn't have is extra time. All departments are fighting for the students' time.

3. **Lack of instructors.** Another reason that writing is not taught in medical school is a lack of qualified instructors. Although

this is beginning to change, teachers of medical writing are not easy to find. Most physicians who are writing and editing medical articles and chapters learned to write and edit the hard way—by trial and error.

4. **Composition under pressure and negligence.** Competition to get published is often intense. Nowhere are deadlines more important than in medical publishing. All too often the result of intense competition and deadlines is sloppy, mistake-ridden writing, such as references that don't jive, tables that don't add up, patients unaccounted for, and errors in grammar, punctuation, and syntax. Poor writing can hurt your chances of getting published. Some editors consider sloppy writing a sign of sloppy thinking. A few extra minutes spent proofreading can mean the difference between getting published or getting panned. Of course, even if a manuscript is technically flawless, it can be worthless if the author doesn't have something worth saying.

Medical Writing: The Facts and the Myths

It is not necessary to be a "writer" to write well. Clear writing is the logical arrangement of thought.
William Zinsser (1988, viii)

There are many myths surrounding medical writing. Before you can begin to improve your writing, it's important to recognize the truth from several common myths.

1. Myth: "I'm a doctor, not a writer."
   Fact: Writing is not a career. Writing is a skill necessary for physicians to do their jobs. In fact, many times the only thing a person knows about you is what you put on paper. For that reason writing should be at the top of your list of skills.

2. Myth: "I don't have any talent for writing. I've always been bad at it."

Fact: Writing is a skill, not a talent. Any physician can and should learn to write effectively.

3. Myth: "Writing has nothing to do with science."
   Fact: Effective medical writing requires the same qualities of thought that are needed for the rest of science: logic, clarity, organization, and precision.

4. Myth: "If a piece of writing gets published, it's a good piece of writing."
   Fact: Many published medical papers are badly written.

5. Myth: "My (chief, chairman, supervisor) is well published; he or she is a good writer."
   Fact: Bad writers do get published. Frequently, the people in your department or institution who are editing your papers have no more knowledge of good writing than you do.

6. Myth: "Most medical writing is poorly written, but that's just the way it is."
   Fact: Medical writing doesn't have to be poorly written. As physicians, you should not accept mediocrity. Your time and that of your readers is too valuable to waste on poorly executed, rambling, disorganized writing.

7. Myth: "I know what I want to say, but I can't seem to get my thoughts organized. Until I have my ideas clearly organized in my head, I shouldn't start writing."
   Fact: The best way to clarify thinking is to start writing. To put a puzzle together you need to see all the pieces. Research shows the act of writing helps to clarify and organize thinking.

8. Myth: "I'm not going to stay in academic medicine. I'm going into private practice. I won't be writing much at all."
   Fact: All physicians need to write. Here are just a few examples of the writing all physicians have to do at some time:

◆ Write-up of history
◆ Progress notes
◆ Discharge summary
◆ Letter to referring physician
◆ Operative report
◆ Laboratory report
◆ Outpatient records
◆ Consultation reports
◆ Communications to patients (letter reporting, test, examination results, instruction sheets)
◆ Academic/administrative correspondence (cover letter, memo, job application)

Writing Well

All doctors need to write, and write well. Why? Because many times the only thing other physicians, patients, and insurance companies know about a physician is what he or she puts on paper. The sentences below are taken directly from physicians' letters.

"The patient is a fourty four year old women."

"This is a 75 year old man who lives with his wife who is alive."

"To adequately access this patient, it was necessary to . . ."

"We are in the process of updating our computer files, please bare with us."

"Irregardless of your decision, we will . . ."

"Between you and I, . . ."

"While inspecting the liver, the lesion was found."

"The patient was put on a regime of gentamicin plus . . ."

"Most importantly, . . ."

Don't fool yourself into thinking that these examples are the fault of someone's secretary. The fact is if your name is on it, it belongs to you.

The Benefits of Writing: Clear Up Your Thinking

We write to find out what we know and what we want to say.
William Zinsser (1988, viii)

Writing is a great way to share useful medical information with your colleagues. It's a great way to be viewed as an authority on a particular subject. But there are other less obvious benefits to writing: Writing stimulates and clarifies thinking.

Have you ever started writing something and found that the more you wrote, the more ideas you developed? The actual act of typing or writing seems to have the effect of activating new understanding on a subject. Freewriting, the practice of writing nonstop for several minutes, without worry about grammar, punctuation, or style, is based on the fact that writing can stimulate thinking.

In addition, the process of writing forces you to examine your views in detail and to put them into a coherent and sequential structure. That process of writing leads not only to a completed product, such as a letter, newsletter, or manuscript, but also to a greater understanding of the subject.

Essay

◆

Read To Write Better

Richard M. Caplan, M.D.

Why discuss reading in a book that deals with effective writing? Because crafting a piece of good writing requires much rewriting, and that obliges authors to read and edit their own material. Secretaries and software programs can help but they can't prevent or repair all the problems, especially the crucial ones that deal with *meaning*. Does the sentence, passage, or article make sense, and is it the sense you wish to convey to the reader? Does it omit needless words?

Throughout this century in the United States, reading has clearly topped any survey that asked how physicians gain their continuing education, and how they wish to gain it. Even with the affinity that Americans feel for technical progress, the impressive array of satellite broadcasts, audio and video recordings, and the diverse instructional uses of computers have not usurped the lead enjoyed by reading—mainly medical journals. After all, words appear on computer screens as well as on paper, and must be read. Accurate communication, via the written or spoken word, therefore remains paramount.

Poets, novelists, and dramatists sometimes strive for uncertainty or ambiguity, specifically to allow the richness of interpretation that characterizes great art. Thus, metaphors and double meanings abound. But good scientific writing, even though it cannot totally avoid similes and metaphors because they are a necessary component of thinking, still seeks exactness of meaning. Not only must writers make themselves understood, they must also eliminate or reduce the possibility of being misunderstood. Accurate communication, however, requires effort by the

Richard M. Caplan, M.D., is Coordinator, Program in Medical Humanities, University of Iowa College of Medicine, Iowa City, Iowa.

receiver (reader/listener) as well as the sender (writer/speaker), effort that needs much practice and reinforcement. Thus, I've long thought that drills in proofreading would yield valuable payoff. Your eye must spot malapropisms and typos, for example. Your text must not say "evaluation" when you mean "evolution" or vice versa. Can one learn or improve the skill of being sharp-eyed? I think so. It is especially useful to study writing closely enough that the mind attends fully. One must do what Sherlock Holmes did or what any good clinician does—examine with closeness, seeking to notice both the broad themes and the details. Yes, that takes time, but woe to the writer who doesn't read what he releases to the world, whether an article, a grant application, a report, or a legal document. Such close examination justifies and provides the content of journal clubs—reading an article carefully enough to join a discussion about it. Book groups provide similar training. Formal course work in literature, history, or philosophy offers good practice at learning to read and write with the diligent care that I am describing.

Being a careful reader means you, as writer, must mentally interact with your own text (not necessarily a textbook); you must be able to respond as would your reader, receiving what you read with a fresh eye. Have you been sufficiently clear, without ambiguity? Does your punctuation perform well its crucial job of serving as guideposts to your thought?

It is useful to read aloud to yourself, or perhaps to a friendly listener, any text you think to publish. Your ear may guide you to modify words, syntax, or punctuation. Reading your text aloud helps emphasize the substantial difference between written language and spoken language.

A written text can and usually does have greater formality and complexity than extemporaneous speech; it can be more compact and contain self-reference. A reader can, if necessary, glance back to reread a passage that produces mental uncertainty or inattention. On the other hand, a listener at a live presentation cannot backtrack that way. Therefore, an effective speaker must be highly sensitive to the need to speak the language that people are used to hearing. And a speaker must more frequently repeat key ideas, or spotlight a transition. ("Now that we've considered those first events of the coagulation mechanism, we can move on to consider the corresponding clinical manifestations.") In other words, the speaker makes audible the outline or organization of the presentation. Anyone planning to give a talk who has not read it aloud, preferably to a sympathetic audience for critique, is either very experienced, or a successful gambler, or a poor speaker!

Chapter One

◆

The Physician as Writer

People do not deserve good writing; they are so pleased with bad.

Ralph Waldo Emerson (Winokur, 134)

Qualities of Good Medical Writing

Good medical writing is so clear and exact that every intended reader is able to pinpoint the author's message. Below are some of the qualities of good medical writing.

- ◆ Reader-based
- ◆ Purposeful
- ◆ Clear
- ◆ Concise
- ◆ Accurate

- ◆ Simple
- ◆ Without invented words
- ◆ Free of jargon
- ◆ Few, if any, abbreviations

Reader-based

When you write, you should be thinking, *Who is my reader? Are they colleagues, medical students, nurses, lay readers? What do they know? What do they need to know? How can I best present the material to these readers?* When editing and proofreading your writing, always read it from the perspective of your intended reader. Recently I edited a book chapter written by a physician for a lay audience. After reading the first

11

paragraph, I was lost in medical jargon, Latin names, and obscure abbreviations and acronyms. I called the physician-writer and said I was having a hard time understanding what he was trying to say. His answer was, "Well, it's perfectly clear to me." Being perfectly clear to you is not good enough; your writing needs to be perfectly clear to the intended readers.

Purposeful

Your second question when sitting down to write should be, "Why am I writing this?" Today, we live in an overcommunicative society. We're drowning in memos, letters, ads, promotional materials, newspapers, books, magazines. Our way of dealing with this glut of words is to "not see." In fact, most of what we write no one reads—not our letters, memos, patient histories, notes.

Right now, there are about 40,000 biomedical journals worldwide. And most of what is written in the medical journals is not particularly newsworthy. In fact, the last thing we need is more ho-hum articles. So why is everyone racing to get published? If an academic physician wants tenure, a promotion, an appointment, he or she must publish. Unfortunately, for many medical writers, that is the sole purpose for writing. But there should be another purpose, one having to do with the reader.

As a medical writer, you should ask yourself these questions: What do I want my reader to do after reading this article or chapter? Do I want to inform, motivate, educate, convince, provoke? You want your article or chapter to strike a chord with your audience. Readers want something in exchange for their time.

When reading an article, aren't you frequently thinking to yourself, "How does this relate to my research?" "How can I use this information to improve my clinical skills?" If you are investing time writing a memo, a letter, or a journal article, make sure it is useful and relevant to your audience.

Start writing with a reader and a purpose in mind—whether it's on a patient's chart, a letter to a referring doctor, a letter to an insurance company, an abstract for a meeting, or an article for a journal. Without a clear idea of a reader and purpose, you won't be able to determine what and how much detail you need, what level of diction to use, where to start, and where to end.

Clear and Concise

Without doubt, lack of clarity is the number one problem in medical writing. As a result, the most frequent question I ask an author after reading a sentence or paragraph in a manuscript is, "What exactly do you mean?" Often, I can guess what the writer is trying to say, but guessing isn't what medical writing is about. Interpretation should be left for poetry. Medical writing should be absolutely clear to every one of its intended readers. Readers don't have time to wade through superfluous words in search of your ideas.

TIP: *Many writers will read a long, rambling sentence they've written, and if they think it's unclear, they'll write another long, rambling sentence to clarify it. That's a mistake. If a sentence is unclear, begin taking words* out, *not putting more in. When you revise, the best thing you can do is "word weed." Pull out all words that are strangling your message. Evaluate every word. Is it absolutely necessary to your message?*

Look at the following example:

> *The gastric secretions are a necessary part of the digestive mechanism that plays an important part in the normal function of digestion* (22 words).

Now, take out all unnecessary words. What's left? *Gastric secretions are necessary for digestion* (6 words). If your audience consists of physicians, do you need this sentence at all? Probably not. In fact, when you start taking out superfluous words, sometimes you'll find there really isn't any necessary message at all.

How about this sentence?

> *The essential purpose of the current study by investigators focused chiefly around the individual body and head movements of each patient while he or she was in bed in a sleep mode* (32 words).

After word weeding:

> *Study investigators focused on patients' movements during sleep* (8 words).

The obvious question is, Why would someone use thirty-two words to communicate when eight would do? Think back to high school. The teacher has just assigned a paper. What is your first question? Certainly not, *Who is my reader? What is the purpose?*, but rather, *How long does it have to be?*

Most of us have learned to write for quantity: a ten-page paper, a twenty-five page paper, a 500-word essay. And somehow, we began to equate quantity with quality. Nowhere is quantity less related to quality than in writing. Avoid ten words if you can say it in five. Don't use *at this point in time* if you can say *now*. And don't believe that a long piece of writing is necessarily better or more scholarly than a shorter one.

Another reason that writing lacks clarity is the use of vague, imprecise words. Translate the following sentence:

> *Information on interdisciplinary operations and facilities helps to impact the viability and clarification of actual microbiology data restructurization.*

Not possible, is it? This sentence can't be translated because there are too few concrete words. You could read this sentence every day for the rest of your life and probably have no better idea as to what the writer is trying to say. You could guess, but again, medical writing is not about guessing.

We understand the spoken or written message through precise, concrete words—words that we can know through our senses. For instance, you hear the words, "decubitus ulcer." Instantly you have a mental picture of a decubitus ulcer. The same is true for words such as *sputum, Marfan syndrome, hydrocephalus, purulent, conjunctivitis*. But try to visualize the following words: *information, empathy, implementation, facilitation, compilation*. You can't. These words are abstract words, and used too frequently, they work against clarity.

TIP: *One red flag for an abstract word is the suffix -ion. The -ion words often appear when a writer takes a strong verb (such as inform, implement, facilitate, compile) and turns it into a wimpy noun (such as implementation, facilitation, compilation). Scrutinize nouns ending in -ion to see if you can substitute a concrete word.*

Abbreviations and Jargon

> *Employing CCD measurements to modify the well-accepted BPD, AC generated greatly improved prediction of LGA.*

Unless you are a perinatal obstetrician, this sentence probably doesn't mean anything to you. Medicine has become so high-tech and so specialized that more and more new words, acronyms, jargon, and abbreviations are being used to communicate ideas. Unfortunately, they can cost readers time and understanding.

A physician I know, a native of India, tells about the time he was a first-year intern in the United States. One night when he was on call and sleeping in the doctors' lounge, he got a call from a nurse on the floor asking him to come down and pronounce. Still half-asleep the young Indian doctor couldn't imagine what the nurse wanted him to pronounce. When he arrived on the floor, the nurse pointed down the hall and said, "Room 349." Still confused the young physician went into Room 349. A few moments later, he came back to the nurse and said in his most careful English, "I don't know what you want me to pronounce, but you should know the gentleman in 349 is dead." A good way to determine if you should use an abbreviation or jargon is to ask yourself, "Would someone outside my specialty or from a foreign country know what I'm talking about?" If not, spell it out.

TIP: If it's too pretentious to say, it's probably too pretentious to write. *Pretentious language is often used to sound scholarly or intelligent. Would you ever call someone on the phone and say, "At this point in time, implementation of the new, innovative plan will be done on the managerial level prior to others." Let's hope not. Instead, you'd probably say, "Managers will implement the new plan first."*

Ways to Improve Your Writing

To my knowledge, there are still only two ways to improve your writing: practice and modeling.

Practice

Because writing is a skill, in order to improve, you need to practice. If possible, set aside some time each day to write. What should you write about? Anything. Write a case report. Write your impressions of a patient. Write a letter to the editor of a journal. Write about a particularly perplexing case. *What* you write is not so important as *that* you write. This will improve your writing and help refine your thinking.

If you work with younger physicians or medical students, have them write often. Make writing a part of their curriculum. I've found that training programs that require students and residents to write at least one publishable paper prepare their students for the real world in which they will be writing all the time. Their writing is organized, and these physicians are generally able to write more efficiently and quickly than those with less practice.

TIP: *To improve writing and critical reading skills, photocopy a journal article and take out the abstract and discussion sections. Have your students read the article and write an abstract for it. This exercise is an excellent way to see how well your students are reading, as well as to see how well they are writing.*

Modeling

The other way to improve writing skills is to model your writing after good writing. The problem that physicians, and scientists in general, have is that much of the writing that they are reading isn't all that good. It's often filled with nonsensical jargon and abbreviations, convoluted syntax, rambling and disorganized structure. Examples of good writing are in *The Annals of Internal Medicine, Journal Watch,* and *Lancet,* and most of the writing of Lewis Thomas. Of course, there are other examples of good writing, and as you become more aware of your writing, you'll begin to differentiate between writing that is easy to read and writing that is painful to read.

Resources for Medical Writing

To diagnose a disease correctly, you need the appropriate tests. To operate successfully, you need the right instruments. Writing is the same. Good writing requires the appropriate tools.

Dictionaries

An excellent general dictionary is *Webster's Collegiate Dictionary*. Physicians frequently ask me to recommend the best dictionary. I usually tell them that if it weighs five pounds or more it's probably good enough. You won't need the dictionary to find the biggest or longest word, but rather the most precise word.

Style Guides

Physicians in the writing seminars often complain that the problem with English is that they're always changing the rules. (I guess "they" are the imagined secret grammar police holed up in some back room arbitrarily changing rules of grammar, syntax, and punctuation in order to drive the rest of the world mad.) The fact is, very few rules have changed. What does change is style. Most publications have style guides—books that answer questions on subjects including grammar, punctuation, word usage, capitalization, abbreviations, references, and units of measure. Each of these has slightly different rules. Which should you use? It's probably best to use one of the two used by most biomedical journals, *The American Medical Association Manual of Style* or the *Council of Biology Editors Style Manual*. Look them both over, choose one, then stick with it. (Other style guides are listed in the Useful Resources at the end of the book.)

Additional References

The Elements of Style, by William Strunk, Jr., and E. B. White. A classic that is distinguished by clarity, conciseness, and good sense. This little gem should be on every writer's desk. This is the book that every student buys as a freshman and sells back as a sophomore. Unfortunately, these same students get into the real world and realize it's one of the few books they really need. If you're looking for a copy, it is now in paperback. Pick one up.

How to Write and Publish Papers in the Medical Sciences, by Edward J. Huth, M.D. This book is the best I know for physicians who want to write for publication. It takes the medical author step by step through the writing and publishing process. It's written by a former editor of *The Annals of Internal Medicine*. Anyone who wants to publish in the medical journals should read this book. It is clear, concise, and organized practically.

The Synonym Finder, by J. I. Rodale. Many years ago I was teaching basic writing to a group of college students. Most of them had never written an essay. Their first assignment was to write about something they really loved. One student, a hulking football player, proudly brought his paper in the following day. He had written about his car, a GTO, I think. About every other word was twelve to fifteen letters, totally inappropriate to the content of the material. "What do you think?" he asked when I'd finished reading the paper. I said I thought he had worked very hard on it, but I was curious: Where had he gotten all the big words? With a beaming smile, he said, "From the Tyrannosaurus."

If you're looking for a big word the dinosaur of books, the *thesaurus*, is a good place to look. If you're looking for the exact word, *The Synonym Finder* is a better choice. It groups words according to meaning, so you have less chance of using a wrong or inappropriate word.

Principles and Practices of Research, by H. Troidl and W. O. Spitzer. This is a helpful, inclusive book for research scholars. It's both a text and a reference book covering the planning, funding, execution, analysis, and evaluation of research, as well as the effective reporting of results. The contributors to this book are international experts in clinical science and research methodology. All of the authors have experience teaching how to execute research projects to students excited about a career in clinical science.

Studying a Study, Testing a Test: How to Read the Medical Literature, by Richard K. Riegelman and Robert P. Hirsch. I particularly like this book because it spends a good deal of time discussing critical reading of the medical literature. Anyone involved in research or who works with medical students, interns, and residents would be wise to review this book.

Interpreting the Medical Literature, by Stephen H. Gehlbach. The amount of medical literature today is staggering. How do you digest it all? And how do you evaluate what's applicable to your daily study, research, or practice? Dr. Gehlbach, in a concise and easy-to-read style, has the answers. This book is an invaluable resource to help you understand the fundamental principles of epidemiology, apply published epidemiologic data to your own needs, develop the skills to effectively evaluate study design and execution, and formulate a dissenting opinion.

Primer of Biostatistics, by Stanton A. Glantz. This is an excellent book designed to provide clinicians and health researchers with an understanding of the most commonly encountered statistical procedures in medical research.

Software Programs

Stedman's/25, published by Williams & Wilkins. Anyone who has ever tried to check the spelling in a medical research paper using a regular spell-check program knows how time-consuming it can be. The software program doesn't recognize most medical terms because they are not in the regular dictionary. So the words you most want to check don't get checked. The *Stedman's/25* software contains the *Stedman's Medical Dictionary*, so all medical terms are included. Obviously, this package can save time and mistakes.

Medical Edition Grammar Check, published by Williams & Wilkins. For any medical writer who is serious about improving his or her writing skills, this is a very helpful program. This is not just a fix-it program. Rather, it alerts the writer to common writing problems, including sentences that are too long, pretentious language, misplaced modifiers, lack of subject–verb agreement, and overuse of the passive voice.

Grateful Med, published by National Library of Medicine. If you have a personal computer and a modem, you can tap in to the vast medical information of the National Library of Medicine (NML). *Grateful Med* is a software package that enables the physician to access more than 15 million medical journal articles, books, and symposium proceedings in various data bases, including MEDLINE, NLM's premier data base. *Grateful Med* is available for both

Macintosh and IBM compatible computers. For more information, call 800-639-8480.

For more resources, see the section of Useful Resources.

Common Problems in Medical Writing

Misused Words

Medical writing frequently includes words that are used incorrectly. Below are a few examples of commonly misused words.

1. Eighty-two four-year-olds were tested utilizing the standard pediatric, audiometry techniques.

   Utilize is not synonymous with *use*. *Utilize* has the specific meaning "to turn to practical use or account," suggesting the new use for something.

2. The disease rarely impacts men before the age of 50.

   The word *impact* is another word that is frequently misused. I think many people use it because they aren't sure if they want *affect* or *effect*, so they use *impact*.

3. The patient was not toxic when he was brought in.

   Patients can't be *toxic*. Their conditions can be.

4. Investigators must look at specific manic symptoms in samples with and without dementia.

   Samples, like cases, aren't manic, with or without dementia. People, patients, participants, or subjects may be.

5. The 33 controls are displayed in the following table.

   Controls cannot be displayed in a table. Data about controls can be.

6. Cases also drank significantly more alcohol than controls.

   Cases can't drink alcohol, nor can they drink controls.

The sentence should read, *Patients drank significantly more (38%) alcohol than did the patients in the control group.*

7. Presently, we have 36 residents and fellows in our department.

   Presently means "in the near future." The writer means *Currently.*

8. The discussion should center around the treatment choices only.

   The correct expression is *center on.*

9. How does diabetes present?

   Diabetes doesn't present; patients with diabetes do.

10. The patient displayed classical symptoms of carpal tunnel syndrome.

    The correct word is *classic,* meaning typical. *Classical* means relating to the ancient Greek and Roman world, especially its literature, art, architecture, or ideals.

11. Please join Dr. Clark, Dr. Weiss, and myself in welcoming Dr. Benedetti to our office.

    It should be *me.* Today, many people are confused about when to use "I" and when to use "me," so they throw in "myself." I tell them if you go with "I" or "me," you'll be right about 50% of the time. If you go with "myself," you'll be wrong about 95% of the time. The word *myself* should be used (1) when subject and object are oneself: *I wrote myself a letter,* and (2) for emphasis: *I, myself, would never have considered that procedure.*

12. We monitored the affect of the medication.

    In this sentence *effect* is correct, not *affect. Affect* and *effect* are probably the most frequently misused words in medical writing and speaking. They sound very much alike and there is a noun version of both and a verb version of both.

13. Tetracycline can affect a cure.

> Yes, tetracycline can *affect* a cure if the patient is being treated for a yeast infection. But tetracycline can also *effect* a cure, meaning "to bring about." If *effect* and *affect* have always been a problem for you, give up trying to memorize their meanings. Instead write out each word and its synonym and tack it up near where you write.
>
> **affect, v.** = to influence. The drug can affect appetite.
>
> **affect, n.** = behavior, outward appearance. The psychiatrist noticed the patient's inappropriate affect; he laughed when she learned her father was dead.
>
> **effect, v.** = to bring about. Fluoxetine can effect dramatic personality changes.
>
> **effect, n.** = outcome. What is the effect of trazodone on sleep?

14. We studied the effect of propranolol on the blood pressure of the spinalized dogs.

> *Spinalized, endorphinized, prophylaxed, surgerized* are not words—yet. While you may be using them in conversations with your colleagues, avoid them in your writing.

15. Biopsy the lesion.

> *Biopsy* is a noun, not a verb.

16. The standard dose is tetracycline 500 mg orally, q 12 for 7 days.

> The correct word is *dosage,* which refers to regulation of the size, frequency, and number of doses. *Dose,* on the other hand, means the quantity to be administered at one time.

17. The patient presented with all the classic symptoms of macroglobulinemia, i.e., fatigue, weakness, skin and mucosal bleeding, visual disturbance, headache.

> The abbreviation *i.e.* is often used in error for the abbreviation *e.g.* The abbreviation *e.g.* stands for the Latin

exempli gratia, and means "for example," and should be used before examples of what has previously been mentioned.

Example: The library has several good books on the subject of writing, e.g., *The American Medical Association of Style, How to Write and Publish Papers in the Medical Sciences, The Elements of Style.*

The abbreviation *i.e.*, on the other hand, stands for the Latin *id est*, and means "that is." Use *i.e.* before amplifications of what has previously been mentioned.

Example: The patient was a vegan, i.e., a vegetarian who also avoids eggs and dairy products.

TIP: *For a discussion of incorrect word usage, take a look at* Medical Usage and Abusage, *by Edith Schwager. It's informative and fun.*

Redundant Words

In an attempt to bulk up their writing, many writers use redundant words. Here are a few examples.

1. Basal reactivity and habituation represent two different kinds of physiological and behavioral processes . . .

    The expression, *different kinds* is common but redundant.

2. There was a consensus of opinion among physicians at the M & M meeting.

    Consensus means "collective opinion."

3. A palliative, noncurative technique was employed . . .

    Palliative means "to make less severe without curing."

4. Rigorously peer-reviewed by experts specifically trained in immunohistochemistry, the *Applied Immunohistochemistry* emphasizes practical application . . .

    Authors and readers hope peers reviewing articles in

an immunohistochemistry journal are experts in the field!

5. In order to make an accurate diagnosis, the physician must very closely scrutinize the patient's history.

   Scrutinize means "to look very closely."

6. With careful advance planning, we should be able to make Grand Rounds a more useful activity for our residents.

   All planning is advance.

Punctuation and Grammar

> *It is not wise to violate the rules until you know how to observe them.*
>
> T. S. Eliot (Safire, 214)

> *Punctuation, to most people, is a set of arbitrary and rather silly rules you find in printers' style books and in the back pages of school grammars. Few people realize that it is the most important single device for making things easier to read.*
>
> Rudolf Flesch (Trimble, 104)

Good medical writing is directly related to correct punctuation, proper word usage, and correct grammar and syntax. Problems in any of these areas can cause confusion. The following sentences are taken from physicians' writings that contain common errors in punctuation. See if you can find the mistakes, and correct them.

1. Patients are often terrified when they hear the word "cancer".

   All journals published in the United States place periods and commas inside the last quotation mark. It doesn't make sense, and it's one of the few rules in English that I can't defend. In the days of handset type, so the story goes, printers discovered that a period or comma hanging out at the end of a sentence after a quotation mark was easily knocked awry, and they solved the problem by putting the period or comma within the closing paragraph regardless of logic. To confuse the issue, if you read *Lancet*, a British journal, you'll notice that the commas and the periods come outside the last quotation mark.

2. The hypertension can probably be controlled either by beta blockers or you may use diuretics.

    Parallelism is the principle that parts of a sentence that are parallel in meaning or weight should be parallel in structure. Parallelism is particularly important for clarity and conciseness. The sentence should read, *The hypertension can probably be controlled using beta blockers or diuretics.*

3. Each patient recorded their temperature.

    Subjects must agree with their pronouns. The word *each* requires the use of *his* or *her*. However, using *his or her* over and over again becomes cumbersome. To solve the problem, whenever possible use the plural, in this case, *Patients recorded their temperatures.*

4. Inspection of the tongue not infrequently yields important clues.

5. This test is not without considerable danger.

    Sentences 4 and 5 use the double negative. Recently, I was working with a group of four residents. At one point in the paper, they had written, *The condition is not infrequently seen in lactating women.* As an editor I suggested, *The condition is frequently seen in lactating women.* "Oh no," they all cried. "It's not that common. It's not frequent; it's just not infrequent." I was confused. So to make a point, I asked each resident to write on a piece of paper the percentage that "not infrequent" represents. They wrote 55%, 60%, 68%, and 75%. Quite a discrepancy, and not particularly scientific.

I suspect there are several reasons that we see so many double negatives in medical writing. One reason is we often don't have the exact number, so we are purposely vague. Another is that it is so common we have come to think it has meaning. Keep in mind, however, that double negatives are not reader-friendly, especially in scientific writing. It requires the reader to stop and translate the writer's meaning. That's good in advertising (Nobody Doesn't Like Sara Lee), but bad in scientific writing.

6. Preconceptional paternal alcohol intake may affect intrauterine growth.

   Frequently, medical writers use a string of adjectives (preconceptual paternal alcohol). Often it can be confusing. Simply stated: *The amount of alcohol a man drinks prior to conceiving a child may affect intrauterine growth.*

7. Prospectively, 92 laboring women underwent clinical estimation of birth weight and concurrent sonographic measurements of four fetal parameters.

   Avoid taking meaningful adjectives (prospective) and making them confusing adverbs (prospectively). The following is shorter and clearer: *We conducted a prospective study of 92 laboring women. We estimated birth weight and measured four fetal parameters by sonogram.*

8. Dr. Kastrup will limit her practice to the older patient.

   Avoid using the comparative *older* when you mean *elderly* or *geriatric*. The sentence should read, *Dr. Kastrup will limit her practice to geriatric patients.*

9. The housing department forms require name, age, sex and transportation requirements.

   It's unlikely that the housing department is interested in your sex requirements. Putting the last comma in a series before *and* is a style question. Some style guides say put it in (*American Medical Association Manual of Style*) while others say take it out (*The Washington Post Deskbook on Style*). Putting it in avoids confusion, particularly when writing about symptoms, e.g., chills, nausea, and vomiting, as well as treatments, e.g., methylprednisolone, cyclophosphamide, plasmapheresis.

10. Cholera is characterized by: profuse diarrhea, vomiting, muscular cramps, dehydration, oliguria, and collapse.

   If a sentence contains a long list, you can help the reader by introducing it with a colon (:); however, you must have a complete sentence before the colon. *Cholera is characterized by the following signs and symptoms: profuse diarrhea . . .*

11. The patient's ECG's were all within the normal range.

   When writing the plural of an all-capital abbreviation or of numerals, do not use an apostrophe, e.g., ECGs, EEGs, WBCs, 1990s.

12. Dr. Swiegart is chief of surgery at the Veteran's Administration Hospital.

   Do not use an apostrophe in the name of an organization in which the qualifying term (Veterans) is used as an adjective rather than a possessive.

13. She was brought to the clinic with a self inflicted knife wound.

   Self-inflicted is correct. Use a hyphen to join two or more words that have the force of a single modifier before a noun.

14. He was moderately-obese.

   Do not use a hyphen when making a compound modifier with an adverb ending in *ly*. Correct: *He was moderately obese.*

15. Use the Richard's retractors.

   Capitalize an eponym but do not use the possessive when it describes surgical and diagnostic instruments, materials, or solutions, for example, Richard retractor, Foley catheter, Liston-Stille forceps, Starr-Edwards valve, DeBakey appliance. Do use the possessive, however, with an eponym that describes a particular treatment or test, for example, Balfour's treatment, Dubois' method, Fliess' therapy, Ebstrein's diet.

16. We removed the diseased Fallopian tubes and ovaries.

    Do not capitalize words derived from eponyms, e.g., fallopian, eustachian, malpighian.

17. The baby weighed six pounds, seven ounces.

    Use arabic numerals with symbols and abbreviations, e.g., 6 lb 7 oz, 2 bid, 2%, pH 6.5, #14 Foley, 1 mm.

18. The ages of the patients in our study were eight, nine, 12, 15, and 16.

    Use arabic numerals when numbers are part of a series, even if one or all of them is less than 10. For example, *The ages of the patients were 3, 6, 12, and 14 years, respectively.*

TIP: *The best sources for answers to questions about spelling, capitalization, punctuation, grammar, and style in medical writing are a good medical dictionary and the* AMA Manual of Style.

Misplaced Modifiers

I've read hundreds of confusing passages in medical papers whose lack of clarity is due to *misplaced modifiers*—phrases that make it unclear who or what is being described. This problem can usually be avoided by placing the describing word or phrase as close as possible to the word it describes. Physicians tend to misplace modifiers when they use the passive rather than the active voice or when they are dictating. Look at the following examples:

Unclear: *By using antipsychotics, Dr. White was able to treat the patient.*
Better: *Dr. White was able to treat the patient with antipsychotics.*

Unclear: *The pelvic examination will be given later on the floor.*
Better: *The attending physician will perform a pelvic examination on Ms. Smith in her room.*

Read the following sentences, and note how placement of modifying words and phrases can confuse (and amuse) a reader, especially a hurried reader.

1. Walking to the hospital, the key was found.

   Keys don't walk.

2. After six hours of labor, Dr. Stein performed a caesarean section.

   Was Dr. Stein in labor?

3. After suturing the incision, the monkey was returned to the lab.

   Who did the suturing?

4. According to medical records, many children are burned in house fires unattended by an adult.

   Are the children unattended or are the house fires?

5. The patient was treated at St. Mark's following the stabbing by the trauma team.

   Who did the stabbing?

6. While doing exploratory surgery, the tumor was found.

   Tumors can't do surgery.

7. For someone who is considered an expert in communication, I would expect your letter to be more straightforward and less circuitous.

   Who is the expert here, the reader or the author?

8. After having been proven incompetent, the psychiatrist on call admitted the patient.

   Was the patient found incompetent or the physician?

9. Mulling over the treatment options, his confusion only increased.

   Confusion can't mull.

10. While reviewing the patient's chart, the error was found.

    Errors can't review charts.

11. After reviewing patient data, headaches, dizziness, flushing, pedal edema, and reflex tachycardia became common side effects.

    Symptoms can't review patient data.

12. However, among other clinical observations, these authors stressed the frequent cutaneous manifestations and acute enteritis.

    Are authors clinical observations?

13. Following the reconstructive surgery, the physician was sued for malpractice.

    Who had the reconstructive surgery?

14. Having been carefully reviewed by our editorial board, I am pleased to inform you . . .

    The manuscript was reviewed, not the author of the sentence.

15. The patient was given treatment for outpatient respiratory tract infection.

    The treatment was outpatient; the infection wasn't.

Long Sentences, Unclear Antecedents, Poor Transitions

> *There is not much to be said about the period except that most writers don't reach it soon enough.*
> William Zinsser (1980, 104)

Many times, medical writing is difficult to understand because the sentences are too long, the antecedents are unclear, or the writer has not made the connections between sentences and paragraphs clear to the reader. Look at the following sentences taken directly from medical journals or textbooks:

1. Though renal artery stenosis has been rarely associated with hypokalemia secondary to hyperreninemic hyperaldosteronism,

there are very few reports that have actually evaluated the pathophysiologic changes in such a patient with renovascular hypertension.

Comment: Medicine is complex enough without using overly complicated sentences to explain it. One enemy to clarity in medical writing is long sentences. I would make two sentences, putting a period after hyperaldosteronism. Then, to help the reader, I would put a transition word or words, possibly *however*, at the beginning of the next sentence. And finally, I would change *in such a patient* to *in patients with* . . .

Revised: Renal artery stenosis has been rarely associated with hypokalemia secondary to hyperreninemic hyperaldosteronism. However, there are very few reports that have actually evaluated the pathophysiologic changes in patients with renovascular hypertension.

2. The problem of separating dementia from the depression can be seen in DSM-III-R by the fact that these criteria allow for a subtype of dementia with coexisting depression and the fact that they require that organic disorders be excluded when making the diagnosis of depression.

   Comment: Meaning can get lost because too much is going on in one sentence, and because of pronouns like *they* that don't have clear antecedents.

3. Incidence and time of onset of germinal matrix/intraventricular hemorrhage (GM/IVH) were prospectively ascertained in 1105 infants weighing < 1 g at birth, a cohort comprising about 85% of births of that weight born from September 1984 to June 1987 in the central New Jersey counties of Ocean, Monmouth, and Middlesex.

   Comment: Qualities that confusing sentences often have are length and the passive voice. To improve clarity, shorten sentences, and avoid the passive voice.

4. Although the Olmsted county findings contradict those of several previous referral center studies reporting higher

risks of acute expansion and rupture for patients with small aneurysms who initially refused operation or who had higher initial surgical risk, they are virtually identical to the findings of recent Canadian, Swedish, and British studies.

Comment: The previous sentence has 51 words, a challenge to the best reader. William Zinsser (1980, 104) says: "If you find yourself hopelessly mired in a long sentence, it's probably because you are trying to make the sentence do more than it can reasonably do—perhaps express two dissimilar thoughts. . . . Among good writers it is the short sentence that predominates, and don't tell me about Norman Mailer—he's a genius. If you want to write long sentences, be a genius."

Lack of Clarity

Writing and rewriting are a constant search for what it is one is trying to say.

John Updike (West, 121)

Lack of clarity can make medical writing bewildering and unintentionally comical. You can often correct such problems if you read your writing out loud. If the passage doesn't *sound* clear, its meaning will be unclear to the reader. As with all the examples in this book, the following were taken directly from actual physicians' writing.

1. In Case 3 the patient's preoperative hearing was significantly worse to begin with, and he had no useful hearing postoperatively.

    The writer would be wise to think this thought through and start again.

2. Sixteen patients died during and after liver transplant surgery.

   They died either during or after surgery, not both.

3. Beginning on January 6, a suicide recovery meeting will be held every Monday evening at 7:00 in Room 272 of the hospital. All are welcome.

   We can assume there aren't many people at this meeting.

4. He came to believe that suicide was the only viable alternative to a lingering death.

   Death doesn't linger, and fetuses are viable; alternatives aren't.

5. The otitis media was treated with amoxicillin, then changed to a cephalosporin.

   The ear infection became a drug?

6. With well over 200 cases now reported in the literature, renal oncocytomas continue to mesmerize urologists because of their benign nature.

   Although urologists might be benign, I think the author was referring to the oncocytomas.

7. At City Hospital, some of our surgeons can add years to your life. Others are equally expert at reversing the process.

   There are good doctors and there are bad ones.

8. Low level of physical activity has been found to be associated with the risk of hip fracture in both prospective studies and retrospective studies.

   Studies don't have hips.

9. The misdiagnosis of his patient pointed out in the clinic yesterday the problem with that procedure to Dr. Carter.

   Too many prepositional phrases can lead to misplaced modifiers.

10. I've included a list of our residents broken down by sex.

    Residents do get broken down but probably not by sex.

Wordiness

Let the words be few.

Ecclesiastes 5:2

In composing, as a general rule, run your pen through every other word you have written; you have no idea what vigor it will give your style.

Sydney Smith (Safire, 48)

There is a difference between providing the details readers need to understand your point and filling a passage with superfluous words. Suggestions for trimming your writing:

- Identify the purpose of every sentence. If a sentence doesn't have a clear purpose, get rid of it.
- After you have written the first draft, cut out all sentences that serve as warm-ups for the main point.
  <u>Let me once again take this opportunity to</u> thank you.
- Cut out words and phrases that serve only to announce the obvious.
  The staff of residents will change in <u>the month of</u> July.
- Sharpen your words with precise meaning or get rid of them. For example, the word *dog* is clear, but the word *Dalmatian* is clear <u>and</u> precise.
- Use transition words when necessary. Medical writing can be complex. Help your reader by using transition words, e.g., *furthermore, however, nevertheless, moreover, in addition, first, finally, in contrast,* to show relationships between sentences and paragraphs.
- Mary Collopy, medical editor, offers this exercise to add clarity and vitality to your writing: Use a colored pencil to try to eliminate one word from every line in your first draft. Examine the results. Next, use another colored pencil to identify every abstract word in your paper, e.g., *functional, concept, implementation.* Now use a different colored pencil to identify every concrete word in your paper, e.g., *lipids,*

adenoma, hyperthyroidism. What is the balance? You should have more concrete words than abstract words. No matter what their backgrounds, readers need concrete words to understand your main points.

◆ Never use a complex word when a simple one will do. Don't say *felicitous* if *just right* will do.

Look at the following examples. Are they as concise and clear as they can be? If not, how might you improve them?

1. Physicians who wish to be more effective in commanding the attention of listeners in order to move them toward the position advocated by their spoken message can accomplish this by learning and using the techniques developed for this powerful form of medical communication.

   Probably what this writer meant to say is, "To sell your ideas, you must be a good communicator." Remember: If it's too pretentious to say, it's probably too pretentious to write.

2. The ear is part of the auditory mechanism that plays an important role in the normal function of receiving and translating sound.

   The ear is necessary for hearing.

3. It was readily apparent to us that the patient was suffering from oxygen deprivation.

   The patient was clearly hypoxic.

4. The book is designed as a monograph concerning the non-invasive diagnostic instrumentation known as Doppler ultrasound.

   The monograph concerns Doppler ultrasound, a non-invasive diagnostic tool. Notice the word *monograph*; it's more precise than the word *book*.

5. Needless to say, acetone-extractable lipids are a requirement for enzymatic activity.

   If it's needless to say, don't say it.

6. The effective implementation of cryopreservation techniques could potentially impact quite positively on the salvage of ischemic extremities into the next decade.

   It is possible, in the next decade, using cryopreservation techniques, we will be able to salvage many more ischemic extremities.

7. This information is potentially viable in the ongoing comprehension of the growing knowledge and numerous functional capacities and pharmacology premises on neurochemical interrelationships.

   We use this sentence frequently in the writing seminars. Although more than 1500 physicians have read it, I've yet to find one who can explain exactly what the writer meant. To find out why it is so obtuse, take a pencil and circle every concrete word in the sentence, that is, every word that we can see, touch, hear, smell, or taste. I doubt you will find any. To be understandable, every sentence must have a majority of concrete, definable words.

8. Although PAP generated by increasing flow rate does not correlate closely with barotrauma as well as plateau pressure, the amount of central airway pressure that is actually transmitted to the alveolus (the actual risk factor for barotrauma) is difficult to judge.

9. In view of the evidence already considered, it would seem unlikely that studies of T cell receptor usage in the inflamed joint would be able to detect a minority population of antigen-specific cells responsible for driving the joint inflammation, even if we were to assume that the same T cell receptor was always used to recognize a particular MHC/peptide complex (which is certainly not always the case).

   Sentences 8 and 9 are difficult to understand because too much is going on in each. To improve clarity, the writers should first get rid of unnecessary words, then break each sentence into smaller sentences, and add clear transition words. Because we, as readers, aren't exactly sure what the writers were trying to say, it would be hard to offer a corrected version.

10. It has long been known that . . .

Avoid this expression. It implies, "I know there are references, but I didn't bother to look them up."

The Passive Voice

> *Active verbs are stronger than passive verbs because they propel a sentence forward.*
>
> William Zinsser (1988, 71)

The term *active voice* means that someone or something in the sentence "does" the action of the verb. Syntactically, that generally means subject, verb, object.

Active voice: *Dr. Peterson wrote the abstract.*
Passive voice: *The abstract was written by Dr. Peterson.*

The active voice gives writing a sense of strength, energy, vitality, and motion. The passive voice slows things down. The active voice is not only stronger than the passive voice, it's 20–30% shorter. Why then are so many physicians and scientists using the passive voice? Recently, I worked with a young oncology resident on a journal article. We edited the article for clarity and conciseness, changing the passive voice to the active voice whenever appropriate. She then gave it to her chief to review. Methodically, with a red pencil, he changed every active construction to the passive. "Why?" she asked. "Because that's the way we do it," he replied.

Here are some common myths about the active voice.

Myth: The active voice is self-promoting and shows a lack of humility.

Fact: If you did the work, there's nothing wrong with saying you did. "We determined . . . " is stronger than "It was determined that . . ."

Myth: It's not good science. The scientist should stay out of the work.

Fact: Good science is logical, well organized, clear, and concise—the same qualities of good writing. Use of the passive voice often results in confusing, obtuse prose because it promotes misplaced modifiers and subjects that are far away from their verbs.

Example: A retrospective study (*subject*) of 301 patients who underwent radical prostatectomy for clinically localized prostate cancer between January 1991 and December 1992 at St. Mark's, City Hospital, and affiliated hospitals was performed (*verb*).

How many times have you read a sentence like that? The main problem is it requires readers to read it twice. By the time readers get to the verb (*performed*) in the last line, they've forgotten what the subject (*study*) is. Without a clear idea of the sentence's subject and verb, the reader has a difficult time making sense of a string of words. For clarity and conciseness it would be far better to have written, "We performed a retrospective study of . . ." Immediately the readers know who did what to whom.

Myth: Using the passive voice makes the writer less accountable, particularly if something goes wrong.

Fact: "The procedure was performed using . . ." doesn't make you any less accountable than saying "I performed the procedure using . . ."

I don't recommend banishing the passive voice entirely. There are occasions when it is preferable. For example:

◆ If the doer is unknown. *The patient was brought to the emergency room.* In this sentence, we don't know who brought the patient, nor do we care. The sentence remains clear, concise, and accurate.

◆ If for discretion, the doer should remain nameless. *The patient was never given her 4:00 AM medication.*
◆ If the receiver of the action is more important than the doer. *Roberta Kurtz, M.D., was named Chair of the Department of Surgery.*

Which of the following sentences would you change to the active voice? Remember, the goal is to make every sentence as clear and concise as possible.

1. A prospective study of 128 women who underwent reconstructive surgery at the same time of radical mastectomies between June 1990 and December 1990 in three midwestern medical centers was conducted.

   We conducted a prospective study of 128 women . . .

2. A recommendation has been made that blood flow be allowed to return to baseline before proceeding with the next occlusion.

   We recommend (or whoever did) . . .

3. It is concluded that this method can detect pulmonary edema and congestion.

   We (or whoever did) concluded that this . . .

4. It has been reported by Smith that Therapy A is more effective against nosocomial pneumonia than Therapy B.

   Smith reported . . .

5. A 45-year-old man with a gunshot wound to the abdomen was brought to the emergency room.

   I would leave this sentence in the passive voice. It is clear, concise, and the focus is on the 45-year-old man.

6. A palliative, noncurative relief of symptoms has been reported in women with rheumatoid arthritis taking the oral contraceptive Enovid by several investigators.

   Several investigators reported that Enovid, the oral

contraceptive, can offer women with rheumatoid arthritis some palliative relief of symptoms.

7. A decision must be made on the part of the chairman of the department in regard to the recommendation to change the format of Grand Rounds in order for there to be adequate preparation by residents and fellows.

   The chairman of the department must decide soon whether to recommend changing . . .

8. Four hundred twenty women who presented for annual Papanicolaou (Pap) screening or follow-up evaluation after an abnormal Pap smear result were evaluated prospectively to determine whether cervicography is an effective method of cervical cancer screening.

   We conducted a prospective study with 420 women . . .

9. A double-blind, randomized trial evaluating the efficacy of 250 mL of 7.5% sodium chloride hypertonic saline, with and without the colloid dextran 70, for the prehospital resuscitation of trauma patients whose systolic blood pressure (BP) was less than 90 mm Hg at any time in the field during transportation was conducted by the Multicenter Group for the Study of Hypertonic Saline in Trauma Patients.

   The Multicenter Group for the Study of Hypertonic Saline in Trauma Patients conducted a double-blind trial of randomly selected . . .

10. There were 19 men in a study conducted by investigators at our institution to determine the efficacy of Drug X.

    Investigators at _____ Medical Center conducted a (what type?) study. . . .

Dictation

A very frequent cause of bad writing in medicine is the dictaphone. Many physicians, because of their busy schedules, prefer to dictate their letters, memos, and manuscripts, then have a secretary transcribe them. The two most common problems with dictated writing are (1) incorrect punctuation, grammar, and usage and (2) long, rambling sentences. Here are a few suggestions to avoid these common dictation errors:

- ◆ **Proofread everything you dictate.** With modems and fax machines, there is no reason any piece of writing should go out unread by the writer. While a good secretary will read a piece of writing to see if it makes sense, most secretaries do not have medical training so they cannot be expected to catch all mistakes. One manuscript I read mentioned a "disconfusion." Another said the patient had a "Sudomonis infection." Remember: If you sign it, you own it.
- ◆ **Think before you speak.** Before turning on the dictaphone, jot down a rough outline of what you want to say. A few moments spent planning can save hours of revision.
- ◆ **Speak slowly, loudly, and distinctly** and don't dictate in places where there is a lot of background noise. Airports and highways don't lend themselves to dictation.
- ◆ **Identify yourself.** Secretaries often work with several physicians. Be sure to state your name, title, department.
- ◆ **State the type of communication.** Give all necessary information about the communication before you start. Is this a memo, letter, manuscript, abstract? Is it a rough draft or final copy? How many copies? Single-spaced or double-spaced? Confidential?
- ◆ **Give the transciber cues.** Spell out names. State "New paragraph" or "All caps." If you want to make sure about punctuation, say it. "After reading the report *comma* I will give you a call *period.*
- ◆ **Specify enclosures,** indicate dictation has ended, and remember to thank the transciber.
- ◆ **Listen to yourself** and imagine you were trying to transcibe your words. Are you enunciating clearly? Are you saying after a fifty-word paragraph, "Delete that last paragraph"?
- ◆ **Use a style guide.** Make sure you and your secretary share the same style guide, so you can agree on questions of punctuation, grammar, and usage.

◆ **Meet with your secretary** on a regular basis to ask how you can make your dictation easier to transcribe.

When and Where to Write

The more a man writes, the more he can write.

William Hazlitt (Flesch, 320)

You've decided to write an article, grant, or poster. You've conducted a literature search, organized your references, and analyzed your prospective reader and purpose. Your next task is to consider ways to make your writing time as easy and productive as possible. Most medical writers underestimate the importance of when and where they write. Good writing takes time. Plan your writing to give yourself enough time for second and third drafts, as well as for careful proofreading.

To make writing time easy and productive, try these suggestions:

◆ **Set up a writing routine and never vary from it.** *The habit of daily writing* helps overcome writer's block, divides writing projects into manageable tasks, and forces you to avoid last-minute overload, a state that can make you feel overwhelmed and out of control. One of the best analogies I have heard about writing comes from Mary Collopy, medical writer and editor. She says knowing you have a writing task in front of you is like wearing a large backpack. Each day that you don't write is like putting a heavy rock in the backpack. After several days of not writing, the weight of the pack is almost unbearable. Writing each day keeps that backpack from overwhelming you.

◆ **Determine what time of day and length of time works best for you.** Use that time every day to devote to a writing task, even if you feel you have nothing to say. That time should be devoted exclusively to writing or thinking about writing. Even 15–30 minutes a day can be extremely helpful.

◆ **Write when your energy is high,** not when you are tired.

Writing requires concentration. If you are tired or have other matters on your mind, you will not be able to give your writing the attention it needs.

✦ **Surround yourself with everything you need** to write efficiently: dictionaries, style guide, user's guide for your computer and software, all the data, drafts of figures and tables, references, pens, paper.

✦ **Give yourself ample time** for rewriting and proofreading. These tasks are too important to be done at the last minute. Many physicians develop a time line, which is essential if you are working with several authors.

✦ **Work in a quiet place** where you will not be interrupted. For many of us, finding a quiet place is almost impossible with phones, faxes, colleagues, and families. But separating ourselves from people and things for a few minutes each day is probably good not only for our writing but also for our spirits.

You Are Not Alone: Getting Help with Writing and Editing

> *No passion in the world is equal to the passion to alter someone else's draft.*
>
> H. G. Wells (Winokur, 115)

Medical Editors

Medical centers from which many papers get published, (e.g., Johns Hopkins, Mayo Clinic, Lahey Clinic, University of California at San Francisco, Cleveland Clinic, Massachusetts General, and Dartmouth), have one thing in common: medical editors. Medical editors do more than just "fix it up." If they are good, they advocate for physicians with publishers. Cathy Coffin, a former medical editor at Dartmouth-Hitchcock Medical Center, defined her role as medical editor:

> *When reading a medical manuscript, I'm another pair of eyes looking for meaning, organization, and consistency. In addition, I'm the*

reference checker, software critic, and attender to details and directions, as well as a coach.

Medical editors must be excellent wordsmiths and coaches, and also clever marketing specialists. Before they send a manuscript to a journal, good editors know (1) journal editors, (2) possible reviewers, (3) journal specifications for manuscripts, (4) intended readers, and (5) recent articles on similar topics. One editor believes that the more you know about the journal and its readers, the more you can tailor your manuscript to their needs.

Freelance Editors

If a staff medical editor is not available to you, try a freelance editor. Here are some hints on selecting one:

- ◆ Anyone can call himself or herself a medical editor; there is no license, board certification, or specific training required to set up a medical editing business. Choose carefully and be sure to check references, particularly those from other physicians.
- ◆ A good medical editor should see the revision process as a joint effort; avoid the editor who merely wants to "clean up" your article.
- ◆ Choose the editor with a thorough grounding in English and some medical background instead of the editor with a solid scientific background and little grounding in language.
- ◆ Ask your peers if they have used an editor they could recommend.
- ◆ Call the American Medical Writers Association or Council of Biology Editors for a list of their members.
- ◆ Work with an editor early in the writing process. You'll save yourself time and money later on. A good medical editor can pinpoint problems in the study design that could cost you months of work.
- ◆ Agree on tasks and wages before you begin work with the editor. Consider what level of editing you want. Do you want just a proofreading to check tables and references, or are you

looking for a detailed review and revision? Once you have decided exactly what you want, then determine whether it is best to pay an hourly rate or a project rate.

Writing Groups

Several hospitals have writing groups, similar to journal clubs. Participants, often under the direction of the faculty, meet once a month and bring photocopies of their current drafts to review with other physicians. At these meetings, participants work on their introductions, abstracts, study designs, conclusions, graphics, and posters. Participants report that time spent working and listening to other writers is time well spent. As one resident from a hospital writing group said, "Love is blind. After working for months on a manuscript, I often can't see the inconsistencies or problems. I'm too close to it. Having others review and discuss my manuscript gives me valuable perspective. It's one of the few meetings I try never to miss—or sleep through."

Undergraduate Interns

Writing for publication requires a great deal of time and energy. The ideal situation would be if the physician could attend to the research, data analysis, and actual writing, and let someone who isn't necessarily a physician attend to tasks such as cross-checking references and proofreading tables and charts. Today, when jobs for recent college graduates are hard to come by, many students are looking into internships in order to get work experience. Check with local universities to find out if there are students in your area who would be interested in working in a medical setting. Students in pre-med, chemistry, biology, statistics, English, and journalism often intern in medical centers. These students generally are hardworking and more than willing to do those time-consuming and tedious tasks related to writing for publication. It's a nice arrangement for everyone: you, the physician, get to spend your time on the more important tasks and the intern gets work experience. The price is often right, too.

Whether you use an editor, a writing group, or writing intern, be sure to ask one or two other physicians to read your manuscript or grant application before you submit it. They can tell you if there are sentences or sections that are wordy, unclear, or redundant.

Essay

Lessons Learned

Anand B. Karnad, M.D.

Tidal waves of words, both written and spoken, overwhelmed me early in medical school. Anatomy was taught in a century-old red brick building that housed close to fifty cadavers and rows of skeletons in a massive dissection hall. It was here, faced with the daunting task of memorizing *Gray's Anatomy*—a prerequisite to pass the gruelling written examinations—and having to attend endless hours of lectures, that I learned the importance of writing and speaking well. The experience was so profound that now, seventeen years later, I can still close my eyes and quote my favorite passage from *Gray's*: "Ontogenetically, phylogenetically, structurally, and functionally, the cortex and medulla of the suprarenal gland are distinct from each other, but together they constitute a single topographical entity" (p. 1456).

Large amphitheaters adjacent to the dissection hall reverberated with the sound of lectures, as row upon row of medical students sat breathing in the formalin-laden air. Boring lectures—dull, verbatim recitation from textbooks—were common, their soporific effect mercifully put me out of my misery. Good lecturers, on the other hand, made time stand still. Professor Cooper, who taught me anatomy, lectured with an impish sense of humor, supplementing his careful choice of words and measured diction with colorful works of art on the blackboard; and, like magic, could make the blue cloth-duster—which he draped over his hand—go from a morula to an embryo in seconds. Professor Shanmugasundaram, who taught me orthopedics, delivered his lectures

Anand B. Karnad, M.D., is Associate Professor of Medicine, Division of Hematology-Oncology, Department of Internal Medicine, James H. Quillen College of Medicine, East Tennessee State University, Johnson City, Tennessee.

in a stern, booming voice with a clipped Indo-British accent, and paced the floor like a caged animal, slamming the long wooden pointer on the nearest desk with a sharp *rap* as a signal to move on to the next slide. He snapped chalk in his right hand in mid-sentence as he illustrated fractures—oblique versus transverse, simple versus compound. His style, the *rap-rap* of the pointer, and the flying pieces of chalk commanded attention and nobody slept. Finally, the late Professor K. V. Thiruvengadam, a brilliant physician and inspiring teacher, who, during bedside rounds would gently admonish, "Make it crisp and to the point, Anand; it is better to say 'the abnormal findings were confined to the right hemithorax,' rather than be repetitious and verbose about the normal half of the chest."

Later, I often found myself quite matter-of-factly using the "too busy" excuse instead of taking the time to craft a perfect paper, or to practice meticulously for a talk—until I read Richard Asher's *Talking Sense*. Richard Asher, an outstanding British clinician and teacher, best known for his witty essays and inspired lectures, wrote: "Both in writing and lecturing clear style and short words are best. Obscurity is bad, not only because it is difficult to understand but also because it is confused with profundity, just as a shallow muddy pool may look deep." At the peak of his career, he spent many hours writing and rewriting his lectures and papers. He said, ". . . if I am talking about words, I must say something about style. I don't care a fig for schoolroom stuff on the difference between phrases and clauses or the distinction between metaphors, similes, and hyperboles. But I do feel strongly about style. It is only a matter of putting down what you have to say in the neatest and most palatable form. And it cannot be done except by taking a lot of trouble" (p. 89).

Even more inspiring to me are the talents of Harvey Cushing, founder of modern neurosurgery, and Pulitzer prize-winning author of *The Life of Sir William Osler*. A prolific writer, he penned 5,000 to 10,000 words a day during his last twelve years at the Peter Bent Brigham Hospital in Boston. While writing Osler's biography, he would, at times, spend eighteen hours a day at the desk for six weeks straight; at other times, he operated by day and wrote by night. In the five years it took to complete the two-volume biography, he saw an increasing number of patients who flocked to his clinic from all over the world and published fifty major papers, about an average of one a month. Virtually all drafts of papers were handwritten including the entire Osler manuscript. His eloquent addresses were carefully prepared and typed on small cards that he would partially conceal in his hand as he spoke. Many of these were corrected and copied a dozen times, as he, no doubt, practiced his speech. Cushing's biography of Osler should be required reading for physicians who are just too busy to take the trouble to write and speak well.

In this era of rapid communication, when I am tempted to dash off a manuscript with cursory revisions, I remember Quentin Gibson's story of writing a paper with his mentor Francis Roughton, who once returned a heavily edited version of the *fourth* draft of a manuscript with the words, "Come Gibson, remember, we are writing a classic."

Throughout medical school, and then during residency and fellowship training, I was constantly reminded of the need to write and speak well. I now realize that I have to learn to speak in several styles, a task akin to learning completely different languages—simple, nontechnical language in talking to patients and their families; acronyms and jargon when talking to fellow physicians; the conscious attempt to be grammatically perfect on the dictaphone; and finally, brevity, clarity, diction, and style, all required to lecture to students and speak at professional meetings. As for writing, well, a callus on the third finger of my right hand is proof of the voluminous writing required in the world of medicine today; writing in patients' charts; writing memoranda, letters, prescriptions, and papers; writing notes to students, residents, fellows, secretaries, nurses, and at times to myself. It is not surprising therefore, that I have had to look to my teachers and to the great figures from the history of medicine to help me understand the undeniable fact that writing and speaking well is hard work, but well worth the effort.

Chapter Two

◆

Getting Published

The Journal Article

Many Are Sent; Few Are Chosen

Competition for space in journals is fierce. Major clinical journals in the United States reject 60%–70% of the papers submitted. *The New England Journal of Medicine* and the *Journal of the American Medical Association* report a rejection rate of close to 90%. And as more and more physicians from foreign medical centers and in private practice get into publishing, competition will only get greater.

Generally, journals don't reject good articles because they have too many. Good articles describing quality studies are accepted even if they cannot be published immediately. Why, then, are so many rejected? Following are the three most common reasons that journals reject articles.

1. **The manuscript is inappropriate** for the particular journal and its specific audience. What this tells me is that many writers are not doing their homework. Every journal has an "Information for Authors" page. In some journals it's in every issue; in others it's in the January and July issues. The Information for Authors page tells authors:

   - The journal's mission
   - The type of articles the journal accepts
   - Who its readers are
   - How to format the manuscript
   - Specific instructions on abstracts and keywords,

copyright, tables and figures, references, any author's charges

Recently, a resident in urology asked me to review a manuscript for publication. I asked him to which journal he was planning to submit it. "I haven't decided yet; probably one of the urology journals," he replied. To his surprise, I told him I'd have a hard time editing it without a clear audience in mind. Even though there are many similarities among the urology journals, there are also differences. I suggested that he review several back issues of each, then decide to which his manuscript was best suited. After analyzing the two top journals and their readers and purposes, he decided on Journal X. He then rewrote and formatted his manuscript specifically for Journal X. He cleverly took it one step further: he contacted a member of the urology staff at his hospital, who occasionally reviews manuscripts for Journal X, and asked him to review his manuscript before he submitted it.

We often suggest to physicians planning to submit a manuscript to a journal that they call that journal to ask the editors if they have suggestions for manuscript preparation. Some journal editors flatly refuse to talk to prospective authors; others offer helpful suggestions and advice. Try it. All you have to lose is the cost of a phone call.

2. **The manuscript describes poorly designed or conducted studies.** The editors of biomedical journals report that the major problems with unacceptable clinical studies are the following:

    - ◆ Insufficient information
    - ◆ Inadequate samples
    - ◆ Biased samples
    - ◆ Confounding factors
    - ◆ Vague endpoints
    - ◆ Straying from the hypothesis
    - ◆ Poor control of numbers

As you review your manuscript, look closely for these problems. Have a colleague in your department, as well as a physician in another department, review your manuscript before you send it off.

3. Manuscripts are poorly written. Many editors and reviewers have received manuscripts so filled with errors that they were not possible to evaluate. In fact, one editor said, "I was so appalled at one manuscript that I received, I called the chairman of the department from which the manuscript came. I told him I'd be sending the manuscript back and suggested he sit in front of a nice fire, with a cold drink, and page by page burn the manuscript." How can you prevent your manuscript from ending up in the inferno? Proofread. Proofread. Proofread. The more eyes that see your manuscript before it goes out, the less chance it will have of being rejected.

TIP: One particularly helpful way to pick up errors and inconsistencies is to read your manuscript aloud. We often underestimate how skilled our ears are at picking up errors. Often when I have writers read me their manuscripts, I don't have to say a word; the author hears his or her mistakes.

Taking It Step by Step

The prospect of writing a manuscript for a medical journal can seem like an insurmountable task for the novice writer. Researching, collecting data, organizing, and writing can be time and energy consuming. What is the most efficient approach? How can you get the best manuscript with the least amount of wasted time and energy? Ask yourself the following questions:

1. **Should I write an article for a journal?** Only if you have something worth saying. Many articles and presentations today are "show and tell," because the author merely tells an audience what he or she is doing at his or her institution. Most physicians don't have time to read show-and-tell articles. As a medical researcher and writer, don't waste your time or anyone else's with a rehash of old news. Make everything you write worth your reader's time. When planning an article, keep these five criteria in mind:

- ◆ new
- ◆ true
- ◆ important
- ◆ comprehensible
- ◆ useful

2. **Why do I want to write this article?** To have a published article on my curriculum vitae (CV) is probably the first answer that comes to mind if you're in academic medicine—and with good reason. A study conducted at Johns Hopkins University School of Medicine found that clinician-teachers who were promoted had about twice as many articles published in peer-reviewed journals as those who were not promoted. Whether for good or ill, the "publish or perish" mentality is alive and well. But there are other reasons to write a publishable article:

   - ◆ to communicate useful information to colleagues
   - ◆ to be viewed as an expert in an area
   - ◆ to clarify and expand your thinking on a topic

3. **What are the major pitfalls I might run into?** Before jumping into a research project, every new researcher–author would be wise to read *Studying a Study, Testing a Test* by Richard K. Riegelman and Robert P. Hirsch. It covers the major problems with unacceptable clinical studies: insufficient information, inadequate samples, biased samples, confounding factors, vague endpoints, straying from the hypothesis, poor control of numbers. If you truly want to publish, be on guard for such landmines on the way.

4. **Did someone beat me to the punch?** No one wants to spend months on a project to find out later it's already been done. Before beginning a study, do an in-depth review of the literature. If you need help, check with a medical librarian.

   Two indispensable tools for the researcher are (1) *Index Medicus*, a printed index, alphabetized by subject and author, of more than 3200 journals and periodicals. *Index Medicus* is published monthly by the National Library of Medicine; and (2) *Medline* is the on-line literature storage, analysis, and retrieval system of the National Library of

Medicine. There are 3646 biomedical journals on *Medline.* Finally, don't make the mistake of searching the literature only in the beginning of a project. Make several searches during the process to see what shows up.

5. **What is the most suitable journal?** Take a few hours and look through several journals. See how each journal differs. Who is the audience? What is the journal's statement of purpose and mission? Does the journal accept unsolicited manuscripts? What is the quality and prestige? What is the journal's impact factor (formula that determines the number of times that journal is cited in other journals). What is its circulation? For more information, you can call the journal and speak to an editor.

6. **What is the best format?** A case report? A letter to the editor? Most journal articles are either original research papers or review articles. Most original research articles follow the IMRAD format, that is

Introduction:	Why did you start? (present tense)
Methods:	What did you do? (past tense)
Results:	What did you find? (past tense)
Discussion:	What do your results mean? (present tense)

Once you have answered these questions, you can proceed to these steps suggested by F. Peter Woodford (1986, 9):

1. **Begin your research.** Take five differently colored index cards; use one for each of five sections: Introduction, Methods and Materials, Results, Discussion, References. You can use a computer to separate sections as well. As you do your research, record brief facts, experiments, thoughts, and observations that belong in each. Make sure you keep accurate records of references for each note, including source, page, author, title. You'll be glad you did when the time for submission arrives.

2. **Choose or design appropriate graphics.** The main points of the paper will probably be made in the tables and figures. Make the tables and figures fully informative in

themselves. Keep in mind that most of the information in your Results section should be displayed in a table, graph, or figure.

3. **Construct an outline.** Arrange topics in a logical order. In the Methods, use a chronological format. In the Results, put the most important and explicable findings first, and the less important later. Use headings and subheadings to guide readers through your ideas.

TIP: I've never met a physician who doesn't have something valuable to say to someone. The trick is knowing what it is and to whom you should say it.

A Look at Each Section

After you have organized your research and designed a good writing routine, you're ready to start writing the first draft, a difficult task because you may have only a rough idea of what you want to say. It's only as you are writing a first draft that you discover exactly what you want to say. So expect to spend a fair amount of time and energy on this draft. Which section should you start first? I suggest novice medical writers start on the one they know best. Confidence and comfort are great allies in the writing process. A brief description of the contents of each section and suggestions about each follows.

The Introduction

The Introduction should answer the question, *Why was this work done?* It should describe the general problem of interest, prior work that has been done, and the research question (or hypothesis) you hope to answer. Keep it short. With the proliferation of review articles, the necessity for extensive introductions has passed. Mimi Zeiger (1993), medical writer and lecturer, suggests that the Introduction state a question.

> *Why should the question be stated? The reason is that the question is the anchor of the paper. For the story to be clear, every sentence in the paper should relate to the question. Thus, Methods tells what was done to answer the question; Results tells what was found that answers the*

*question; and Discussion states and explains the answer to the question . . .
The question can be introduced with a question word, such as* whether,
as in we asked whether, *or as a hypothesis to be tested:* In this study
we tested the hypothesis that . . . *The question is not the first statement in the Introduction. Before stating the question, the Introduction
should lead readers to the question, by telling them a story of what is known
about the topic of the research and what is not yet known. (p. 457)*

The following are examples of effective introductory sentences in the
Introduction of an article:

*Infection remains an important cause of morbidity and mortality in
heart–lung transplant recipients. We hypothesized that knowledge of the
incidence and timing of infection could help in the prevention, early
detection, and initiation of therapy in these patients.*

*After a pancreatic endocrine tumor has been diagnosed on the basis of
clinical signs and the results of laboratory tests, localization of the tumor by the usual imaging procedures fails in as many as 40 to 60 percent of patients. We questioned whether endoscopic ultrasonography, a
sensitive test for small carcinomas of the pancreas, might be useful in
localizing endocrine tumors of the pancreas that cannot be localized by
conventional methods.*

*Identification of malignant cells in Sézary syndrome often relies on the
identification of the cerebriform nucleus of the Sézary cell, even though
it is well established that this morphologic criterion is nonspecific. We
investigated whether fluorescent in situ hybridization can visualize and
accurately enumerate malignant aneuploid mononuclear cells in a patient with Sézary syndrome.*

Methods and Materials

The Methods and Materials section answers the question, *How did you
carry out the research?* The traditional purpose of the Methods section
of a research report was to provide other researchers a blueprint of
the study so that it could be replicated and the findings verified. Today, the more important use of this section is to provide the information necessary to judge the quality of the study design and procedures
and hence the validity of the findings. There are generally five areas
that should be addressed in the Methods section of an article:

1. **Design.** Include a description of the experimental design (for example, randomized, controlled study, clinical trial, case control study). Knowing the exact design helps readers assess whether bias could have been introduced into the study by way of extraneous variables. Include special techniques (blinding, blocking) used to eliminate bias. State the duration of follow-up, if any.

2. **Study population.** Provide a complete description of the participants (humans or animals) and how they were selected or assigned, for example, 101 hospitalized adults with asthma or chronic pulmonary disease currently using an albuterol metered-dose inhaler.

3. **Setting.** Indicate from where the study population was selected, for example, three Veterans Administration Hospitals in upstate New York.

4. **Interventions.** Describe treatments, therapy, or measurement instruments used, both specially designed ones (e.g., pilot testing, questionnaires) as well as standardized instruments (e.g., Spitzer quality assessment instrument). If you are discussing drugs, use the generic name (diazepam, not Valium).

5. **Main outcome measure.** Provide a complete description of how the data were analyzed (mean scores, serum levels, dual-energy X-ray absorptiometry, heart rate, calcium secretion from 24-hour urine specimens, statistical analysis). Most biomedical journals have adopted rigorous policies to ensure that the statistical tests used by authors are appropriate for the study and are done correctly. If the statistical manipulation of data is complex, consult a biostatistician. Write this section in the past tense.

Here are some examples of strong Methods and Materials statements:

> *We randomly assigned 170 consecutive outpatients treated at six primary care centers for acute maxillary sinusitis to receive oral clarithromycin (500 mg twice daily) or oral amoxicillin (500 mg three times daily)*

for 7 to 14 days. Clinical and roentgenographic responses to antibiotic therapy were determined within 48 hours after the last dose and then 6 weeks later.

We analyzed the effect of age on prognosis in 1551 premenopausal breast cancer patients from one French institution who were followed for a median of 7 years. We grouped the patients by age at diagnosis: younger than 34 years (100 women), 34–40 years (326 women), and those over 40 years (1225).

We randomly assigned 1500 men with diastolic pressures of 85 to 109 mm Hg to take hydrochlorothiazide, atenolol, captopril, clonidine, sustained-release diltiazem, prazosin, or placebo. We followed them for 1 year of treatment.

The Results Section

This section should be the easiest to write. One journal editor says, in his opinion, the best result section would be, "The results of the study can be seen in Table 1." The Results section has two functions: (1) to state the results of the experiments described in the Methods and Materials section; and (2) to present evidence that supports the results or to direct the reader to figures or tables that present supporting evidence. Don't repeat what is already clear to the reader from a cursory examination of the tables and figures. If these have been well constructed, they will show both the results and the experimental design. Present the data or results obtained from the study in a straightforward, factual manner, without commentary or interpretation. The Results section must account for all subjects who actually entered the study and not only those who stayed in it as assigned. Write this section in the past tense.

Here are some examples of strong opening sentences in a Results section:

We found that migraine with aura and migraine without aura were both more common in patients with Raynaud disease than in control subjects (27% compared with 5%; P< 0.001 and 34% compared with 17%; P = 0.008, respectively).

When calculated according to the base-line assumptions, the probability of in-hospital death (after admission) for a patient more than 75 years of

age with a suspected acute myocardial infarction was 21.4% when throm-
bocytic therapy was given and 24.4% without such therapy.

Of the 89 patients who were taking captopril, enalapril, or lisinopril,
25% had a "definite" drug-induced cough (a cough that first appeared
within 6 weeks of starting the drug and resolved within 1 week of stop-
ping it).

Twelve-month abstinence rates ranged from 8% to 25% among smok-
ers using self-help methods, versus 20% to 40% among those using
smoking cessation clinics.

After adjusting for multiple confounding risk factors, we found that the
90 infants born after mothers were transported to university perinatal
centers had marginally lower neonatal mortality than the 241 infants
born in local hospitals.

Discussion Section

The Discussion is the heart of the paper and the one that readers will
turn to after reading the abstract. It is the section in which the author answers the question posed in the Introduction and assesses the
meaning of the results. As a writer, you will find the Discussion probably takes the most time to organize and write. Here are some suggestions from journal editors:

- Begin the Discussion with the answer to the question in the
  Introduction, followed immediately by support for the answer. The reason for beginning with the answer to the question is that the Discussion is a position of prominence and
  therefore should be used for the most important idea.
- Write this section in the present tense; the findings of the paper
  are now considered established as scientific knowledge.
- Discuss controversial issues clearly and fairly.
- Stress, rather than hide, anomalous results for which no explanation is readily available. You can be sure that if you don't
  mention them, a reviewer, editor, or critic will. Keep in mind
  that most interesting and valuable to science are the results
  that open up new possibilities of exploration.

◆ Take the opportunity to speculate and theorize. Such discussion can spark readers' interest. Just make sure that any speculations or theories are appropriate.

◆ Avoid unqualified statements and conclusions not supported completely by the data.

◆ Avoid claiming priority and alluding to work that has not been completed.

◆ Include recommendations when appropriate.

Here are some examples of effective opening sentences in a Discussion section:

> *Splenic radiation can be a safe and effective method to raise the platelet count in older patients with ITP that is refractory to corticosteroids and in whom the risks associated with splenectomy are high.*

> *This study strongly indicates that ACE inhibitors prolong life and prevent cardiac events in patients with ejection fractions below 30% to 40% and no evidence of CHF, including patients without recent MI.*

> *Oral acyclovir appears to provide a modest benefit in adults when started within 1 day of the appearance of chickenpox lesions.*

> *These data suggest that aspirin may reduce diabetic patients' risk of MI.*

> *This study indicates that there is little relation between the use of benzodiazepines and mortality in the elderly.*

> *This study confirms many others that have found an increased risk of leukemia and lymphoma after treatment for Hodgkin's disease.*

Title

Imagine for a moment that you've just picked up the latest edition of your favorite medical journal. What do you look at first? You probably scan the table of contents, and if a title catches your attention, you generally take time to turn to that article.

When writing a title, keep in mind you want to catch your reader's attention at a glance. To do so, titles should be short, specific, and clear. The most effective titles are fewer than 10 words.

Write the title after you have written the heart of the paper. If you have completed earlier steps, you should be able to formulate a title quickly. Titles of most journal articles are indicative rather than informative; they state the subject of the article rather than its conclusion.

Indicative: *A Comparison of Paroxetine and Clomipramine in Obsessive-Compulsive Disorder*

Informative: *Clomipramine Better Than Paroxetine in OCD*

The following are some hints from journal editors on writing effective titles:

◆ Avoid abbreviations, acronyms.
◆ Choose each word carefully. Titles provide information from computerized information storage systems. Titles also determine whether a reader stops to read an article. Think of all possible interested readers and include words to attract them.
◆ Avoid the temptation to use a title that is cute, catchy, misleading, dishonest, or too provocative.

The Abstract

Although the function of an abstract is to provide an overview of an article and to stimulate readers' interest, in fact it is often the only part of an article that is read; therefore, your purpose should be clear both to readers who read the paper and to readers who do not read the paper. Skill in writing an abstract generally translates into skill in writing the whole article.

Most medical abstracts are either indicative or informative. If you are writing a review article, you will probably want to use the indicative (descriptive) abstract. This form of abstract is a brief description of the content of the article that does not include results and conclusions; it is constructed from information derived from the background material, the problem reviewed, and the discussion. The informative (comprehensive) abstract is generally used for original research articles. This form of abstract can be either structured or unstructured and is the most common. It has four distinct parts:

1. The **Introduction** states clearly and concisely the hypothesis or question that you asked.

2. The **Methods and Materials** section states clearly and concisely what you did to answer the question you posed in the Introduction.

3. The **Results** part states clearly and concisely what you found to answer the question.

4. The **Discussion** states clearly and concisely the answer to the question.

The following are examples of each type of abstract.

Indicative or Descriptive Abstract

Otorhinolaryngology is a medical and surgical specialty requiring the use of a number of pharmaceutical products. It is vital to understand the actions, potential adverse effects, and possible drug interactions of these agents. In this article, the author reviews the four most commonly used drug classes: antihistamines, decongestants, corticosteroids, and cromolyn sodium.

Unstructured, Informative, or Comprehensive Abstract

It is now established that angiotensin-converting-enzyme inhibitors retard renal damage in patients with diabetes and hypertension. But does this protective benefit extend to diabetics who are normotensive or have borderline hypertension?

This study randomized 409 type-1 diabetics with early nephropathy to receive captopril (25 mg three times daily) or placebo and followed them for a median of 3 years. Baseline blood pressure was about 140/85 in both groups.

In a multivariate analysis that adjusted for blood pressure, captopril recipients were 43% less likely than placebo recipients to have a doubling of the initial serum creatinine level, and were 46% less likely to die or require dialysis or transplantation. Patients with more advanced renal dysfunction at baseline benefited the most from captopril.

Comment: This conclusive, landmark study shows that insulin-dependent diabetics with nephropathy should be treated with ACE inhibitors even when they are normotensive. How ACE inhibitors slow the progression of nephropathy remains unclear. Two important questions have yet to be answered: whether insulin dependent diabetics should take ACE inhibitors even before evidence of nephropathy, and whether ACE inhibitors also benefit patients with adult-onset diabetes.—*ALK* (Lewis, E. J., et al. "ACE inhibitors slow nephropathy even in normotensive diabetes." Reprinted by permission of *Journal Watch*, 1993. Dec. 1; 12(11): 81.)

Structured, Informative Abstract

Objective.—To determine the effectiveness of carcinoembryonic antigen (CEA) monitoring in detecting surgically curable recurrence of colon cancer.

Design.— Clinical data were collected from a national surgical adjuvant trial in which CEA monitoring was elective.

Setting.—Cancer centers, universities, and community clinics.

Patients.—A total of 1216 patients with resected colon cancer, 1017 (84%) of whom had CEA monitoring.

Main Outcome Measures.—Sensitivity and specificity of ECA testing for cancer recurrences and CEA-motivated diagnostic and surgical interventions and their end results.

Results.—Among 417 monitored patients with recurrence, 59% had a preceding elevation of CEA concentration. Sixteen percent of 600 patients without recurrence showed a false-positive test result. Carcinoembryonic antigen testing was most sensitive for hepatic or retroperitoneal metastasis and relatively insensitive for local, pulmonary, or peritoneal involvement. Surgical explorations were performed in 115 patients with CEA elevations, and 47 recurrences, usually hepatic, were resected with curative intent. On the other hand, 38 patients with normal CEA concentrations and 23 patients not monitored also underwent such resections—usually for pulmonary or local recurrence. Of all CEA-monitored patients, 2.3% are alive and disease free more than 1 year after salvage surgery (2.9% of those with CEA elevations and 1.9% of those with no elevations). Of patients with no CEA monitoring, 2.9% are also alive and disease free more than 1 year after salvage surgery.

Conclusions.—Cancer cures attributable to CEA monitoring are at best, infrequent. It is questionable whether this small gain

justifies the substantial cost in dollars and physical and emotional stress that this intervention may cause for patients. (Moertel,
C. G., et al. "An evaluation of the carcinoembryonic antigen (CEA)
test for patients with resected colon cancer." *JAMA,* 1993; 270: 943–947)

Note that the structured abstract uses *Objective* for *Introduction,*
Conclusion for *Discussion,* and has several parts to the Methods and
Materials. Although the headings differ, the content is the same. Most
journals limit the length of the structured abstract (usually to 250 or
fewer words). "Uniform Requirements for Manuscripts Submitted to
Biomedical Journals," which appears in every issue of *The New England
Journal of Medicine,* specifies 150 words. If no limit is stated, make your
abstract no longer than the abstracts in recent issues of the journal.

Journal editors offer the following suggestions for writing an
effective abstract:

◆ Beware of the three most common errors of all types of abstracts: (1) no clearly stated question or hypothesis, (2) too
  long, (3) too detailed.
◆ Write nonstructured abstracts as one paragraph.
◆ Use verbal signals to indicate the parts of the abstract. Example: *We hypothesized* (Introduction); *We conducted* (Methods
  and Materials); *We found* (Results); *We conclude* (Discussion).
◆ Use the present tense for the question (Introduction) and the
  answer (Discussion), past tense for what was done (Methods)
  and what was found (Result).
◆ Choose simple, concrete words. Write short sentences. For the
  sake of readers outside your specialty and foreign physicians,
  avoid jargon.
◆ Use the active voice. It's shorter and generally more clear than
  passive voice. "We found that" is clearer than "It was found that."
◆ Avoid abbreviations except commonly understood ones like DNA
  and AIDS. Abbreviations make an abstract hard to read. If you
  must use an abbreviation, define it the first time you use it.

Constructing the Abstract

In the writing seminars, we spend a good deal of time working on
abstracts. The most frequent problem we see is that ideas from one

section are put in another, for example, Discussion in Results, Methods in Introduction. Look at the following abstracts written by physicians.

Abstract 1

Colonoscopic removal of large, sessile polyps is a challenge for the endoscopist. "Piecemeal" resection with an electrocautery snare was performed in 108 patients with 132 such lesions. The mean size of the unresected polyps was 3.0 cm, and there was good correlation between endoscopic and pathologic size determinations. Complications occurred in 3.0% of polypectomies (3.8% of patients), with bleeding necessitating transfusion in 2.3% of polypectomies (2.8% of patients), and microperforation in the remainder. No patient required emergency surgery due to a complication. In 65 patients (60%), exclusively colonoscopic resection and follow-up was carried out. Of these, adenomas recurred in 28%, most of which were successfully re-resected. Nearly half of all recurrent polyps occurred after at least one negative intervening exam. Carcinoma later appeared in 17% of the recurrences despite apparent initial complete resection of a previously benign polyp. Cure was ultimately achieved in 88% of endoscopically managed patients. Surgical resection was required in 27% of patients, mostly following the initial polypectomy when invasive carcinoma was found in specimens from these patients. Ninety-one percent of cancers were favorable stage, whether discovered early or late. Follow-up colonoscopy was achieved in 77% of patients over an average of 3.7 years. Metachronous polyps were excised in 52 patients (63%), and metachronous carcinoma was diagnosed in three patients (3.6%). An aggressive regimen of surveillance colonoscopy is warranted in these patients to detect and manage local recurrences, and to remove subsequent adenomas. When performed by an experienced endoscopist, resection of large sessile adenomas is safe and effective.

Abstract 2

In this study of 60 patients with documented blunt splenic trauma, 18 patients ages 12–16 years (Group I) were preferentially managed nonoperatively while 42 patients ages 17–21 years (Group II) were preferentially managed by surgery. Comparison of Groups I and II reveals a similar distribution of patients with respect to class of splenic injury and hemodynamic status (p = 0.365 and 0.744, respectively) indicating that these are comparable groups of patients. A significantly greater number of patients were treated operatively in Group II as compared to Group I (p = 0.027) yielding an overall splenic salvage in Group I of 61.1% (11/18) versus 35.7% (15.42) in Group II. Comparison of both Groups with respect of outcome reveals a slightly higher transfusion requirement in Group II as compared to Group I which did not reach statistical significance (p = 0.150), but a significantly longer length of hospital stay in Group II as compared to Group I (p = 0.048). Comparison of treatment groups reveals those patients treated by splenorrhaphy to have the highest transfusion requirements (p = 0.003) followed by splenectomy, with those treated nonoperatively having the lowest transfusion requirements. Length of stay is not significantly different between these treatment groups. We conclude that young adults with blunt splenic trauma may be safely managed nonoperatively based on CT scan and clinical findings with no higher transfusion requirement or hospital length of stay than those managed operatively.

Abstract 3

Selective decontamination of the digestive tract with topical nonabsorbable antibiotics has been reported to prevent nosocomial infections in patients receiving mechanical ventilation, and the procedure is used widely in Europe. However, it is unclear whether selective decontamination improves survival. We conducted a randomized, double-blind multicenter study in which 445 patients receiving mechanical ventilation in 15 intensive care units were given either prophylactic nonabsorbable antibiotics (n = 220) or a placebo (n = 225). Topical antibiotics (tobramycin, colistin sulfate, and amphotericin B) or placebo was administered through nasogastric tube and applied to the oropharynx throughout the period of ventilation. The main end points were the mortality rate in the intensive care unit and the mortality rate within 60 days of randomization. A total of 142 patients died in the intensive care unit: 75 (34%) in the treatment group and 67 (30%) in the placebo group (P = 0.40), even after adjustment for factors that were either unbalanced or individually predictive of survival in the two groups (P = 0.70). Pneumonia developed in 59 patients (13%) in the intensive care unit within 30 days of enrollment in the study (33 in the placebo group and 26 in the treatment group, $P = 0.42$). Pneumonia acquired in the intensive care unit and due to gram-negative bacilli was less frequent ($P = 0.01$) in the treatment group than in the placebo group. The total charges for antibiotics were 2.2 times higher in the treatment group. Selective decontamination of the digestive tract does not improve survival among patients receiving mechanical ventilation in the intensive care unit, although it substantially increases the cost of their care. (Adapted from Gastinne, H., et al. "A controlled trial in intensive care units of selective decontamination of the digestive tract with nonabsorbable antibiotics." *The New England Journal of Medicine*, 1992; 326:594. Copyright © 1992 by the Massachusetts Medical Society. All rights reserved. Reprinted with permission.)

Notice how no section (Introduction, Methods and Materials, Results, Discussion) is clearly delineated in abstracts 1 and 2. Abstract 3, however, has clearly defined sections, so clear in fact you could easily box each one off from the other. (In fact, this abstract was published in a structured form in the *New England Journal of Medicine*.) One way to help keep each section together and complete is to use a structured format, favored today by many journals, including *JAMA, New England Journal of Medicine,* and *Annals of Internal Medicine*. Even if your final abstract will be unstructured, initially putting it into a structured form may help you organize ideas.

Frequently in the writing seminars, physicians bring in abstracts they are working on. Many of the abstracts are unstructured. We shuffle the abstracts around so everyone has someone else's abstract. I then give each participant four differently colored highlighters (yellow, pink, blue, green). I then ask physicians to read each sentence in the abstract very closely. Next, I ask them to highlight every sentence that belongs in the Introduction with the yellow highlighter, every sentence that belongs in the Methods and Materials with a pink highlighter, every sentence that belongs in the Results with the blue highlighter, and finally, every sentence that belongs in the Discussion with the green highlighter. Problems become immediately visible: a pink sentence with yellow sentences, no yellow sentences at all, or more than half the sentences in one color. If the abstract was done correctly, every sentence has a color, there are four distinct blocks of colors.

(*I*) Gentamicin is usually given three times daily for serious infections, but animal studies suggest that once daily dosing may be equally effective and less nephrotoxic. (*M*) This randomized trial compared a single dose of intravenous gentamicin (4 mg/kg once daily) with three divided doses (1.33 mg/kg 3 times daily) in 123 patients with a variety of infections. Treatment was stopped in 56 patients within 72 hours as dictated by culture results. The remaining 67 patients received a full course of gentamicin adjusted according to criteria developed by the researchers (based on serum drug levels). Most patients also initially received amoxicillin and none were neutropenic. (*R*) The two gentamicin regimens did not significantly differ in clinical or microbiological efficacy. However, significantly more patients who received thrice-daily gentamicin had a 0.5 mg/dl or greater rise in serum creatinine (24% vs 5%). The frequency of ototoxicity was similar in the two groups. (*D*) This study suggests that in serious infections, once-a-day gentamicin is less nephrotoxic and does not compromise efficacy. (Prins, J. M., et al. "Once versus thrice daily gentamicin in patients with serious infections." *Lancet*, 1993. Feb 6; 341: 335–9. Copyright © 1993 by *The Lancet Ltd.* Reprinted with permission.).

Organizing the Abstract

As you've seen, the most common problem when writing an abstract is keeping each sentence in the correct section, that is, **Introduction** (objective, hypothesis), **Methods and Materials** (design, setting, patients, interventions, outcome measures), **Results**, and **Discussion**. The more you study the abstracts you read, and the more you practice writing your own, the better you will become at organizing one. The following is an exercise we frequently use in the writing seminars to practice recognizing which sentences belong in what section of an abstract. As you read the sentences, you may notice that occasionally one sentence fits in more than one section, for example, *To determine efficacy of current MI therapy, we randomly selected 108 patients seen at the City Hospital within 12 hours of MI onset to receive angio-plasty or t-PA after treatment with aspirin and beta blockers.* This sentence has covered hypothesis, design, patients, setting, interventions.

Exercise

Read each sentence below and determine in which section or sections of the abstract it belongs. Use *I* for Introduction, *M* for Methods and Materials, *R* for Results, and *D* for Discussion.

___I___ Anxiety heightens the trauma of suturing even simple wounds in small children.

_____ **1.** We assessed efficacy using a standard depression scale.

_____ **2.** Several recent studies have shown that myocardial infarction is a major cause of perioperative morbidity and death.

_____ **3.** Normal term nulliparous patients entering labor spontaneously were randomly selected to receive either narcotic or epidural anesthesia for labor analgesia.

_____ **4.** More study is needed to determine how best to further evaluate these women with cervical atypia, and whether a more aggressive strategy is warranted.

_____ **5.** Transient ischemia was detected in 45 of the 116 patients during 48 hours of ambulatory ECG.

_____ **6.** The patients were identified from 132 eligible candidates, excluding those who were less than 13 or more than 70 years old, were morbidly obese, or had other serious medical conditions.

_____ **7.** The two gentamicin regimens did not significantly differ in clinical or microbiological efficacy, and the frequency of ototoxicity was similar.

_____ **8.** We compared 175 Japanese patients with angiographically documented coronary-artery spasm to 176 control subjects without coronary disease or inducible spasm.

_____ **9.** Some data suggest that smoking and Graves' disease are related.

_____ **10.** The tamoxifen group had slightly fewer admissions for breast cancer and immunologic disease and slightly more admissions for benign gynecological disease.

_____ 11. Midtrimester 24-hour blood pressure monitoring reliably predicts isolated intrauterine growth retardation.

_____ 12. Six institutions throughout the United States participated in the study.

_____ 13. Although a large body of literature addresses the topics of dog and human bites, there is scant information available regarding the management of these injuries to the male genitalia.

_____ 14. Complications decreased with increasing experience, to 0.98% after a surgeon's 75th procedure.

_____ 15. Using fetal SaO_2 monitoring for reassurance during nonreassuring FHR patterns may decrease unnecessary intervention.

Answers to this exercise appear at the end of this chapter.

The following examples are abstracts for (1) a result paper, (2) a methods paper, and (3) a meeting. In what ways, if any, do they differ?

Abstract for a Result Paper

The objective of the present study was to determine if patients with COPD who were taking Theo-Dur *bid* or *tid* (total dose 400 to 900 mg per day) could be safely switched to Uni-Dur, 800 mg given *qd* at bedtime. Twenty-eight patients were enrolled in the study, and 23 completed the study. The mean daily dose of theophylline prior to the study was 828 mg, while the mean dose after three weeks of Uni-Dur therapy was 783 mg. The mean serum theophylline level 10.5 + 3.6 h after the last Theo-Dur dose was 10.5 mg/L. After three weeks of Uni-Dur therapy, the mean theophylline level at 8:00 A.M. was 14.6 mg/L, while the mean theophylline level at 8:00 P.M. was 9.9 mg/L. This latter level did not differ significantly from that obtained at the start of the study 10.5 + 3.6 h after the last dose of Theo-Dur. After three weeks of Uni-Dur therapy, the peak expiratory flow rate, the FEV1, and the FVC were not significantly changed from those at the initial evaluation. Twenty-one of the 23 patients ended up receiving 800 mg Uni-Dur *qd*. From this study, we conclude that once daily theophylline dosing with Uni-Dur compared with *bid* or *tid* dosing with Theo-Dur, produces similar theophylline levels and pulmonary function, and most COPD patients who are taking 400 to 900 mg Theo-Dur daily can be managed with 800 mg Uni-Dur once daily at bedtime. (Chetty, K. G., et al. "Conversion of COPD patients from multiple- to single-dose theophylline: serum levels and symptom comparison." *Chest*, 1991; 100: 1064–1067)

Abstract for a Methods Paper

Double pigtail ureteral stents have proved to be useful adjuncts to extracorporeal shockwave lithotripsy. Although formerly introduced using a rigid cystoscope using a general anesthetic, currently, flexible cystoscope provides better results when the guidewire is passed up the ureter to the desired level with the use of local anesthesia. The cystoscope is removed and replaced by the passage of a stent that is well lubricated with a topical anesthetic agent. The ureteric stent is left in situ, two coils in the renal pelvis, with the distal end in the bladder. Roentgenographic examination provides confirmation of stent placement. Success was achieved in 30 of 34 patients. All 14 patients had successful removal of stents with the use of local anesthesia. Local anesthesia allows reduced risk. It is also a cost-effective alternative and a safe and reliable technique for the insertion and removal of double pigtail ureteric stents. (Mark, S. D., et al. "Flexible cystoscopy as an adjunct to extracorporeal shockwave lithotripsy." *British Journal of Urology*, 1990, 66: 245–247.)

Abstract for a Meeting

Title: The Effect of Intrapartum epidural analgesia on nulliparous labor: A randomized controlled prospective trial

Objective: To determine the effect of epidural analgesia in nulliparous labor on the incidence of cesarean section (CS) for dystocia

Study design: Normal term nulliparous patients entering labor spontaneously were randomized to receive either narcotic or epidural for labor analgesia. Randomization was performed in early labor. Data are reported as mean ± SD or %.

Results: $^*p < 0.05$

	Narcotic N = 45	Epidural N = 48
Cerv dilation on admit	2.5 ± 1.0	2.3 ± 1.0
Admit analgesia (min)	258 ± 204	316 ± 246
Cerv dilation at analgesia	4.1 ± 1.2	4.0 ± 1.2
First stage (min)	519 ± 279	676 ± 394*
Second stage (min)	54 ± 45	115 ± 71*
Birth weight (gms)	3416 ± 396	3467 ± 460
Visual pain score in labor	8.0 ± 2.0	3.5 ± 2.9*
Instrumental delivery	11.1%	18.8%
CS for dystocia	2.2%	16.7%*
CS for fetal distress	0	8.3%
TOTAL CS	2.2%	25%*

Conclusions: In a randomized prospective trial with nulliparous patients, epidural analgesia resulted in a significant increase in cesarean section for dystocia. Epidural provided superior pain relief.

(Thorp, J. A., Department of OB/GYN, St. Luke's Hospital and University of Missouri, Kansas City. Reprinted with permission.)

In writing any type of abstract, (results, methods, or meetings), always state concisely the question, what was done to answer the question, what was found to answer the question, and the answer to the question. Notice that in the abstract for a meeting, it is acceptable to give more details of methods than in an abstract of a paper. It is also more acceptable in a meeting abstract to display data in a table or a graph so that the reader can evaluate the validity of the work. In addition, implications are included in abstracts for meetings more often than in abstracts of papers to indicate the importance of the work. The next time you have to write an abstract, whether for a journal, presentation, or poster, try using the abstract form in Figure 2.1.

Other Formats for Medical Writing

When we consider writing for publication, we often think only in terms of research articles. But there are other types of formats physicians

Figure 2.1 Abstract Writing Form

Title (short, specific, clear)

_____

_____

Objective (a clear statement answering why the study was under-taken)

_____

_____

Methods and Materials

(a) **Design** (length of study, type of study)

_____

_____

(b) **Setting** (general community, primary care, ICU, private)

_____

_____

(c) **Participants** (clinical disorders, sociodemographic features, eligibility)

_____

_____

(d) **Main outcome measures** (experimental approach or protocol, including independent and dependent variables, essential features of interventions)

_____

_____

Results (What happened?)

_____

_____

Discussion (What is the meaning of what happened?)

_____

_____

should consider. Which format you choose will be determined by the journal and its content. For information about each format, always check specific journals.

Case Reports

The case report is one of the best ways new physician-writers can get exposed to the process of reporting research, medical writing, and publishing. It's a great way for residents to improve critical thinking skills, reading and analyzing skills, and organizational skills. But a case report should be more than just an exercise to improve these skills. A good case report should be informative and clinically useful to its readers. You, as the author, should have a clear idea of your purpose in writing the report. Edward Huth in his excellent book, *How to Write and Publish Papers in the Medical Sciences*, writes that the central point of interest in a case report is likely to be one of four kinds:

- ◆ The new or never reported disease or condition
- ◆ The unexpected association of two or more diseases or disorders that may represent a previously unsuspected causal relation
- ◆ A new and important variation from an expected pattern
- ◆ An unexpected evolution that suggests a therapeutic or adverse drug reaction (pp. 69–70)

All four kinds of case reports include the following first-level headings:

- **Introduction:** Start with a short introductory paragraph that justifies the reasons for reporting the case and states why the case is important to readers.
- **Case description:** Include participants, pertinent medical history, initial examination findings, laboratory and other diagnostic findings, and subsequent clinical events.
- **Discussion:** State why this case is significant. Assess the validity and strength of the evidence for and against the conclusion, evidence derived from both the case and relevant literature. Discuss how the conclusions are useful for clinical application or research.

Review Articles

Several months ago, a resident in California asked if I could look over a review article he had written that had just come back to him with a rejection. "I spent so much time researching the topic," he said. "I'm surprised the journal rejected it." Before reviewing the article, I asked how he came to write it. "Well," he said, "I'd just finished a grant proposal on the same topic. I got the grant, so I decided to send the review of the literature I'd done for the grant to the journal." His mistake was a common one—writing a review article from the annotated bibliography of another project.

Review articles are written to give perspective to previously published work. They can be spin-offs from grant proposals, grand rounds presentations, case presentations, poster sessions, meetings, or even from a letter the author has written to a journal; however, the author will need to tailor the content and format for a specific journal. You can't hope to photocopy sections of a grant proposal or grand rounds presentation, send it to a journal, and expect it to be published.

Before beginning a review article, decide to which journal you will submit it. Then look carefully at review articles published in that journal. Ask yourself who are the readers? What do they already know? What do they want and need to know? Try to strike a balance between essential explanations and leading-edge information. The review article must catch the interest of readers quickly, provide useful clinical information, and be understandable to those who are not experts on the topic. There are two basic types of review article:

◆ **Descriptive.** This type of review brings readers up to date on clinically useful concepts in a constantly changing field. For instance, a review entitled *Tamoxifen: Who should be taking it?* would probably discuss all the current research on tamoxifen in relation to breast cancer, osteoporosis, and heart disease.
◆ **Evaluative.** This type of review answers a specific question. For instance, *Should tamoxifen be given to women at risk for heart disease?* Chances are, you already have an opinion on the subject. Watch that your biases don't determine your choice of which articles to review and which articles to dismiss.

Before beginning work on a review article, it's a good idea to call the editors of the journal to which you plan to submit it. Ask whether the topic is suitable for their journal, and whether you, the author, have the credentials required to write such an article. Unlike the research article, there is no standard format for review articles, but each must include the following:

◆ Reasons for choosing the topic, that is, what was the question you were trying to answer?
◆ Methods and parameters used in searching the literature, for example, all *Medline* articles on tamoxifen for the last two years
◆ Rationale for article selection, that is, why did you choose to include article A and B and exclude article C?
◆ Limitations of the articles cited
◆ Conclusions, that is, what does it all mean?

Be aware the reviewers will be looking for bias on the part of the author. The review article must be an objective assessment of the literature and not just support for your opinion. It should also be a means of stimulating ideas. Because review articles are generally longer than research articles, it's a good idea to include headings. Headings help readers follow the article's content and sequence. Headings may include Introduction, Literature Search, Etiology, Epidemiology, Pathogenesis, Pathophysiology, Clinical Manifestations, Diagnosis, Treatment, Prognosis. If your review article is short, you probably won't need subheadings.

The abstract for a review article should include introduction, findings, and conclusions. The following is an example of an abstract for review article.

Although a cure for Alzheimer's disease and other related, progressive dementias has so far eluded the medical community, there is much that the clinician can do to improve the quality of life for both patient and care giver. Behavioral manifestations of dementia, such as anxiety, agitation, sleep disturbances, and depression, can be managed successfully using a carefully designed program of environmental and pharmacologic interventions. Care givers need to be advised of the wealth of community resources available for the dementia patient, as well as the necessary legal steps to take when the patient loses decision-making capabilities. The recent approval of tacrine for Alzheimer's disease patients marks the first step in the search to halt the cognitive decline that characterizes dementing illnesses. (Segal-Gidan, F. I., Chui, H. C. "Alzheimer's disease and related dementias: therapeutic options." *Clinician Reviews* 1994; 4(1):65)

Finally, a review article for a biomedical journal is as much a scientific endeavor as an original research article, and it must pass the same rigorous editorial standards. To ensure that your review meets these standards, you may want to use the following checklist before submitting your manuscript to a journal.

1. Who is your intended reader?

2. What is your purpose?

3. Does the review address a question that is relevant to this reader's clinical practice or interest? If so, how?

4. Are the questions and methods stated clearly?

5. Did you describe the explicit criteria you used to determine which articles you chose?

6. Did you include your methods for assessing the validity of the primary studies?

7. Were the primary studies free from bias?

8. Was *your* assessment of the studies free from bias? Did you include negative findings?

Case Series or Case Reviews

A frequent type of article in clinical journals reports an analysis of cases, usually a number of cases sufficient for reasonable conclusions on the variety of manifestations in a particular syndrome or disease. A well-written introduction clearly justifies the analysis and indicates the question, or questions, it aims to answer. A case series or case review may use the format of the single case report, the research paper, or the review article. Which format you choose will be based on two issues: (1) your purpose, that is, to answer a question or to merely report findings, (2) the guidelines of the journal to which you plan to submit your article. Note the difference between a case series and a case review.

> *Case series: If all of the cases have been drawn from the experience of the authors or their institutions, the term* case series *is appropriate.*

> *Case review: If some or all of the cases analyzed have been drawn from published reports, the term* case review *is appropriate.*

Editorials

It used to be that editorials were a forum for the journal editor to express his or her views. Today, editorials in biomedical journals are often short essays written by guest authors on a timely topic. Editorials are often the most influential and most interesting articles in medical journals. Unfortunately, they are generally thought not to be as prestigious as research. Academic and promotion committees often place little weight on editorials, possibly because they are cited less often than original research. Editorials are difficult to write; as a result, there is a scarcity of good models. The author must be clear, organized, convincing, and concise. A good editorial does one of the following:

- ◆ Present new information
- ◆ Summarize material in a clear and concise style
- ◆ Highlight a conflict
- ◆ Make a reasoned judgment

In most journals editorials are short enough not to need headings to subdivide text. Author's name, affiliation, and address should come at the end of the editorial. Check with specific journals to determine format and style.

Letters to the Editor

Letters to the editors are usually the best-read section of the general medical journal. Good letters are lively and succinct. You may want to write a letter to the editor commenting on a recent article or expressing a new idea. The most valuable letter, in the opinion of editors, is one that challenges, supports, or adds to published scientific articles. Spodick and Goldberg (1991) regard the exchanges of letters on published articles as a check on the peer-review system. The following are some guidelines for writing a letter to the editor:

- ◆ Decide whether the letter is just for the editor or for publication. Indicate this to the editor.
- ◆ Make only one point, and make your position absolutely clear. Cut out all unnecessary repetition and detail.
- ◆ Put your topic into perspective with two or three sentences that give the reader adequate background information.
- ◆ Make the tone of the letter objective. Avoid ranting or preaching.
- ◆ Check the journal's format in regard to references and length of letter.

If you are writing a letter that refers to a previously published article, make sure all facts, names, numbers, and quotations are accurate. The journal editor will probably give the author of the original article a chance to respond to your letter. The comment or rebuttal may be published with your letter. As always, check for grammar, punctuation, clarity, and conciseness. *Note:* Most journals do not notify the authors if their letters will not be published.

The Process of Revision

Whether you choose to write an article, letter to the editor, or case report, you should always spend adequate time in the revision process. Below is a list of steps to check whether your article is ready for the mailbox.

- ◆ Identify the purpose of every sentence.
- ◆ Identify the relationship between each sentence, each paragraph, each section. Have you used appropriate transition words to aid the reader in comprehension?
- ◆ Ask yourself, *Am I saying what I mean? Could there be any misunderstanding?*
- ◆ Delete every useless or redundant word or phrase.
- ◆ Limit the number of abstract words. Give your reader concrete, specific words.
- ◆ Look for punctuation errors, misplaced modifiers, overuse of the passive voice.
- ◆ Check figures and numbers. Does every table add up? Is every patient accounted for?
- ◆ Check to be sure you have used abbreviations and acronyms sparingly, if at all. Give your writing the jargon test: Can readers from outside your specialty or from another country understand every word?
- ◆ Check subject–verb agreement.
- ◆ Check spelling of proper names, particularly all references.
- ◆ Combine or simplify tables where necessary. Take out of the text anything that is evident in the table.
- ◆ Take a break from the writing. When you've finished writing something important, put it aside. Let it sit for a day or two, if possible. You'll come back to your copy with a fresher point of view.

Here are some hints to help proofread accurately:

- Increase the type size of your proofing copy on your computer or copy machine. Mistakes show up more easily in larger print.
- Read your work out loud. Your ears are great proofreaders. Occasionally I'll ask a physician to read me his or her manuscript. As the author reads, I generally say nothing. I don't have to. The author hears the mistakes or inconsistencies before I do. He or she might say, "That doesn't sound right." or "Let me put that sentence before the last one."
- Read your work backward (from last word of sentence to first); this overcomes the tendency of speed readers to skip syllables and words.
- Have at least one more pair of eyes proofread your paper. If you wrote it, rewrote it, edited it, and proofread it, you'll find love is blind.
- Look closely around any error you find. Mistakes seem to run in groups.

Submitting Your Manuscript

Articles based on shoddy research rarely get published. Articles based on good or mediocre science written by a principal investigator with a strong background almost always get published. Between these extremes lies the largest group of manuscripts. Some will be published; some will not. Editors refer to these manuscripts as being *in the grey zone*. All articles could be stronger if they were written better, that is, easier for the reviewer to read and to understand.

Suggestions from the Editors

- Introduce your manuscript with a cover letter, addressed to the current editor, not the one who died or retired two years ago.
- Include in the cover letter why you have selected this particular journal and suggest who might be interested in reading

the article if it is published. Show the editor that you've done your homework.

◆ Include a transfer of copyright signed by all the authors.

◆ Check the cover letter for correct spelling, grammar, punctuation. One reviewer told us that if a cover letter is filled with typos, grammatical errors, and rambling prose, he doesn't even look at the manuscript. He just sends it back to the editor with a terse note saying, "Please don't waste my time."

◆ Always read the *Instructions for Author* section in the journal to which you are submitting an article. Prepare title page, abstract, text, tables, figures, key words, and references in accordance with the journal's instructions. Several editors have told us it's a pleasure to get manuscripts from the Mayo Clinic; the manuscripts are generally well organized, appropriate for the intended journal, and formatted correctly.

◆ Check to see that all references are correct, including authors' names, dates, and page numbers.

◆ Include only tables, graphs, and charts that display data more efficiently and clearly than you can explain in the text.

◆ Make captions clear and concise so that the reader will have a quick understanding of the numbers in tables, graphs, and charts.

◆ Check every table against the text; validate points in figures; add numbers in every table or chart one last time for accuracy. Delete expressions such as *the table on the following page* or *the figure below*. When your manuscript is published tables and figures often get moved. Number each table, graph, or chart, for example, Figure 2.3.

◆ Include a list of authors' affiliations with or financial involvement in any organization with a direct financial interest in the subject discussed in the submitted manuscript. Generally, this information is confidential during the review process. If the manuscript is accepted for publication, the extent of disclosures will be determined by the editor-in-chief. If in doubt, list everything that might be considered a financial interest.

◆ Include key words for indexing. Some journals ask authors to supply a list of key words or phrases, to guide indexers in selecting terms for the journal's index. Indexing terms are sometimes printed after the abstract or after the title in the journal's table of contents. Select terms that you would look up to find your own paper and that would attract your intended readers. To select current, specific terms, use the MeSH, an acronym for medical subject headings, which are used by the National Library of Congress. You can find these medical headings in the January issue of *Index Medicus*.

Once the editor-in-chief receives your manuscript, he or she will send it to an outside consultant from the journal's referee file. Occasionally, the editor will ask the author to include the names of two or three particularly qualified reviewers who have experience in the subject of the submitted manuscript. The manuscript will be sent to one from your list and one from their list. If you are in doubt as to whether to send a list of referees, check with the journal.

Ethics in Publishing

Authorship: Will the Real Author Please Stand Up?

No discussion in the writing seminars is more heated than the one about authorship. Everyone seems to have an opinion. One thing everyone can agree on: The decision on authorship should be made *before* writing the first draft. All potential authors should agree who will be the primary author and the order of the other names on the published paper. The primary author should be responsible for setting a schedule for all authors to follow.

With the profusion of articles with 10, 12, even 15 authors, the question often comes up: What are the criteria for claims of authorship? The writer and all his friends and relatives? Although one might not know it, there are strict criteria for claims of authorship. The decisions should be guided by one central principle: Any one whose name is listed as an author should be able to publically defend every part of the article. According to the "Uniform Requirements for Manuscripts Submitted to Biomedical Journals":

> All persons designated as authors should qualify for authorship.
> The order of authorship should be a joint decision of the coauthors.

Each author should have participated sufficiently in the work to take public responsibility for the content.

Authorship credit should be based only on substantial contributions to

(a) conception and design, or analysis and interpretation of data
(b) drafting the article or revising it critically for important intellectual content
(c) final approval of the version to be published

Conditions (a), (b), and (c) must all be met. Participation solely in the acquisition of funding or the collection of data does not justify authorship. General supervision of the research group is also not sufficient for authorship. Any part of an article critical to its main conclusion must be the responsibility of at least one author.

Note: If you use the services of biostatisticians, plan to either pay them or include them on the authors' list. Biostatisticians, like physicians, are evaluated by the number of publications on their CVs.

Plagiarism, Fraud, Duplicate Publication

Any system in which advancement, fame, and fortune await a successful practitioner will tempt a certain number of individuals to cut corners.

Daniel E. Koshland, Jr.
Editor-in-Chief, *Science**

Everyone involved in the publishing process, including the author, reviewer, and editor has a responsibility to maintain the highest standards of behavior. As an author, be alert to the following:

1. **Plagiarism.** Plagiarism is the act of submitting the work of others as your own work, in whole or in part. I think much of the plagiarism that goes on is unintentional. Anyone who

---

*Reprinted with permission from D. E. Koshland, Jr., "Fraud in Science." *Science* 1987; 235 (4785): 141. Copyright © 1987 American Association for the Advancement of Science.

writes knows how easy it is to pick up the words of others. To avoid unintentional plagiarism, when you get to the writing stage, close all your books, turn over all your research notes, and tell the story in your own words. This method of writing not only helps you avoid mistakenly taking someone else's words, but also helps you locate your own "voice." Another guard against unintentional plagiarism is to keep meticulous notes.

2. **Fraud.** Fraud can take many forms. It's fraud if you fabricate a report of research in whole or in part. It's fraud if in your overzealousness you suppress data that doesn't support your hypothesis or report only the good news and omit the bad. Fraud seems to occur more frequently when individual parts of a research project take place in several laboratories without one investigator overseeing the whole process. Fraud also seems to occur more frequently when the senior personnel, often because of time constraints, delegate laboratory projects to others. If you are involved in research, in order to avoid any possibility of fraud, insist on reviewing all protocols and data. *Be aware*: Once you put your name on a report, you become both responsible and accountable for every part of that report, whether you wrote it or not.

3. **Duplicate publication.** How many times have you picked up a journal, began reading an article, and thought, *I've read this before*. If you're really curious, you may go to the library, search the literature and find the same author, with a similar title and topic, in another journal. Unless the author had informed both journals of his attempt to publish a second article, he or she would be guilty of duplicate publication. *Be aware*: If a journal unknowingly publishes a previously published article, and readers complain, the journal's editor will make a statement, in an editorial or the letters to editor column, giving the title of the offending article and listing all authors.

Responsibility of Reviewers

Authors are not the only ones who must maintain high ethical standards. Reviewers and editors have responsibilities also. As a potential reviewer, you should **not** review a manuscript

♦ if you do not have adequate time to devote to the review; you should be able to review and return the manuscript within two to three weeks
♦ if you have a conflict of interest, such as that you are working on a similar project or have financial interests related to the project
♦ if you do not feel qualified to judge the manuscript

If you accept the task of reviewing a manuscript, you will be obliged to

♦ make a duplicate copy of the mauscript on which you will write your comments and return the original manuscript to the editorial office unmarked
♦ review the manuscript fairly and consistently, using objective criteria; when writing the advice to authors, be constructive, specific, polite, and considerate
♦ report to the journal editors any questions of possible fraud, plagiarism, or duplicate publication
♦ keep all parts of the manuscript confidential; if you ask the opinion of a colleague on any part of the manuscript, inform the journal editors of the consultation
♦ obtain direct written permission from the editors and authors to cite any part of the original work
♦ obtain editorial consent to communicate directly with the authors

As for editors, they are responsible to see that each manuscript receives a confidential, expert, critical, and unbiased review, and they are expected to make public any fraudulent, plagiarized, or previously published research reports.

Answers to the exercise on pages 70–71:

1. M, 2. I, 3. M, 4. D, 5. R, 6. M, 7. R, 8. M, 9. I, 10. R, 11. D, 12. M, 13. I, 14. R, 15. D.

Chapter Three

◆

Graphics

Sometimes words are not the best way to communicate an idea. A graph, table, chart, map, or photo might inform more effectively and more economically. In medicine, however, a visual representation needs to be more than just effective; it needs to be absolutely accurate.

Anyone who has looked at enough charts and graphs, whether in a journal, textbook, poster, or presentation, knows that graphics can be used to slant or distort facts and figures. There are several shortcomings of graphics:

- ◆ Graphics are often not explicit. For the most part, charts and graphs lack the precision of plain numerical data.
- ◆ Graphics can't be quoted. Except for some broad generalities like up or down, high or low, bigger or smaller, or percentages of the whole, there is little that can be quoted.
- ◆ Graphics can be overdone. Invariably too much of anything will spoil the appetite for more. Transmit everything and you will communicate nothing.
- ◆ Charting requires know-how. Conceiving graphics is not a simple matter. Many people try but not all succeed. It takes design skill to translate raw data into visual form.

Before putting any data into visual form, ask the advice of a graphics designer or statistician. And always follow the format of individual journals and meetings.

Tips on Using Graphics for Publication

Graphics are used in biomedical articles to transmit information in a lucid, rapid, and memorable manner. If done well, they can emphasize, expand, and summarize the author's message. It is vital, therefore, that they be carefully planned. And the planning should begin very early in the writing of the article. As an author, you have several graphic formats to choose from. Attempt to strike a balance between simplicity and function. The following are suggestions to help make your graphics as effective as possible:

- ◆ Write your text around your graphic evidence. Use a minimum number of graphics. Pick only those that save long, involved explanations and help the reader better understand your message.
- ◆ Make all parts of the graphic legible. Remember the graphic may have to be reduced for publication.
- ◆ Use terms in the graphic consistent with the terms in the text. For example, don't use *nosocomial* in the text then use *hospital-acquired* in the graphic. Be consistent in format, size, and terminology.
- ◆ Aim for clarity and conciseness. The point of using a graphic is to show your reader quickly and clearly what you could have said in the text.
- ◆ Tell the reader early in the discussion that the graphic exists so that the reader can refer to it while reading.
- ◆ For the first citation, refer to the graphic by number and title. A reference to a graphic in another part of the document should include its number and general location, for example, (see Figure 6.2 in Chapter 6).
- ◆ Put the graphic as close as possible to its first mention in the text. *Note:* Raw data and supplemental material are generally placed in the appendix. If you have a graphic in an appendix, tell your reader it's there.
- ◆ Don't refer to "the table below" or "the graph on the next page." When the manuscript is printed, the table may not be below, or the graph may be several pages later.
- ◆ Use guidelines from the specific journal to number your graphics.

Tables

A table has at least two columns, a title, and a number. The title of the table should be succinct but informative. The purpose of a table is to highlight actual numbers. Use a table

- ◆ To summarize research findings, particularly in a review article or case series
- ◆ To group specific data sets to compare and relate
- ◆ To document an account of experimental procedure and result
- ◆ To enable the reader to make calculations from experimental data
- ◆ To enable the reader to reproduce the experiment

A good table is

- ◆ **Complete.** It must be understandable without detailed reference to the text.
- ◆ **Accurate.** Data in a table must not only be accurate, but also pertinent and understandable.
- ◆ **Logical.** Make groupings logical.
- ◆ **Appropriate.** Design the table to fit the format of a published article—not a slide, overhead, or poster. Always refer to the *Information for Authors* for a journal's specifications for tables.
- ◆ **Clear.** Keep the format clear and simple. Common abbreviations that are not acceptable in the text are generally acceptable in tables. If, however, you use an abbreviation that is not standard, use a footnote to explain it. Avoid using horizontal and vertical rules; they can be distracting. Capitalize only the initial letter of each word or phrase entry, and avoid using boldface or italics to indicate statistical significance. Finally, type no more than one table on each page and double space the entire table, including title, headings, and footnotes. If the whole table doesn't fit on a page, don't reduce the type size; use two pages, repeating headings. (See Figure 3.1.)

Figure 3.1 An Effective Table

Table 6-3 Percentage of People with Access to Affordable Contraception, 45 Countries

| Country | Type of Contraception | | | |
	Condoms	Pills	Male or Female Sterilization	Abortion
Argentina	50	45	2	5
Canada	100	100	100	83
China	84	84	92	92
Cuba	100	100	98	100
Egypt	84	97	53	58
Ethiopia	30	30	3	NA[a]
Guatemala	65	60	50	NA
Guinea	2	2	NA	NA
Jordan	20	30	25	NA
Kenya	58	54	21	NA
Lebanon	28	29	25	29
Nepal	9	14	29	NA
Nigeria	29	24	6	15[b]
Pakistan	39	30	3	NA
Uganda	6	22	6	NA
United States	100	90	80	78
Former USSR	20	10	NA	90

Data Source: From Population Crisis Committee, "Access to Affordable Contraception." 1991 Report on World Progress Towards Population Stabilization (Washington, D.C.: 1991: Population Crisis Committee, 1991).

[a] Method not used, or no data available.
[b] Figure is for menstrual regulation, rather than abortion.

SOURCE: P. Revelle and C. Revelle, *The Global Environment: Securing a Sustainable Future* (Boston: Jones and Bartlett Publishers, 1992), p. 144.

Graphs and Charts

Graphs of data are the most widely used means of research communication. Graphs are especially useful for showing trends, changes, and relationships between and among variables over time. If you have a choice of presenting your information in tables or graphs, choose the graph. A graph conveys the information more quickly and easily than a table. It also shows the information more impressively and memorably. Each type of graph can present information in a different way, so know what you want to say and make sure the kind of graph you select is appropriate for your message.

Pie Chart

A pie chart is used to show parts of the whole (100%). As the number of components required to constitute the sum of the circle increases, the size of each segment gets smaller. The following is a good rule of thumb: When the segments of the circle are so small that they cannot be visually differentiated from each other, there are probably too many components. Generally the size of a segment should not be less than 6 or 7 percent of the pie. When using a pie chart, have the largest piece of the pie start at the 12 o'clock position. The second largest piece should come next in a clockwise direction, and so forth. Like tables, pie charts should have brief but descriptive titles. And remember, all pieces must add up to one whole pie, 100%. (See Figure 3.2.)

Bar Chart

The bar chart measures amounts. In a bar chart the items to be compared are listed on the vertical axis and the quantity, or amount scale, is placed on the horizontal axis. The length of the bar is drawn to correspond to the item's value, or amount, on the horizontal quantity scale. The moment that a second, third, or fourth bar is entered a comparison becomes possible.

Figure 3.2 A Pie Chart

Extramural Awards Make Up 83% of the NIH Budget
Fiscal Year 1992

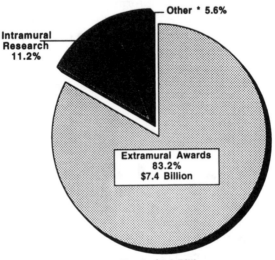

Total - $8.9 Billion

*Includes Management Costs, Buildings and Facilities, Interagency Agreements, etc.   4/9/93
Source: NIH, DRG, ISB, SAES   E1cg3

4

SOURCE: National Institutes of Health, *NIH Extramural Trends: Fiscal Years 1983–1992*
(Bethesda, MD: NIH, November 1993), p. 4.

The axis of the bar chart should include zero, and neither the
bars nor the axis should be interrupted. You can enhance differences
among bars by using shading or color. Specific types of bar graph
are illustrated in Figures 3.3 to 3.8.

- ◆ **Simple bar chart.** This is one of the most useful and widely
  used forms of graphic presentation. The simple bar chart
  compares two or more items and the bars are usually
  arranged according to magnitude of items. (See Figure 3.3.)

Figure 3.3 A Simple Bar Chart

Chart D-31
Out-of-Pocket Expenses for Prescribed Medicine per Person per Year by Population
Groups of Specified Characteristics (USA, Civilian Noninstitutionalized Population, 1980)

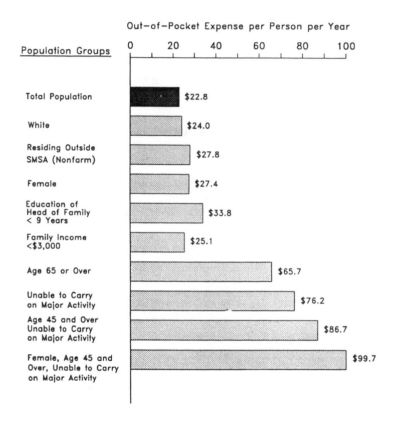

Out–of–Pocket Expense per Person per Year

Population Groups	Value
Total Population	$22.8
White	$24.0
Residing Outside SMSA (Nonfarm)	$27.8
Female	$27.4
Education of Head of Family < 9 Years	$33.8
Family Income <$3,000	$25.1
Age 65 or Over	$65.7
Unable to Carry on Major Activity	$76.2
Age 45 and Over Unable to Carry on Major Activity	$86.7
Female, Age 45 and Over, Unable to Carry on Major Activity	$99.7

Source:

National Center for Health Statistics. National medical care utilization and expenditure survey (NMCUES). Washington DC, 1980. Unpublished data based on analysis performed at the Department of Medical Care Organization, The University of Michigan.

SOURCE: L. Wyszewianski and S. S. Mick, Eds., *Medical Care Chartbook*, 9th ed. (Ann Arbor, MI: Health Administration Press, 1991), p. 141.

Figure 3.4 A Subdivided Bar Chart

Chart F-53

Percent Distribution of Home Health Visits Under the Medicare Program, by Type of
Service Provided, for Selected Types of Agencies (USA, 1976, 1982, and 1988)

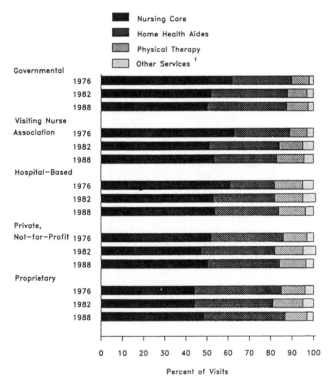

SOURCE: L. Wyszewianski and S. S. Mick, Eds., *Medical Care Chartbook*, 9th ed. (Ann
Arbor, MI: Health Administration Press, 1991), p. 271.

◆ **Subdivided bar chart.** This chart is also known as the
segmented bar or *component bar chart*. The scale values of the
subdivided bar chart are shown in absolute numbers. To
portray percentage distribution of components, the 100% bar
chart should be used. (See Figure 3.4.)

Figure 3.5 A Subdivided 100% Bar Chart

Chart E-2

Percent Distribution of Selected Health Care Practitioners, by Gender
(USA, 1986, 1988)

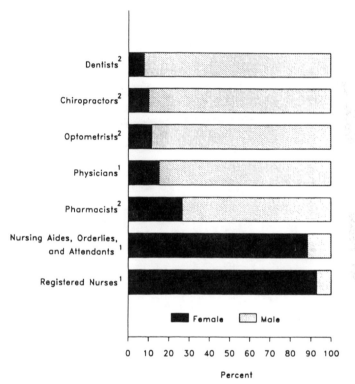

SOURCE: L. Wyszewianski and S. S. Mick, Eds., *Medical Care Chartbook*, 9th ed. (Ann Arbor, MI: Health Administration Press, 1991), p. 150.

◆ **Subdivided 100% bar chart.** This type of chart consists of segmented bars, each of which totals 100%. The various divisions of the bars represent percentages of the whole. (See Figure 3.5.)

Figure 3.6 A Grouped Bar Chart

Chart H-45
Medicaid Expenditures per Beneficiary, for Total Medicaid Beneficiaries
and by Specified Eligibility Status (USA and Selected States, 1986)

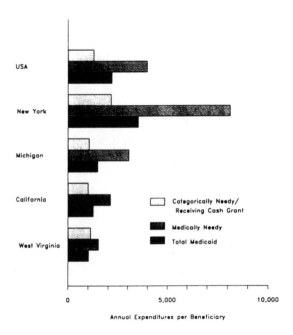

SOURCE: L. Wyszewianski and S. S. Mick, Eds., *Medical Care Chartbook*, 9th ed. (Ann Arbor, MI: Health Administration Press, 1991), p. 361.

◆ **Grouped bar chart.** This type of chart is also referred to as a *multiple* or *multiple-unit* bar chart. Comparison of items in two, and sometimes three, respects can be made on such a chart. (See Figure 3.6.)

Figure 3.7 A Deviation Bar Chart

Chart A-1
Aged Persons by Age Groups: Number and Percent of Total Population
(USA, Selected Years, 1900-2040)

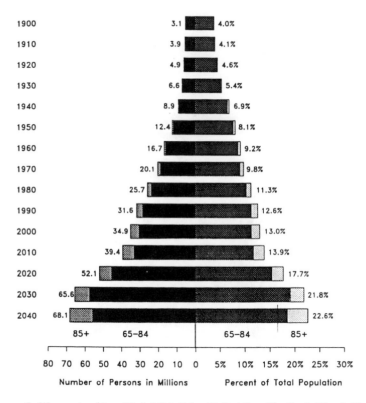

SOURCE: L. Wyszewianski and S. S. Mick, Eds., *Medical Care Chartbook*, 9th ed. (Ann Arbor, MI: Health Administration Press, 1991), p. 3.

◆ **Deviation bar chart.** In this chart, bars extend either to left or to the right of the same baseline. This type of bar chart is especially valuable for presentation of positive and negative data. (See Figure 3.7.)

Figure 3.8 A Paired-bar Chart

Chart A-7

Percent Distribution of Families, by Income Level and Race
(USA, 1987)

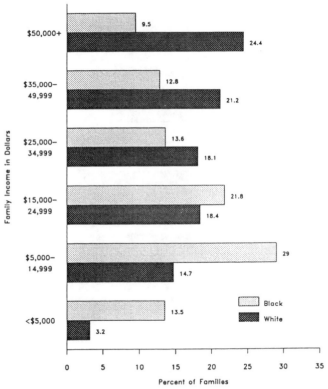

SOURCE: L. Wyszewianski and S. S. Mick, Eds., *Medical Care Chartbook*, 9th ed. (Ann Arbor, MI: Health Administration Press, 1991), p. 9.

◆ **Paired-bar chart.** This chart, along with the deviation bar chart and the sliding bar chart, is a special type of bilateral, two-way, or two-directional chart. Different units and scales can be used for each set of bars. (See Figure 3.8.)

Column Charts

The column chart has many of the same qualities as the bar graph, except for one distinct difference: The column chart is used to compare similar items at different times (time series), and the bar graph is generally used to compare different items at the same time. For example, you might choose a column chart to show the number of cases of pseudomonas aeruginosa pneumonia in Hospital X during 1985, 1986, 1987, and 1988. In contrast, you might choose a bar chart to show the number of newly diagnosed cases of pseudomonas aeruginosa pneumonia at Hospital A, Hospital B, Hospital C, and Hospital D during 1988.

A grouped-column graph can show up to three bars in each group to indicate magnitudes of different items at each time. For clarity and ease of reading, use shading for different items. If you use striped patterns to show differences, avoid optical illusions by designing all stripes at a 45-degree angle to the baseline, running from left to right. Always keep your reader in mind and make sure that the contrast among columns is distinct enough to avoid confusion. Figures 3.9 to 3.13 illustrate specific column charts.

Figure 3.9 A Simple Column Chart

Chart D-21
Percent Increase in Medical Care and Other Major Components
in the Consumer Price Index[1] (USA, 1960-1988)

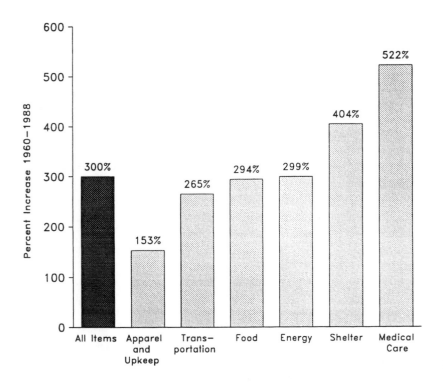

SOURCE: L. Wyszewianski and S. S. Mick, Eds., *Medical Care Chartbook*, 9th ed. (Ann Arbor, MI: Health Administration Press, 1991), p. 131.

◆ **Simple column chart.** This is a time series that compares just one item over time. The baseline is drawn horizontally, and should never be omitted. (See Figure 3.9.)

Figure 3.10 A Connected-column Chart

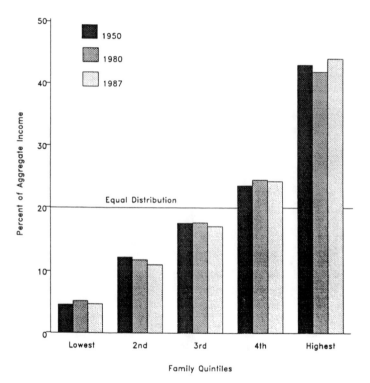

Chart A-5
Percent of Aggregate Income Received by Each Quintile of Families
(USA, 1950, 1980, and 1987)

Source: L. Wyszewianski and S. S. Mick, Eds., *Medical Care Chartbook*, 9th ed. (Ann Arbor, MI: Health Administration Press, 1991), p. 7.

◆ **Connected-column chart.** This type of chart, also known as a *staircase surface chart*, is different from the simple column chart in that there is no space between columns. The connected-column chart is particularly useful as a space-saving device. (See Figure 3.10.)

Figure 3.11 A Grouped-column Chart

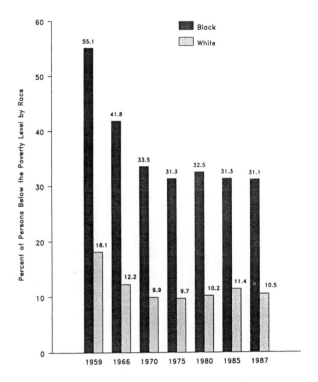

Chart A-9
Percent of Persons Below the Poverty Level by Race
(USA, Selected Years, 1959-1987)

SOURCE: L. Wyszewianski and S. S. Mick, Eds., *Medical Care Chartbook*, 9th ed. (Ann Arbor, MI: Health Administration Press, 1991), p. 11.

◆ **Grouped-column chart.** In this chart two, or occasionally three, columns representing different series or different classes in the same series can be grouped. The groups of columns may be joined or separated by narrow spaces. (See Figure 3.11.)

Figure 3.12 A Subdivided Column Chart

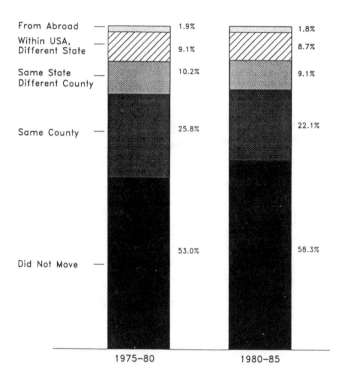

Chart A-3
Percent of Population Having Changed Residence in Two Five-Year Periods
(USA, 1975-1980 and 1980-1985)

From Abroad — 1.9% / 1.8%
Within USA, Different State — 9.1% / 8.7%
Same State Different County — 10.2% / 9.1%
Same County — 25.8% / 22.1%
Did Not Move — 53.0% / 58.3%

1975–80   1980–85

SOURCE: L. Wyszewianski and S. S. Mick, Eds., *Medical Care Chartbook*, 9th ed. (Ann Arbor, MI: Health Administration Press, 1991), p. 5.

◆ **Subdivided-column chart.** This chart shows a series of values with respect to their component parts. Shading or crosshatching is ordinarily used to differentiate the various subdivisions of the columns. (See Figure 3.12.)

Figure 3.13 A Deviation Column Chart

Chart G-22

Standardized Physician Performance Scores[1] for Episodes of Care That Included
Hospitalization, for 15 Diagnostic Categories, by Specialty Status and Domain
of Practice (Hawaii, General Hospitals, Care Initiated in 1968)

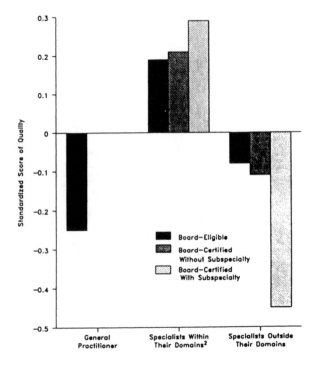

SOURCE: L. Wyszewianski and S. S. Mick, Eds., *Medical Care Chartbook*, 9th ed. (Ann Arbor, MI: Health Administration Press, 1991), p. 306.

◆ **Deviation column chart.** This chart emphasizes positive and
negative numbers, increases and decreases, and gains and
losses. In the deviation chart the column extends either above
or below the referent line, but not in both directions. (See
Figure 3.13.)

Figure 3.14 A Line Graph

Chart A-6
Median Income of Families, by Race of Family Head, in Constant 1987 Dollars
(USA, Selected Years, 1950-1987)

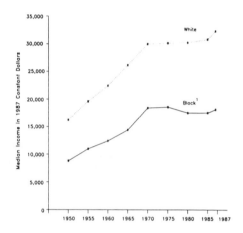

SOURCE: L. Wyszewianski and S. S. Mick, Eds., *Medical Care Chartbook,* 9th ed. (Ann Arbor, MI: Health Administration Press, 1991), p. 8.

Line Graphs

The line graph is probably the most familiar form of graphic. It's easy to design, extremely flexible, and can be adapted to a wide range of applications. The line graph, originally borrowed from mathematicians, gives a "picture" that describes relative movement of its data. Line charts are used for the simplest comparisons and for the most complex. The curve on a line chart can follow almost any pattern from a straight trend line to a fluctuating up-and-down line showing drastic changes in the data. Use a line graph when data covers a long period of time or when the emphasis is on the movement rather than on the actual amount. For example, imagine you want to emphasize how the incidence of prostate cancer increases in men over age 60. A simple line graph would be comprehensible, compelling, and memorable—certainly more so than a list of numbers in the text. (See Figure 3.14.)

Figure 3.15 A Distribution Map

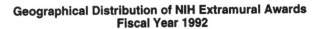

**Geographical Distribution of NIH Extramural Awards
Fiscal Year 1992**

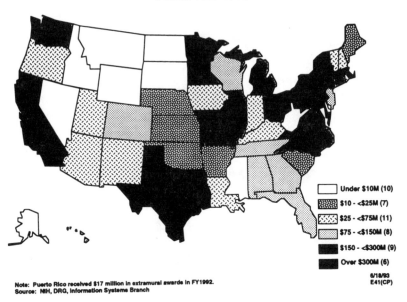

Under $10M (10)
$10 - <$25M (7)
$25 - <$75M (11)
$75 - <$150M (8)
$150 - <$300M (9)
Over $300M (6)

6/18/93
E41(CP)

Note: Puerto Rico received $17 million in extramural awards in FY1992.
Source: NIH, DRG, Information Systems Branch

SOURCE: National Institutes of Health, *NIH Extramural Trends: Fiscal Years 1983–1992*
(Bethesda, MD: NIH, November 1993), p. 92.

Distribution Maps

Maps are probably the oldest form of charting known to humans. A
distribution map displays spatial relationships of data. This type of
graphic uses tones of gray or different colors to indicate geographical areas in which various attributes are located. For example, an author might use a distribution map to show where cases of rabies in
humans have been reported. (See Figure 3.15.)

Figure 3.16 An Algorithm

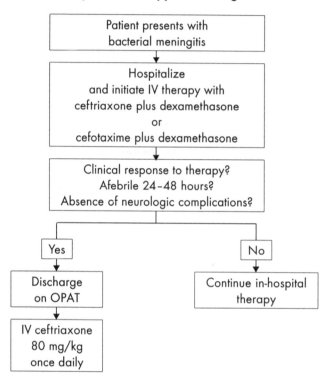

Outpatient Therapy for Meningitis

Algorithms

An algorithm is a diagram of procedures that leads, by a series of choices, to a correct answer. They are very helpful in determining the best treatment. Algorithms follow a logical sequence, left to right or top to bottom. (See Figure 3.16.)

Flow Charts

A flow chart is a diagram that displays processes or sequences. Flow charts are helpful in describing successive stages of a disease or procedure. (See Figure 3.17.)

Illustrations

An appropriate illustration can eliminate pages of text, give insights, and be an exciting and memorable part of the information. In addition to concise description, it adds interest to an article. Medical illustrations should be functional, not ornamental. Studies show that illustrations facilitate readers' understanding and retention of the accompanying text. Average readers remember only 10 percent of what they read, but 30 percent of what they see. The weakness of illustrations is that if they are poorly done (confusing, blurry, inappropriate, too ornamental), they can damage readers' understanding of the text. Obviously, the cheapest way to get an illustration or a photograph is to do it yourself. Unfortunately, the do-it-yourself approach often looks like a do-it-yourself job. If your budget dictates that you do your own illustrating, be sure to consult one of the excellent books listed in Useful Resources.

Photographs

Photographs are the best way to show exactly what something looks like. Photographs can clarify, validate, and document. For example, you may want to show X rays, photomicrographs, photographs of patients, or specimens. If you hire a professional medical photographer, meet with him or her early in the planning stage to discuss purpose and expectations. Often it helps if you can show the photographer journal examples of the kind of reproduction you want. It is also helpful to give the photographer articles related to your topic. The more he or she knows about the subject, the more likely you will get the exact photo you were planning. You will want to

Figure 3.17 A Flow Chart

Steps in Evaluation and Treatment of Osteoporosis

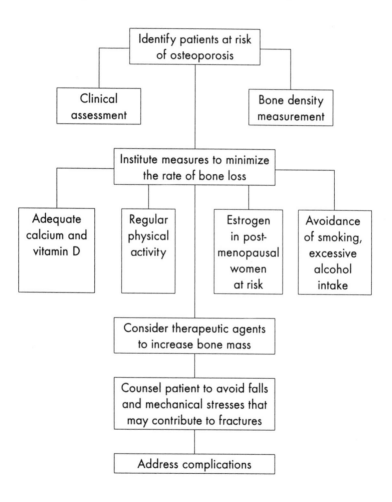

emphasize to the photographer fidelity to the original, that is, no en-
hancements or manipulations that may distort the original image.
Specify also exact directions concerning reductions.

If you plan to do your own photography, you would be wise to
consult a professional photographer about lenses, lights, films, and
filters. There are unique problems to photographing medicine, for
example, adjusting for surgical lights and reflection off tissue. When
submitting your photographs to the journal, mark on a tissue overlay or on a photocopy where you want the photo to be cropped. Do
not mark directly on the photograph.

Chapter Four

◆

Other Writing Projects

Cover Letter and Curriculum Vitae

Writing is a skill that requires training and practice. Unfortunately, many physicians don't get either. The irony is that what and how a physician writes often determines whether he or she gets a residency, a fellowship, a grant, a position, a promotion, or tenure. If a cover letter or curriculum vitae (CV) looks sloppy, because of incorrect grammar, incorrect word usage, and faulty punctuation, or is filled with spelling and typographical errors, it is unlikely the candidate will go any farther with that committee. As one physician in charge of a fellowship program said, "When I'm looking for a candidate for a fellowship, I look very carefully at his or her cover letter and CV. If either is hastily put together, filled with errors and poor grammar, I don't even consider that candidate." Patricia Hoffmeir and Jean Bohner state in *From Residency to Reality*:

> *When asked how they ever made their way through the 750 applications for the general surgeon job, every member but one of the search committee admitted having followed a two-part, rapid weeding-out process. If the cover letter contained even the slightest error or was sloppy, the application went into the "round file," the equivalent of the trash basket. If the letter was obviously a form or if it was "cute," the application went into a "probably not" pile. Said one member of the committee, "You'd be surprised at how quickly it's possible to reduce the number of applications that way. You have to wonder what they're thinking about. One guy even applied for the wrong job." (p. 79)*

Don't underestimate how your credentials are presented. Be sure to spend adequate time putting together your cover letter and CV. Readers expect them to be clear, concise, correct, and well organized. Before you begin writing, spend some time analyzing the reader or readers. For example, let's say you'd like a fellowship in Department Y. What do you know about Department Y? How many fellows do they take? Where have previous fellows come from? What are their backgrounds? Is Department Y known more for their research or for their clinical work? Do you know anyone who has trained at Department Y or who is currently working there? If so, what can they tell you about it? Is there anyone at your current institution who might know someone or something about Department Y? If so, could you make an appointment to speak with him or her?

As you answer these questions, two things will become clear. First, you will begin to have a better idea exactly what type of person Department Y is looking for. Second, you will begin to see how well you would fit into Department Y. It should be obvious that, in order to write an effective cover letter, you need to know your audience, inside and out.

Now you are ready to put pen to paper. In the cover letter, answer clearly and concisely certain questions: What is the position for which you are applying? What is it about Department Y that made you decide to apply for a fellowship there? How will the position help you? In what ways will you help Department Y? Basically, show Department Y that you know exactly what they are looking for and convince them that you are it. Before you put your cover letter and CV in an envelope to mail off, have someone who has experience reviewing cover letters and CVs review it. It will be worth the extra time it takes. Finally, remember these two rules: (1) Keep it short. A reviewer may have as many as 100 applications to read for residency or fellowship positions. (2) Avoid the temptation to sound scholarly. You'll probably end up just sounding pretentious.

For further reading on CVs and cover letters, I recommend *From Residency to Reality*, by Patricia Hoffmeir and Jean Bohner (see Useful References). It is a wonderfully down-to-earth and comprehensive guide to planning and managing your career in medicine.

Grant Applications

> *Failure is the beginning of wisdom.*
>
> William Zinsser (1988, 50)

According to the National Institutes of Health (1992), there are six primary sources of funds which amounted to over $28 billion in 1992, for research in the life sciences. Thirty-three percent (33%) of support comes from the National Institutes of Health (NIH); 12% comes from other federal sources, including the military; 45% comes from industry; 10% comes from all other sources, primarily private foundations. There are four essential elements to a grant application:

- ◆ You—the applicant
- ◆ Your sponsor or mentor
- ◆ Your research environment
- ◆ Your research project

NIH Organization

The National Institutes of Health (NIH) consist of three divisions and thirteen institutes of interest to the biomedical researcher. Proposals are initially reviewed by the Division of Research Grants (DRG), then reviewed again and funded by the appropriate institute. There are basically three types of NIH grants:

1. **Training grants:** These grants, such as the NIH Clinician-Investigator Award (KO8 series), are targeted to physicians with 2–7 years of clinical training who are interested in academic careers but lack training in appropriate basic research. Training grants usually require applicants to commit 75% or more of their time to their training effort over the course of 3–5 years. The goal is to train a clinical investigator to be capable of functioning independently. The award is made to the trainee and to the training institute.

2. **Investigator-initiated research projects:** These grants, including the NIH RO1 and R29, presuppose that the applicant is fully trained and capable of functioning independently. The award is made to the individual investigator in conjunction with his or her institution; funds can be transferred if the investigator moves to a new department.

3. **Program projects (NIH PO1 series):** Applications for these grants are submitted by senior RO1-funded investigators with established track records. A younger investigator may have the opportunity to participate as a co-investigator in a project covered by a larger program grant. The program project is developed around a unified, defined research goal encompassing a number of sound individual complementary projects that will be strengthened by being part of the overall program. Such applications are reinforced by a convincing demonstration of the significant cost savings that will accrue from creating the facilities to support the PO1-related projects. The strength and unity of the program stems from the excellence of its component projects, the focus on a common goal, and collaboration among the project investigators.

Grant writing is time- and energy-consuming work. A typical NIH grant application usually takes at least six months to be acted upon, and a well-prepared grant application can take two months to prepare. Before beginning the process, select the appropriate study section; your medical library should have a list of all agencies. Once you have determined to which study section you will submit an application, look for special announcements and selective requirements relating to it. You may even want to call the NIH section head directly to be placed on their mailing list.

Why Proposals Fail

An analysis of why applications to NIH for clinical research grants fail was made by Janet Cuca (1987) of the Division of Research Grants at the NIH. She found the reasons most grants are disapproved or receive low-priority scores are:

◆ **Experimental design.** (1) Technical methodology is questionable, unsuited, or defective, 66%. (2) Data collection procedures are confusing or use inappropriate instrumentation, timing, or conditions, 41%. (3) Study groups or controls are of inappropriate composition, number, or characteristics, 40%. (4) Data management and analysis are vague, unsophisticated, and not likely to provide accurate and clear-cut results, 31%.

◆ **Research problem.** (1) Hypothesis is ill defined, lacking, faulty, diffuse, or unwarranted, 47%. (2) Proposal is unimportant, unimaginative, or unlikely to provide new information, 30%.

◆ **Investigator.** Principal investigator lacks expertise or familiarity with literature in the research area, poor past performance or productivity on an NIH grant, or insufficient time to devote to the project, 17%.

◆ **Resources.** Inadequate institutional setting, support staff, laboratory facilities, equipment, or personnel; restricted access to appropriate patient population; insufficient collaborative involvement of colleagues and co-investigators, 4% (p. 55).

Grant reviewers offer the following suggestions to consider as you navigate your way through the grant-writing process:

◆ Request a copy of the *NIH Data Book*. It is free and lists basic data relating to the NIH. You can also get copies of the *NIH Guide for Grants and Contracts* for ideas about current interests at the NIH. This is a weekly publication and there is no charge for being on the mailing list. The address is:

> *NIH Guide for Grants and Contracts*
> NIH Distribution Center
> National Institutes of Health
> Room B3BE07
> Building 31
> Bethesda, MD 20892
> 301-496-5366

- Call the funding agency to see if your topic is considered high priority.
- Choose your PI (Principle Investigator) and co-investigator carefully. Both should have appropriate expertise and experience in grant writing. Determine early the percentage of work for which each will be responsible. Keep in mind reviewers will look very closely at the credentials of the PI, particularly prior related work, so enclose a brief CV that indicates your solid training, steady productivity, and recent publications pertinent to the proposed research. The tone should be self-confident but never arrogant.
- Design a concise, yet inclusive title. Request a copy of the titles of recently approved applications. Look closely at format and style. For an NIH grant, make sure that the title is oriented to a study section. Abstracts, like titles, need to be concise and inclusive. Wait until the proposal is complete before writing the abstract or summary. This is the section all reviewers will read, so make it well organized and logical. Reviewers will be looking for lapses in logic. In the abstract, make sure you state the exact research question you plan to answer, stressing any prior related work. Don't leave anything to the reviewers' imaginations. Although the assigned reviewers will read the proposal in detail, most of the reviewers will merely scan it, looking for red flags. Avoid the temptation to sound overly scholarly. Reviewers read hundreds of applications a year; they don't have time or patience for obtuse writing.
- Stay within the maximum page allowance. Reviewers may penalize your application for exceeding it.
- Enclose references related to the research subject or methods. You will want to convince the reviewer *you* know the most relevant and pertinent information on your research question.
- Avoid saying the PI is "to be determined later." Reviewers frown on TBA (to be announced) investigators.
- Be realistic and explicit when it comes to the budget. The average institute-wide RO1 award in 1992 was $154,900 (direct plus indirect costs). Don't pad the numbers to be on the safe side. Rather, itemize costs exactly, including animals, housing, supplies, equipment, and salaries and wages.

◆ Be wary of asking for computer hardware that is very expensive. Such a request is often a red flag to reviewers.

◆ Discuss in the Methods of Procedure your approach to answering each research question or specific aim. Organization and logic are the keys here. Describe alternatives if the initial experiments are not productive, and describe the specific roles of your consultants and collaborators. Enclose a realistic time line.

◆ Use a biostatistician if you don't fully understand statistics. A biostatistician is an excellent investment, particularly when you are designing your experiment or if the significance of your study hinges on statistical design and analysis.

◆ Include in the appendix such items as graphs, pictures, supporting data, submitted manuscripts, letters from consultants and corroborators, IRB (institutional review board) approval, and animal use forms.

◆ Make sure your references are honest and accurate. Many reviewers check them.

◆ Spend adequate time on designing diagrams in the Significance section. They should reveal at a glance the general theory, hypotheses and their tests.

◆ Avoid the temptation to pad the proposal with hundreds of pages in the appendix or lengthy biosketches of co-investigators.

◆ Type everything double spaced using no smaller than a 12-point font. Use bold for diagrams and paragraph titles for easy scanning.

◆ Be innovative, but always remain within the bounds set by proposal guidelines.

◆ Make figures attractive, clear, and simple to understand without complex legends and explanations.

◆ Remember, appearances do count. You want your proposal to stand out from all the others in the two-foot-high pile to be reviewed.

◆ Meet all deadlines for approval letters from the Human Experimentation Review Committee or letters of support from your chairperson or collaborators.

◆ Follow all directions exactly.

◆ Proofread carefully. Misspelled words, typographical errors, and poor grammar reflect a careless attitude; not something reviewers are looking for in investigators.

Both early in the process and just before submitting a grant application, ask one or two senior investigators in your institution to review it. Remember, competition for funds is fierce. If your application is not accepted, don't get discouraged. Take the lessons you have learned and apply them to the next application.

Two excellent sources of information on grant applications are *Writing a Successful Grant Application* by Liane Reif-Lehrer, Ph.D. and *Research Proposals: A Guide to Success* by Thomas E. Ogden, M.D., Ph.D. (see Useful References).

Patient Education Literature

Most physicians and their staffs would agree that patient education literature, if attractive and well written, is beneficial. If done well, patient education literature:

- **Saves time and money.** Planning, writing, rewriting, working with a designer, illustrator, and printer all take time, energy, and money. But think for a moment. How much time do you spend answering calls from patients who misunderstood your instructions or forgot to ask you a question? How many times do you see patients with repeat problems as a result of their not having finished a prescription or, worse yet, not having ever picked up the prescription? Add that amount of time to the time your staff spends taking care of these issues, and you may find the numbers are alarming. Being able to give patients information that is both accurate and readable will probably cost you less in time, money, and energy than you are already spending not using educational literature.
- **Improves compliance.** The statistics on noncompliance are startling. Vaughn Keller, a physician/patient consultant, reports that the general mean rate of noncompliance in all illnesses in the United States is about 50%. However, some believe that the figure is even higher in more serious disorders that require

profound revisions in lifestyle, such as diabetes. Patient education addresses the problem of noncompliance with the belief that informed patients are better able to cooperate in their health care, may have fewer anxieties about their conditions, and have fewer complaints about their physicians. In fact, studies have shown that good communication between patients and physicians results not only in better compliance but also in fewer malpractice cases. In short, good patient education literature is practical as well as time- and cost-effective.

♦ **Reduces patient anxiety.** Patients who come into your office bring with them a host of emotions: anxiety, apprehension, fear, confusion, anger, sadness, hopefulness. As a result of these emotions, many of them are unable to listen and comprehend what you are telling them. Consequently, many of them leave your office more confused, anxious, apprehensive, and fearful. Patient education literature, if well done, can reiterate what you have already told them, and it can be read in the safety and comfort of their own homes. Having this reinforcement of your message is particularly helpful to elderly patients, who may have short-term memory loss.

♦ **Improves public relations.** Patient education literature that is attractive and well written reflects positively on you and your staff. Patients like to take something away from their visits to the doctor. Patients feel special when they can say to their relatives and friends, "See what the doctor gave me to explain my illness."

There are basically two types of patient education literature: general office policy and specific disease states. In the **general office policy brochure**, you may want to include:

♦ **Physician information.** In this section, include your education, training, specialty, associations, awards, hospital positions, and possibly, outside activities and interests.
♦ **Philosophy.** Include a mission statement that confirms dedication to patient health and well-being.
♦ **Hours.** List your regular hours, including lunch hours and days that your office is usually closed.

- **Location.** Include a map with clear directions on how to get to your office plus parking information and fees.
- **Fees and insurance.** Explain to your patients exactly what forms to bring, whether payment is required at the time of service, and if you take credit cards.
- **Staff introduction.** Tell patients who is on your staff and exactly what each person does.

A copy of the general office policy brochure can be given to each patient as he or she comes in for an appointment. You may also want to consider mailing patients a copy *before* their first appointments. Leaving them around the office, hoping each patient will take one, is probably not the most effective way to get your message out.

The second type of patient education literature concentrates on a specific disease or condition such as the nursing mother, prostate problems, bipolar depression, or duodenal ulcers. Currently there are three sources of this type of patient education literature.

1. **Industry.** This type of literature is usually high gloss, four-color, reader friendly, and often free to you, the physician. However, it is frequently inaccurate, biased, or downright promotional.
2. **Nonprofit organizations**, like the American Cancer Society or Heart Association. The information in these brochures is often accurate but not particularly attractive, colorful, or reader friendly. They, too, are usually free.
3. **Your own tailor-made patient education literature**. The advantage of doing your own patient education literature is that you know your patients best. You know their concerns, fears, and the questions they most frequently ask. You also know how you best like to answer each of their questions, concerns, and fears. The disadvantage of writing your own patient education literature is that it will take time, money, and some staff cooperation.

What should you include in patient education literature? The answers to the questions most patients have.

- **Diagnosis.** What do I have?
- **Cause.** How might I have gotten it?

- ◆ **Incidence.** How many other people have it?
- ◆ **Symptoms.** How do you know I have it?
- ◆ **Diagnostic tests.** How can you be sure I have it?
- ◆ **Suggestions.** What can I do to relieve my symptoms?
- ◆ **Treatment options.** How are you going to make me better?
- ◆ **Medications.** Is there anything I can take to feel better? What are the common side effects of this medicine?
- ◆ **Surgical treatments.** Will I need an operation? Is it dangerous?
- ◆ **Outcome.** What can I expect?
- ◆ **Assurance.** How can I be sure I am getting the best medical attention?

Now that you have some idea exactly what to include, keep in mind some basic facts about today's readers. It is estimated that there are twenty-five million American adults who cannot read. A recent study in a public hospital found that 40% of the patient sample could read at the sixth-grade level (Walker, 1987). And many of those who do read are reading *Reader's Digest, TV Guide, People, National Inquirer,* and *USA Today.* The reading level of these publications is generally lower than ninth grade. Here are some suggestions on how to design and write patient education literature that will be read.

- ◆ **Never assume your patients are unintelligent** just because they do not read well or do not understand medical terminology. Several years ago, I wrote a weekly current affairs newsletter for men and women incarcerated in U.S. prisons. Because most of my readers were extremely streetwise, they were interested in topics such as AIDS, gangs, wars, and current movies. Easy enough, I thought—until I learned that the average reading level of a person in prison was second grade. As I wrote, I had to be constantly aware that my readers, although reading on a child's level, were not children.
- ◆ **Make it useful.** Adult learners generally tackle learning projects because they want or need the information to solve real-life problems. What's interesting to you about their condition may not be what's interesting to them. Make patient education applicable to their lives. For example, include in the literature on benign prostatic hyperplasia that, by taking

the drug you prescribe, the patient will probably be able to sleep through the night without having to go to the bathroom several times. This information is far more useful than including the complete pharmacokinetics of the drug. *Note:* For patients who want to know more about their conditions, you can include a "For further reading" section.

◆ **Keep it short.** We're already an overcommunicated society. We can't go anywhere without being bombarded with written information. Don't overload your patient with useless information.

◆ **Make it reader friendly.** Remember when you were in first grade and the teacher marched the class down to choose a book from the library in order to write a book report? Remember the book you were looking for? What did it look like? If you were like most of us, the book you chose to do a report on had lots of pictures, few pages, and big type. Design your patient education literature so that it is attractive and nonthreatening. Nothing turns off the average reader faster than a page gray with type from margin to margin and from top to bottom. You can increase your white space by using shorter paragraphs (3–5 sentences). Remember, most of your patients would rather get their information from *USA Today* than from *The Wall Street Journal*. For those patients who do prefer *The Wall Street Journal*, you have the "For further reading" section.

◆ **Use short sentences.** Keep your sentence to no more than seventeen words. When determining readability, experts use sentence length as one of the criteria—the longer the sentence, the higher the reading level.

◆ **Use short, simple, understandable words.** If you have a choice between a big word and a small word, use the small one. Readability levels are also determined by how many multisyllabic words appear in a piece of writing. The more multisyllabic words, the harder the reading. Remember to use language that your readers use and understand. *Urinate* and *void* may be perfectly acceptable to you but may not be to your patients. *Pee* may be a better word choice. If you must use a medical term, be sure to define it in simple terms.

- ◆ **Use photos, diagrams, and illustrations** whenever possible. Readers remember more what they read *and* see than what they just read.
- ◆ **Keep in mind your elderly patients.** You may have to increase your type size from 10 or 12 points to 14 points.
- ◆ **Tell a story.** Provide real-life examples of people who have problems like theirs. Use metaphors and analogies they can understand, for example, the garden hose and faucet as an analogy for hypertension.
- ◆ **Ask your patients and staff for suggestions on topics.** Patients and staff are a valuable resource when it comes to putting together useful patient education literature. You'd be surprised how many questions about medicine and symptoms your staff are getting. Ask your medical librarian to help also.
- ◆ **Proofread carefully.** Make sure spelling, grammar, and punctuation are correct.
- ◆ **Provide an opportunity for patients to discuss** what they read. People learn better when they are given the opportunity to discuss what they read. Encourage them to tell you how you can improve the next edition. Ask them if there were parts that were unclear, boring, or too elementary.
- ◆ **Never expect patient education to take the place of one-to-one dialogue.**

Posters

A poster at a scientific meeting is an enlarged graphic display containing a title, the authors' names and institutional affiliations, and text and figures explaining the research. This form of presentation was developed as a way to handle the increased size of meetings, the growing number of presenters, and the lack of time slots for slide presentations. Now those who would like to present their work, but do not want to use the ten-minute talk format, have poster sessions. Posters are a great way to stimulate dialogue among colleagues and, as a result, are becoming more and more popular even at smaller meetings and in-house symposiums.

Unfortunately, many poster presenters seem to think they can slap a written paper up on a colored piece of poster board and it will become a poster.

What Bothers You Most?

At several national and regional medical meetings, physicians were asked to give their main complaints about posters they had just viewed. Here are some of their comments.

- **Type too small or hard to read.** Solution: Use 36-point bold type for titles. Text type should be 24 to 30 points. The font should be a simple sans serif typeface, such as Helvetica. It is easy to read, does not distract from the information, and yet is appealing to the eye. Use boldface type for special emphasis, such as titles. Text that is all bold is tiring to read. It also can overshadow the figures and graphs. Test for readability by standing back five feet. If you can't read the poster, your type is too small.
- **Too much unnecessary data.** Solution: Limit your information. Get to the heart of the matter and leave out the rest. Choose two or three points and focus on them. If you want to provide details, make printed summaries for viewers who are interested in more information. The poster medium is made for graphics. Remember that posters are not enlarged papers.
- **Organized in a confusing manner**. Posters are designed like newspapers, in columns. Solution: Follow the format that is set in your instruction package from the meeting organizers. Keep in mind that we learn more quickly and easily from pictures than from words alone; use figures to tell the story and plan the poster around the figures.
- **Lack of headings.** Solution: Use headings as road signs for your viewers. Viewers want to know instantly what they are looking at.
- **Distracting glare**. Solution: Avoid lamination. Although it is great for protecting your posters, it can be a problem when reflected light makes it hard to read.

◆ **Ho-hum research.** Solution: Make sure that the material displayed in your poster is really newsworthy. Time is valuable; both yours and the viewers'.

Advantages of Posters

Poster sessions enhance collegial communication and stimulate dialogue among researchers. I think poster sessions offer several advantages over the ten-minute talk.

◆ **Posters can be studied at the viewers' leisure.** You can only be in one place at a time. Consequently, if you would like to hear the talk in Salon B at 10:00 A.M. and you are giving a talk in Salon A at 10:00 A.M., you're out of luck. Poster sessions, on the other hand, allow you to browse on your own schedule. You can spend as little or as much time on one poster as you like.

◆ **Posters offer personal contact with presenters.** If you are interested in a specific study displayed on a poster, you will have greater opportunity to talk one-to-one with the presenter than if he or she had merely given a talk on the topic. Many poster sessions have times listed when presenters will be with their posters to answer questions viewers have. This is also a good time for younger presenters–researchers to network with viewers who may be working on similar projects in other institutions.

◆ **Posters are more comprehensive and informative than a talk.** If designed well, a poster can be extremely inclusive and informative. Posters are a visual medium. If information is displayed accurately in a table or in a graph, it doesn't need to be explained in the text. Posters show rather than tell. As a result, posters can explain a good deal of data in a relatively small space.

◆ **Posters can be more memorable than a talk.** People retain more when they see the data than when they just hear it. In addition, posters can be photographed. Some people like to photograph parts or whole sections of posters. They can then retain these photos in their files. Presenters can also photograph their posters, photocopy the prints, and give them as handouts to viewers.

♦ **Posters can be fun.** Because they are a visual medium, posters offer many options from which to choose, including colors, typefaces, charts, graphs, tables, illustrations, and photographs. Just be sure you don't get too carried away. Use design principles to communicate, not dazzle.

Although there are many advantages to posters, there are a couple of limitations. First, the viewer is not comfortably seated. He or she must walk around and stand to view posters. This can be tiresome. Second, if many of the other posters are boring, viewers may not stick around to see all the posters. Try to position your poster close to the entrance.

Poster Instructions

Poster instructions, provided by meeting organizers, have information that is vital to planning, such as size, location, length of time for viewing, information to be included, and layout suggestions.

♦ **Poster size.** Careful graphic planning is the key to a successful poster. The size of the poster is the first indication of how much to limit the information. It also determines the layout. Don't assume all posters are six feet wide by four feet tall. Many are eight feet wide by four feet tall; some are four by four; others may be taller than they are wide. Check the instructions carefully. Once you know the exact dimensions, you can design a scale model layout on graph paper. Using a scale layout will save you costly mistakes along the way.

♦ **Poster session location.** I've seen poster sessions in hotel and hospital hallways, hotel ballrooms, hotel rooms, and in convention halls. Occasionally the rooms are crowded, too hot or too cold, badly lighted, noisy, or set up like mazes. Design your posters with these possible conditions in mind. Make them clear, orderly, easy to follow and to read.

♦ **Length of time for viewing**. The length of time for viewing varies, an hour being the minimum. If the poster will be up for more than a few hours, the presenter is not usually expected to be there the whole time. This means that the essential points should be clear and easily understood without personal explanations. Most people attend poster sessions the first day of the meeting. Consequently, if you are presenting a poster, and would like to talk with colleagues, make sure you are with your poster as much as possible the first few hours of the first day.

◆ **Colors.** A single background color unifies a poster and clearly distinguishes it from other posters. Gray or muted colors offer a more restful background than do bright colors. Choose matte board because it is less fragile and easier to handle than poster board. Generally matte boards come in a wider assortment of colors than do poster boards. Art supply and frame shops carry a variety of matte boards.

◆ **Typefaces and sizes.** Do not use all uppercase type. We read by recognizing shapes. If all the letters have similar shapes, it will take longer to distinguish them. Use upper- and lower-case and a sans serif type like Helvetica. Type in uneven line lengths (justify left, ragged right) to avoid gaps between letters and words. The following type sizes are for posters between 3-by-4 feet and 4-by-8 feet.

> **Titles** should be in bold type between 30 and 36 points. Select a title that will catch your reader's attention and make it clear and concise. A clear border around the title makes the title more eye-catching. Viewers should be able to read your title standing fifteen to twenty feet away.
> **Author's affiliation** should be in bold type 30 points.
> **First-level headings** should be in bold type 30 points.
> **Second-level headings** should be in bold type 24 points.
> **Body copy** should be 20 points.

◆ **Content.** Graphics should dominate. Include about fifty percent white space to show breaks between sections and help prevent the chaotic appearance of a cluttered poster. For clarity, remove all nonessential information. Edit for conciseness. Use the active voice; it's shorter and more direct. Be consistent with terms used in text and figures—don't use *parenteral therapy* in the text and *I.V. therapy* in the figure.

Essay

◆

Writing for the Lay Audience

Neil Baum, M.D.

How many referrals or new patients do you get from the publications you have written for peer-reviewed professional journals? There's a good chance that your answer will be "None." My CV lists the titles of several dozen articles that I have written for professional journals. I have not seen a single referral or a new patient as a result of these articles.

Anyone who has published in professional journals knows that an article may require hundreds of hours of time and energy. Although these efforts add to your prestige within the medical community, the return on your investment, marketingwise, is very low. Writing an article for a local magazine or newspaper, however, can generate dozens of new patients. For example, an article I wrote, "The Prostate Gland—A Gland of Pain and Pleasure," appeared in a senior citizen bulletin and generated nearly fifty office visits, five transurethral resections of the prostate (TURPs), one radical prostatectomy, and one penile prosthesis surgery.

By writing articles for local newspapers and magazines, you can effectively promote your practice and make known your areas of interest and expertise.

Why Write for the Lay Press?

Published by-lined articles in the lay press increase your visibility, your credibility, and ultimately, your profitability. People are more likely to believe what you say if you have written it down first. Statistics have

Neil Baum, M.D., is Clinical Assistant Professor of Urology at Tulane Medical Center and Louisiana State University of Medicine, New Orleans, Louisiana.

demonstrated repeatedly that when someone hears information, they retain 20% of it. However when they hear and see the information, the retention is nearly 50%.

By writing articles for the local press, you can easily become a media resource. Other reporters and editors will notice your pieces. Often they will contact you for articles or ask you for quotations to be included in articles they are writing. You can promote this relationship between you and the reporters. For example, when President Reagan had his prostate surgery, I contacted the local paper, the *Times-Picayune*, and offered to provide information about prostate surgery. Several years later, when Reagan had his colon polyps removed, the newspaper contacted me for information for a story on the operation. Because this was not my area of specialization, I contacted a colleague who was happy to be quoted as the local expert on the subject. Local newspapers are always looking for the local angle and, by offering advice and being available, you can be that resource.

How to Select a Topic

Today, topics of interest to readers in your community undoubtedly include wellness, nutrition, cancer prevention, sexually transmitted diseases such as AIDS, and sports medicine. You can create an interesting article about a new procedure, a new treatment, a unique case with an excellent result, or the use of new technologies such as lasers or shock waves.

Do some research before you select your topic. Note what medical stories receive local and national attention on television. When a public figure, such as an athlete, entertainer, or politician, has a medical problem that is making national news, you might contact the local print media and offer to serve as a local expert on the subject. In most instances, newspapers will prefer to print an article with a local twist rather than use wire service articles.

I also suggest that you study the health news section of your local newspaper. Consult national women's magazines, such as *Redbook* and *Family Circle*, which often have excellent coverage of health issues. The print media are interested in personality profiles of health-care professionals and exceptional people coping with disability, illness, or the unique circumstances surrounding an illness. Several years ago, I was involved in the urologic care of a lady from Mexico City after an earth-quake devastated many of its hospitals. As a result of the local short-age of hospitals and medical supplies, the lady came to New Orleans for her care. I contacted the newspaper about this unusual circumstance and they ran a nice article about her, our hospital, and the doctors who were involved in her care.

Ideally, you should try to select a topic that is both familiar to you and identified with your practice. Then find a new angle that will excite the readers in your community or tie the subject matter to a current event. The purpose of any article is to inform, entertain, or persuade the read-ers. The best articles will do all three. Characteristically, physicians are capable of writing to inform the reader. Your challenge will be to arrive at a style and content that elevate the information above the level of simple explanation. Articles that contain appropriate anecdotes and humor are more likely to attract and hold the reader's attention. One caution in selecting a topic: Avoid subjects that are controversial unless you're willing to take the heat.

Making a Pitch to the Editor

Of course, it helps if you know the editor of the paper or the magazine and you contact that person with your story or suggestion for a story. If this is not possible, the standard approach is the query letter—a short let-ter of introduction that contains the vital information that you want the media source to review. The query letter is sent to the decision maker, usually the editor of the magazine or paper. This letter needs to have immediate impact because editors may receive dozens of queries every day. The beginning has to have a "hook" or unique opening to attract the reader. After all, if your query letter is dry and uninteresting, how can they expect the story to be any different? One of the best hooks I ever read was a query letter by an executive from Chemwaste Corporation, a recycling company that was concerned with environmental issues. The letter began with: "It takes 75,000 trees to provide the paper for a single edition of the Sunday *New York Times*. Perhaps we should take a picture of the forests so our children can see what they look like. Better yet, if we recycle, we can preserve the trees and our children can even climb one" (Ailes, 1988). Now that beginning captures your interest and attention and motivates you to read the rest of the letter.

Start your letter with the most interesting aspect of what you want to write about. Use an eye-opening statistic such as the number of people in the community affected by the health problem that you are going to discuss. The next paragraph might describe the benefits of reading the article. The third paragraph should mention your qualifications to write the article. (In most cases, the *M.D.* after your name will qualify you.) The last paragraph offers additional information and how and when to reach you. The query letter should be no longer than one page. Figure 4.1 is a sample of a query letter.

If you are serious about getting published, the query letter is only the beginning. Unless you have a scientifically proven cure for cancer, a follow-up call is a necessary part of the getting-published game. In many cases, your query letter won't be looked at for weeks, so you need to find out if they received the information and have had a chance to look at it. If they are "still thinking about it," offer to provide additional information. Make the call short and then call back in a few weeks.

Remember, there are other print media besides the local newspaper. If you are targeting senior citizens, contact the local American Association for Retired Persons (AARP) and offer to write an article for their local newsletter. If your target is children, target parenting and children's magazines that are published in the community. Many metropolitan communities have local and regional magazines that take articles written on health-care issues. Finally, keep your eyes open for writing opportunities. For example, I was asked to give a talk at a health club on urinary tract infections. I went to the club and no one was there to hear my talk. As I was walking out, I noticed their newsletter. I asked the director if they published articles by physicians. He said no one had ever asked him before. I suggested an article on testicular examination, because the most common cause of cancer in men between the ages of 20 and 40 is cancer of the testicles. The article was published in their newsletter and went out to 5000 members between the ages of 20 and 40. It resulted in ten office consultations . . . and lots of phone calls from scared young men!

Getting Started

Once the print media is interested in your article, how do you write it? I believe the easiest way to start is to tape-record a discussion with a patient (with his or her permission, of course), in which you explain the

Figure 4.1 A Query Letter

January 25, 1996

Mr. Michael Lafavore
Executive Editor
Men's Health
Box 114
Emmaus, PA 18099-0114

Dear Mr. Lafavore:

I am a urologist in private practice in New Orleans, Louisiana. One of my areas of interest and expertise is the diagnosis and treatment of impotence.

I have written a number of articles on this subject for both professional and lay literature. I have co-authored, with Dr. Steve Wilson, a book for men and their partners entitled *ENCETOPMI: (IMPOTENCE) It's Reversible.*

Dr. Wilson and I would like to suggest an 800- to 1000-word article for your publication, *Men's Health*. We are suggesting an article that is positive and upbeat, and that reassures men that help is available for nearly all men who suffer from this problem. Our message is that, in the 1990s, "no one needs to suffer the tragedy of the bedroom."

I am enclosing my CV, several articles that I have written, and our book.

I look forward to hearing from you.

Sincerely,

Neil Baum

Neil Baum, M.D.

illness or medical problem. A grateful patient with an excellent result will often agree to provide an interview for you or the media. Any local story or visuals will bring life to the article.

A 3- to 5-minute discussion with a patient will serve as a basis for an article for most newspapers and magazines. After you have the discussion transcribed, ask the hospital marketing or public relations department to assist you in editing the article for the print media. Another resource for help is the local college or adult-education department. Either the teachers or the students will provide editing assistance at a nominal fee. Once the article is written, personally deliver it to the editor in order to establish a face-to-face relationship. If you don't hear from him or her in two weeks, follow up with a telephone call.

Writing the Article

The writing style in the article is very important. Write the article as if you were talking to your patients. To hold the reader's attention, use short sentences, short words, and short paragraphs. Avoid technical terms unless you define them. Develop an informal, relaxed style. Make it personal and use words such as *you*, *we*, and *us*. Remember *you* is the second most pleasant word in the English language. (The first is a person's own name.)

The readers want the newest information in your field, quick answers, and new ways to enhance their physical and mental health. The goal should be to seize the reader's attention quickly and maintain it while he or she reads your article.

Don't write anything you can't back up. Avoid overstating or making guarantees and false claims. As salespeople know, it is best to "underpromise and overdeliver." Failure to follow this rule can result in a deluge of calls and letters to the editor of the paper and even a loss of existing patients.

You can make an article more attractive by adding a little levity and spice. The public's perception of physicians is that we are stuffy, cold, and straitlaced. A newsletter is an opportunity to show we have a sense of humor by relating some of the funny things that happen to us in our practices.

After your article is written, have someone review and edit it for content and style. Most hospitals have public relations and marketing departments with staff members willing to do this for you. Many universities and teaching hospitals have public relations departments with a staff of freelance writers experienced in medical writing and editing. These writers can also assist you with getting your articles published.

After you write a number of articles and find that you get positive feedback and important results, consider writing a regular column for a local newspaper or magazine. I approached a local magazine, *New Orleans Health and Home*, that accepts health-related topics. I sent them four articles that appeared in other publications as samples of my writing. As a result I now have a monthly column, "Man to Man." In this column I write about the unique health-care problems of men. These articles generate dozens of calls and requests for more information.

What Do You Do with the Articles after They Have Been Published?

You can achieve additional marketing mileage from your articles long after they have been published. For example, if the articles appear in magazines and have color photographs, I have had them framed and placed on the walls of my examination rooms. I have found patients will read and appreciate these wall coverings more than any diplomas. Copies of the articles can be sent to patients with their monthly statements and to referring physicians. If you wrote the article and you have retained the copyright, you can send the articles to other publications for a second printing. Add the articles to your CV. I also have had the articles laminated in plastic and placed in a bound book in the reception area and exam rooms. I have a note on the plastic indicating that copies are available by asking the receptionist or the nurse. Finally, you can send copies to the local radio and TV stations and suggest that you be interviewed for a story on the subject. It has been my experience that you can't take an interview from the radio/TV and approach the newspapers for an article. The reverse is usually more successful. One of the advantages of writing articles is that they have a long "shelf-life" compared to radio and TV presentations to which only those who were listening or watching were exposed.

Be Prepared for Rejection

Not every suggestion you make to the media will be published. After all, Louis Lamour, the accomplished writer of western novels who published 100 books that sold more than 1 million copies each, had 350 rejections before his first piece was published. Everyone, particularly doctors, hate rejection and failure. We are programmed to get people well and to see good results. It is this obstacle that prevents many of us from seeking the print media as a method of marketing our practices. This need not be the case if we can accept the built-in rejections that are sure to come with the job of getting published. Like medical skills, writing skills can be learned and honed. The more you do, the better you get.

Part II

Speaking for Excellence

◆

Introduction

Why Do We Give Presentations?

To bore each other to sleep.

A medical resident's response to,
"Why do physicians give presentations?"

Like you, I have listened to hundreds of presentations. Few are memorable; many are dull. Most physicians learn to present by watching their peers, and the result is perpetuation of bad habits. Frequently in the speaking seminars, I ask participants what would they identify as their main speaking flaws. "Nervousness" is the most common answer. And yet, when I ask, "What bothers you most about *other people's* presentations?" the answer is "Boring." In the next few chapters, we'll look at this discrepancy between the perception of the speaker and the reaction of the audience, which, in many cases, is the reason speakers and audiences don't connect.

Giving a presentation is an anxiety-producing activity. In a national survey, Americans were asked to name their greatest fears. Speaking before a group topped the list. Death placed seventh. If public speaking is a fear greater than death, then *Why do we give presentations?* There are many reasons, including wanting to share information, gain prestige, meet a requirement, or earn some money. In truth, though, it seems many physicians give presentations because superiors require them to do so. Why? Residents frequently tell me they give presentations because most of the staff don't want to. I'm sure that's true in some cases, but I think in the majority of cases the boss has other motives in asking residents to give presentations.

141

- **Physicians need to communicate effectively.** Whether you are in academic medicine or in private practice, you will be communicating daily with colleagues, staff, and patients. In fact, communication is the most frequent procedure a physician performs. Practice is the best way to improve this skill. Like writing skills, your speaking skills can only get better the more you use and practice them.
- **Public speaking is a good exercise in "thinking on your feet."** Physicians, probably more than other professionals, need to be able to read a situation quickly and accurately, and then determine how best to proceed. Effective speakers have the ability to adapt to different situations, to react to an audience, and to be flexible.
- **An effective presentation forces presenters to know and organize their material.** I often tell physicians who teach that if they want their students to learn a subject, don't give them a quiz or test; rather, ask them to give a 15-minute presentation on the subject. Chances are the students will not only learn the material better but also retain it longer. And, in the process, they may be developing better speaking skills.

Most physicians would agree that medical speaking, like medical writing, is a neglected skill. No medical school, to my knowledge, offers students a class on presentation skills. And yet a physician's career is filled with speaking and listening situations—grand rounds, morning report, lectures, ten-minute talks, poster sessions, talks to the lay audience, and one-to-one discussions with patients and colleagues. When you consider the time and energy that go into each of these speaking efforts, and the mediocrity with which they are so often done, you may find yourself asking, *What's wrong here?* And if you haven't yet thought something might be wrong, consider these sobering figures: A one-hour presentation to 100 people represents approximately:

- 100 hours of audience time
- $10,000 worth of audience time (at $100 an hour per person)

Next time you give a one-hour talk to 100 people, ask yourself, *Was that talk worth $10,000?*

Excellence, not mediocrity, should always be your goal when giving a presentation. Physicians with excellent clinical skills would never think about being in a position where they would have to say, "I'm sorry that I'm not doing such a great job with this operation, but I really didn't have time to prepare." Yet I've listened to hundreds of speakers begin their presentations by saying, "I know some people in the back can't read my slides, but . . ."

Writing and Speaking: A Comparison

To give an effective presentation, the presenter needs to recognize the difference between communicating through writing and communicating through speaking. In many ways, writing and speaking are similar. A good presentation, like a well-written article, must be:

- ◆ Purposeful
- ◆ Audience based
- ◆ Clear
- ◆ Concise
- ◆ Accurate
- ◆ Well organized

But a speaker often has to deal with problems the writer doesn't have to worry about:

- ◆ **Poor listening skills.** Studies show that approximately 45% of an adult's day is spent listening. For many physicians the percentage is even higher. Yet many physicians have not learned to listen well. There are several causes for poor listening skills.
  1. *Lack of training.* We do more listening than speaking, reading, or writing, yet we receive almost no formal education in listening. Many people assume they are good listeners; few actually are. Listening well is a skill which must be learned and practiced.
  2. *Listening is hard work.* Most people believe that listening is a passive activity. In fact, to listen effectively requires concentration.

3.   *Competition.* Every day, we are bombarded with competing stimuli—radio, advertisements, TV, movies, reading material, family, colleagues. To cope with all the stimuli, we have learned to tune out what we think is irrelevant. Unfortunately, we often tune out important information as well. The consequences of poor listening are misunderstandings, misdiagnoses, and missed opportunities.

4.   *Speed difference.* The difference between listening speed and thinking speed creates a listening gap. The average person speaks about 135–175 words a minute, but can listen to 300–400 words a minute. Poor listeners often spend the extra time daydreaming, planning a reply to the speaker, or mentally arguing with the speaker.

5.   *Fatigue.* Listening is an active process, which requires energy. If your audience is tired, as many physicians often are, they will not be able to concentrate as well as if they were well rested.

◆ **Finite attention span of the listener.** Listening to a speaker, unlike reading a book or article, has a time limit. As you listen to a presentation, you are unable to go back over a difficult sentence or to request that an inaudible one be repeated. Likewise, there are times when the speaker makes a particularly interesting point and you would like time to jot down some notes or just ponder for a moment. Unfortunately, while you have stopped to contemplate, the speaker is galloping ahead without you.

◆ **Frequent distractions.** Anyone who has been a dinner speaker at a convention in a hotel ballroom knows first-hand about competing with external distractions: waiters clanging silverware, people talking, beepers beeping, noise from adjoining rooms, the constant hum of the air conditioner or audiovisual equipment. In addition to these external distractions, there are speaker distractions: speakers who pace, speakers who jingle their change or jewelry, speakers who constantly say *er* or *uh*. All these distractions can take the audience's attention off the purpose of the presentation. And once that attention is lost, so too is the message.

The Seven Deadly Sins of Speaking

> *The secret of being a bore is to tell everything.*
>
> Voltaire (Safire, 122)

Ask physicians who sit through medical presentations on a regular basis what their main complaint about these presentations is and you'll probably get the answer, "Boring." As a speaker, your cardinal rule should be, Never bore your audience. Easier said than done, you're thinking. Well, not necessarily. Usually the source of the audience's boredom is related to one of what I call the seven deadly sins of speaking:

1. **Not meeting the needs of the audience.** The number one complaint on medical talk evaluations is, "Not relevant to my needs or practice." Every person who walks into your presentation comes with an agenda, or questions he or she wants addressed or answered. Your goal is to find out what that agenda is and make sure you address it. The more you know about your audience, the closer you will come to meeting their needs and agenda. Unfortunately, most presenters come with an agenda or purpose totally unrelated to their audience, for example, to meet a requirement, to impress the chairperson of the department, to bulk up a CV. Keep in mind that a successful presentation is useful to the audience—not just to the presenter.

   Each audience is different; tailor-make every presentation to meet the individual needs of each audience. For instance, a talk on attention-deficit disorder to a group of school teachers should have a different focus and purpose than a talk on the same topic to a group of family practice residents, parents, or social workers.

2. **An unclear purpose.** Many presenters never set clear communication objectives. Before giving a presentation, ask yourself, *What exactly do I want to accomplish? What is my purpose? Do I need to inform, teach, stimulate, convince, motivate, or provoke?* Make sure you recognize the difference between the subject, the title, and the purpose. They are *not*

the same. For example, you may have as a subject migraine headaches. Your title might be "Migraine Headaches: Is There Any Relief in Sight?" and your purpose might be *to convince* your audience that today the drug of choice is no longer ergotamine but sumatriptan because sumatriptan offers greater relief and fewer side effects.

3. **Lack of organization.** Rambling, disorganized presentations are difficult for listeners to follow. The result: the audience tunes out. Early in your presentation, give your audience an overview of your purpose with an agenda of your main points. Then stick to it. For example: "Tonight, I'll present a five-step approach to asthma therapy in order to make your treatment decisions more efficient and appropriate." Capture the attention of your audience at the very beginning. An elderly physician I know says, "When I go to Grand Rounds, I give the speaker about 60 seconds to prove he or she is well organized and has something worth saying. If they can't convince me in 60 seconds, I turn my hearing aid off."

4. **Unnecessary information.** Voltaire was right. If you want to bore your audience, tell them everything you know. Contrary to what many people think, the reason that most presentations don't leave a lasting impression with the audience is that the speaker tries to give the audience too much, not too little, information. If you have thirty minutes to give a talk, plan to have no more than three main ideas. The best advice on preparing for a talk comes from Eugene Stead, M.D., former Chairman of the Department of Medicine at Emory University and Duke University, in a letter to a prospective visiting professor:

> *I want to remind you again that your time as speaker on October 24 is limited. In my experience, most people with a broad subject and a limited time do one of two things: either they say nothing at all, which is certainly bad, or they say so many things that the audience goes home not knowing what was said, which is equally bad. The only alternative is to select a few things which you think are really worth remembering and then say each one of them over three times. It is preferable that you not say them with the same*

*words, but there is no doubt that repetition is essential. Now hav-
ing had my say, blessings on you and do what you want to.* (Courtesy of J. Willis Hurst, M.D., from the book *The Bench and Me:
Teaching and Learning Medicine*, New York, NY: Igaku-Shoin
Medical Publishers, 1992, p. 22.)

5. **Monotonous voice and sloppy speech.** Frequently speakers are enthusiastic and excited about their topics, yet when
they get up in front of others, they are lifeless and dull. If
you're not excited about your topic, don't expect anyone
else to be. It is also common for speakers, in an effort to
impress their audiences, to use foreign words or phrases
they are not used to using. The speaker inadvertently may
use the wrong word or pronounce the word incorrectly.
Don't use words that you are not familiar and comfortable
with. Don't choose *jejune* when *childlike* will do or *au cou-
rant* when *up-to-date* will do.

6. **Unnecessary, unclear, or inappropriate visual aids.** Every
slide should have a purpose and be legible and readable—
not just to you but to everyone in the audience. All too often, speakers use slides as teleprompters. Look at each of
your slides and ask yourself, *Is this slide for me or for my
audience?* In other words, is it a speaker's slide or an audience slide? If it's a speaker's slide, get rid of it. (We'll look
at how to design an effective slide for a medical presentation in Chapter 8.)

7. **Reading your talk.** Almost always a talk will be better if it
is not read verbatim. Why? Most people read aloud poorly;
they mumble or race through the text, using no voice inflections. Readers frequently avoid eye contact, use few, if
any, body or facial gestures, and show no enthusiasm. In
short, listening to a poorly read talk is tedious and boring.
In certain instances, you will have to read your presentation. That doesn't mean, however, you won't have to prepare. Reading aloud is a skill. To do it well you will need
to practice, practice, practice. Ronald Reagan always spoke
with a script. Yet audiences rarely knew he was reading.
Years of practice and coaching made him a master at it.

Essay

Effective Presentations

David M. Albala, M.D.

To lecture well, that is, with profit to your listeners and without boring them, requires not talent alone but experience and skill.
Anton Chekhov, in "A Dreary Story"

To describe how a lecturer should set about collecting material means outlining a way of life, including the steady, ceaseless accumulation of observation from research, clinical work, and reading of related literature. Without continuous input of fresh, personally acquired information, there can be no worthwhile output in the form of instructive and lively lecturing. We all have been subjected to the fossilized lecture, delivered by a person who ceased making intellectual effort long ago, and who arouses no enthusiasm because he has none himself. His script has a musty smell and the slides are faded and dusty. Yet, enthusiasm and inquisitiveness alone are not enough either. When this lecturer tries to prepare for a talk, he may find he cannot remember exactly where he read the relevant articles, or that his interesting cases came and went without leaving behind so much as a clinical photograph or slide to demonstrate their uniqueness.

A filing system for material and a collection of personal slides are required. The easiest method of data acquisition is to always carry 5-by-7-inch filing cards and write summaries of interesting articles immediately after you read them. These summaries may be short, but the title of the paper, name of the journal, and exact location should be noted

David M. Albala, M.D., is in the Department of Urology, Loyola University Medical Center, Maywood, Illinois.

carefully for easy retrieval. Periods of regular observations and recording will be interspersed with bursts of greater activity. These should not coincide with the need to prepare an instant lecture, but should arise when accumulated facts suddenly suggest a new idea. When it is time to give a talk, a lecturer who has prepared this way will be bursting with enthusiasm and fresh facts to relate to his or her audience, and there is no better prescription for success.

A lecturer must introduce and conclude, rather than just start and stop talking. Although the beginning and the end are relatively short, they take a disproportionate time to prepare. They must be carefully composed, whereas the rest of the lecture can be, to some extent, improvised. The introduction should grip the audience and immediately arouse curiosity and attention. There are several ways to achieve this:

- A bold, challenging statement that is highly controversial may, in the course of the lecture, be qualified, explained, and altered until it becomes acceptable.
- A rhetorical question arouses interest and can be answered during the lecture.
- An informative, but little-known statement of fact that has special importance for the audience generates interest.

There are numerous variations for opening remarks, but the opening statement must be worded strongly to carry maximum impact. A lecturer should not approach a talk timidly or hide behind false modesty. Define the purpose and keep to appropriate terms of reference. Decide on a limited number of points and present them in logical sequence. Inexperienced speakers err in trying to make too many points and supporting their arguments with too much detail. Take care in selecting and arranging ideas. Technical details and masses of data that can be absorbed by a reader are confusing and out of place in a lecture. Present only the main ideas and, if necessary, references for further reading. The function of a lecture is to survey the field, arouse interest and enthusiasm, and entertain. The steady sequence of ideas should carry the theme of the lecture in much the same way that giant pylons carry high-voltage cables.

Make the point quickly in each aspect of a talk. People listen most carefully, and remember best, what is said in the first fifteen minutes. Therefore, the complex, attention-demanding material should be concentrated in the first half of the presentation, with the second half proceeding more leisurely. Look at the audience to maintain attention. Relate the number of main points presented to the time available, to the needs of the audience, and the time necessary to introduce the subject and round off the lecture. A conscientious speaker will put a great deal of effort into this work, attempting so far as possible to eliminate errors.

Just as with introductions, there are many possible endings, but it is important to make a strong finish. Never wilt or fade away. Work up to a climax and, almost automatically, a burst of spontaneous applause will follow. Talk too long and the audience remembers only that the speaker did not know when to stop. No one minds if a talk ends a few minutes early. Leave a few minutes for questions. Question time can be as testing as the lecture itself. The extent of the speaker's knowledge and the firmness of his or her conviction will be tried and probed, as will ability to stand up to a challenge or perhaps even an irritation. A good impression left by a lecture can be diminished by a poor question-and-answer session.

Slides are the most useful visual aid but they are also the most abused. Well-designed, simple slides can aid understanding enormously; conversely, overcrowded, illegible slides can be a handicap. Here are a few key points in preparing slides for an international meeting:

- ◆ Do not overcrowd.
- ◆ Avoid complex tables and graphs.
- ◆ Use special statistical slides only when appropriate.
- ◆ Use diagrams and cartoons instead of abstract illustrations.
- ◆ Use dual projection; at international meetings, the right slide should be in English and the left slide should be a simple translation in the language of the country where you are speaking.

With longer lectures, the content and personality of the lecturer is always more important than the skill of the presentation. Medical meetings proliferate and provide an increasingly valuable method of postgraduate education. Long lectures go well when speakers are clear and concise, visual aids illustrate and explain lecture points, and the discussion is forthright and constructive. Lectures in which the speakers mutter and ramble and present overcrowded, illegible, or irrelevant slides, can be painful to attend and little is learned. Keeping these guidelines in mind will help make your presentations effective and worthwhile.

Chapter Five

Preparation

There is only one real secret to success in presenting material: preparation.

Lynn T. Staheli, M.D. (1986, 40)

Subject, Audience, Purpose, and Setting

Before you write one word of your speech, or for that matter even go to the library to do your research, you need to consider your subject, audience, purpose, and setting.

The Subject

We assume that if you volunteer or are asked to give a talk, you have a good deal of knowledge about the subject. But just knowing everything there is to know about a subject isn't a guarantee that you will give a first-rate talk. In fact, one of the most frequent complaints audiences have is that the "expert" overwhelms them with either too much information or the wrong information.

Most topics in medicine are very complex: hypertension, diabetes, duodenal ulcers, bipolar disorder, cancer. These are topics, but not subjects for talks. Why not? Because to discuss each of these topics in depth, you would have to talk nonstop for about two days. To put reasonable and appropriate boundaries on topics, ask a few questions. First, if someone asks you to give the talk, ask him or her for specific objectives.

For example, let's say that a colleague, Dr. Smith, calls you and asks you to speak to a group of emergency medicine residents on the topic of subarachnoid hemorrhage. First, you will want to ask Dr. Smith several questions, not the least of which is what are *her objectives* in arranging this talk? Why did she ask you? What does she think is most important for this audience to know? You may already have some ideas about these answers, but confirm them with the person who asks you to speak.

Finally, be sure that the talk you give is the same talk that is described in the literature announcing it. People generally attend talks on the basis of the description of that talk or its title on a poster or in a brochure or program. Too frequently, what they're told they will get and what they get are two different things.

Audience

After you discuss objectives with the person who has asked you to give the presentation, go to the next question: the audience. Who are they? Without knowing something about your audience, you will have a difficult time preparing a meaningful presentation. Find out their needs and interests.

Here's an example: Dr. M is a family practice physician. He has been asked to give a 30-minute talk on depression to three very different groups: (1) members of the women's auxiliary of the hospital, (2) a group of school nurses, and (3) a group of family practice residents. Can he give the same talk? Not if he hopes to give successful talks. Each of these groups has different needs and interests. Dr. M will have to prepare each talk to meet the different needs of each audience.

Why might the members of the women's auxiliary be attending a talk on depression? To learn more about the pharmacokinetics of antidepressant drugs? Probably not. It is more likely that members of this group are interested in depression because they, or someone they know, have suffered from depression. This audience is probably more interested in knowing the answers to the following questions: What is depression? Who gets it? Is there a cure? How can I help a friend or a family member who is depressed?

For his talk to the school nurses, Dr. M may focus on the differences between depression in adults and in children, discussing the common signs and symptoms of depression in children. And finally, to the family practice residents, Dr. M might discuss sex-related differences in responsivity to antidepressants.

The more you know about the needs and interests of your audience, the more you will be able to focus your presentation. Other questions you may want to consider are:

◆ **Age.** Sometimes age is a factor in preparing your presentation. If you are giving a talk to a group of young children, choose a topic that promotes interaction or a hands-on activity. Because you will be dealing with shorter attention spans, keep the talk brief. In a talk to nursing-home residents, you may have to consider their special needs—poor vision, senility, or impaired hearing. Age of the speaker may also need to be considered. If you are a young or merely young-looking physician talking to a group of senior physicians, you may expect more skepticism than a speaker who is older.

◆ **Education or knowledge.** Sometimes this is related to age, but often not. A group of politicians is probably not going to have the same understanding of AIDS as a group of infectious disease specialists or, for that matter, a group of gay men. Know what your audience already knows, and then tell them what they want to know—not necessarily what you want them to know.

◆ **Sex.** Sex of the speaker may be a factor in some speaking situations. A female urologist may have a more difficult time eliciting questions from an all-male lay audience during a talk on impotence and its treatment than her male colleague would. Likewise, a male gynecologist might have the same problem when talking to a group of 12-year-old girls about menstruation.

◆ **Biases or beliefs.** Many topics in medicine are controversial. Know ahead of time, if possible, whether you will have opposition in the audience. The last thing most speakers want are surprises. If you know ahead of time that you might be challenged, incorporate into your presentation responses to probable objections, and you won't be caught off guard. Not long ago, just before we were to begin a writing seminar, one of the residents, with whom I had worked on a manuscript, told me to watch out for Dr. C, who was notorious for changing everyone's manuscript from the active voice to the passive voice. Sure enough as soon as the words *passive voice* came up, Dr. C wanted the floor. Because I had had a warning, I was prepared to answer each of his challenges.

◆ **Reason your audience is there.** Recently, I led a speaking seminar for residents at a large medical center in New York. The chair of the department, who had called me to arrange the seminar, had chosen a convenient time and date, given me a list of topics he wanted covered, and had told his residents the seminar was mandatory and attendance would be taken.

The night of the seminar, I was met by a sign-up sheet, fifteen tired, sullen residents, some of whom had been on call for twenty-four hours—and no chairperson. I later learned he had gone to the opera. Suffice it to say, this was a tough audience. How did I handle it? After wishing I was anywhere but there, I acknowledged their frustration at being made to attend. Second, I asked them what they wanted to know about giving a good presentation. It took a while of probing, but once I got their questions and concerns, I revised the agenda to meet *their* needs. And finally, I told them that although the seminar was scheduled for three hours, we would finish in around two hours. Telling an audience they will be getting out earlier than they thought seems to keep them more focused during the time you do have them. Interestingly, several of them stayed after the seminar ended to discuss specific topics, and the next day I got a call from the opera-attending chairperson asking me to return to do another seminar.

◆ **Size of the audience.** What you say and how you present information is directly related to the size of the audience. A presentation to ten will be different from a presentation to 300. For one thing, small groups offer more opportunity for interaction. With smaller groups, a blackboard may be the only visual aid you need. With a large group, you will probably need a microphone, lectern, slides as visual aids, and possibly a laser pointer. Any interaction will most likely be in the form of a planned question-and-answer period. However, even with a large audience of 150, I try to interact by taking the microphone off the lectern and going down into my audience. Audiences seem to like having the speaker out from behind the lectern, and I know I feel more comfortable. (We'll talk more about lecterns, microphones, and audience interaction in Chapter 6.)

◆ **Mixed audiences.** Occasionally you will have more than one audience, each with a different agenda. For example, a urology resident was competing in a speaking contest for residents in Washington, DC. She came to us for advice on how to improve her speaking skills. We talked about knowing her audience, knowing her subject, making eye contact, talking to—not lecturing at—her audience, eliminating un-necessary or cluttered slides, coming out from behind the lectern, and interacting with the audience. Before the contest, she felt prepared and confident. And how did she do? "I bombed," she said. We, who had coached her, were horrified. Had we made a mistake? Had we given her bogus advice? After listening to her description of the contest, we realized her talk was designed for the wrong audience. She had designed her talk for other residents, not for the judges. Her ratings with the audience had been high, yet her scores with the judges had been low. Probably, we should have designed a talk for the judges. The lesson we learned was that there will be times when there is more than one audience, and you will have to decide which one will be your primary focus.

◆ **An audience filled with people who know more about the subject than you do.** This is a problem many residents run into during their grand rounds presentations or their ten-minute talks at meetings. How can you handle it? Don't make the mistake of thinking that to impress this audience you will have to tell them everything you know about the subject. What you will end up with is an annotated bibliography on the topic. Rather, spend your time discriminately picking and choosing the most important and relevant points about the topic and then present them in a clear, concise, well-organized manner. You will impress this audience, and probably all audiences, more by telling them less but telling them better. If you know for certain that the author of the definitive article on the topic is going to be in the audience, mention that article, particularly if he or she is your chief.

All this advice is fine if you plan and estimate accurately. But what if you arrive at a talk and find your audience is totally different from what you expected? Unfortunately, if you're like most of the medical speakers out there, you'd probably just give the talk you had planned—and you'd be well on your way to boring your audience. The best presenters are flexible and always ready to meet the needs of their immediate audience.

Now that you have analyzed your audience, their age, sex, interests, knowledge and education level, and size, you are ready to analyze your purpose.

The Purpose

Have you ever sat in an audience, listening to a talk, and asked yourself, *Just what is the point?* In many presentations, the subject and title is clear but the purpose isn't. What is the difference between subject and purpose? The title of one of the seminars we offer is "Speaking for Excellence." The subject of the seminar is how to give an effective presentation and the purpose is twofold: (1) to convince the audience that they can and should give effective presentations and (2) to motivate them to make their presentations as excellent as all of their other medical and scientific activities.

A good purpose answers the question, What do I want my audience to do, feel, or know when they leave this room? Your answer may be, "I want *to inform* them of the five-step approach to managing hypertension," or "I want *to convince* them to use Therapy B," or "I want *to motivate* them to use the new protective equipment," or "I want *to incite* them to demand changes in hospital policy." These are audience purposes, and they are the purposes on which you want to focus. Don't confuse the audience's purpose with the speaker's purpose. Think of your last presentation. What was your purpose in giving it? Did you want another entry on your CV? Did your chief tell you to give the presentation? Did you want the $500 honorarium? These are all legitimate purposes, but they are the speaker's purposes not the audience's purposes. When planning a talk, put your own purpose on the back burner and focus your talk on the audience's purpose.

The Setting

To make your presentation successful, analyze your setting and the occasion.

- ◆ **Analyze the occasion.** If you are in academic medicine, you will probably present at a regional, national, or international meeting. Generally, at these meetings, you will be one of many speakers. If the meeting has a general theme, as many national and international meetings do, make sure that your subject and purpose relate to this theme. For example, a physician who specializes in pain management was asked to give a talk to a group of gerontologists at their annual meeting. The theme of the meeting was "Meeting the Health Care Needs of the Elderly in the 21st Century." She decided to present a new pain intensity scale she and her colleagues had devised but to modify it to meet the special needs of the elderly population.
- ◆ **Learn who or what will precede and follow your talk.** Dr. F, a young researcher from the midwest, was giving his first ten-minute presentation at an international meeting of infectious disease specialists. He was the fifth speaker of the morning. "I was fine all morning—not overly nervous or anxious. I'd done my research, planned my talk, and rehearsed many times. Then the speaker just before me got up and proceeded to give a talk that was almost identical to mine—same references, data, and figures. I panicked. I gave

the talk but it was a disaster. I kept feeling compelled to mention the earlier speaker." Knowing ahead of time who is presenting on what topics before and after you may save you from such a predicament. If I am one of several speakers, I often watch the speakers before me to get a feel for the audience.

◆ **Learn about the room, lights, and equipment.** "Does anyone here know how to work the equipment or dim these lights?" How many times have we heard that at a presentation? Then, for the next several minutes, we sit patiently while a group of people fiddle around trying to fix the lights and equipment. Make a point to arrive at the location of your presentation at least one hour before you're to speak, and make sure all the equipment you will need is there and is in working order. If you don't, you may be a victim of Murphy's Law. The slide projector won't have a bulb. The light switch will be broken. The microphone will have a buzz. One other helpful tip: If at all possible, locate the people who are in charge of equipment, learn their names, and ask where they will be if problems arise.

◆ **Learn who will be in adjoining rooms.** Find out what will be going on in the rooms around you. Will there be a meeting of the Primal Scream Association or International Yodelers? Check to see if the walls and partitions are soundproofed, then adjust your microphone accordingly. I find arriving early also allows me to arrange the room in a fashion conducive to my presentation. If there are fewer than thirty people, I arrange the room in a semicircle. A T-shape or U-shape allows more group interaction. Many times I can be found dragging tables and chairs around a room before a presentation. Arriving early also allows you to greet people as they come in. Meeting audience members ahead of time can reduce your anxiety by putting friendly, familiar faces in the crowd.

It should be clear by now that much of the preparation for a successful talk begins even before you go to the library or put ideas on paper. Look at the organizational review, Figure 5.1. Once you have answered the questions, you will be ready for the next step: Topic research.

Figure 5.1 Organization of a Presentation

What?

1. What is your subject? My subject is _____.
2. What is your title? My title is _____.

Why?

3. Why are you giving this presentation? I am giving this presentation because _____.
4. What is your purpose? My purpose is to _____.
5. Is this a "Know this" presentation (to inform or to educate)? A "Do this" presentation (to persuade, convince, motivate, or provoke)? Both?

Who?

6. Who is your audience? My audience is _____.
7. How many people will attend your presentation?
8. Where do they come from?
   a. your department
   b. your specialty
   c. your hospital
   d. around the country
   e. around the world
   f. lay people
9. Why are they attending?
   a. they were required to come
   b. CME credits
   c. they need the information to pass a test or do their jobs
   d. interest in the subject or curiosity
10. How many in the audience are familiar with the subject?
    a. most   b. about half   c. few
11. How many in the audience equal or surpass your expertise on the subject?
    a. most   b. about half   c. few   d. none

(continued)

12. Why do *you* think they need this information?
a. direct contact with them
b. what others say about them
c. general information about their interests and needs

13. Do you have an accent? Will they have difficulty understanding you?
a. too much jargon
b. too many acronyms or abbreviations
c. references to procedures, tests, diseases that are unclear
d. language, accent, or dialect differences

14. Will your talk have more information than the audience needs to hear?
a. yes   b. no   c. perhaps

15. Will your audience be present in mind and body? Is your talk
a. early morning?
b. midday?
c. just before or after a meal?
d. late in the day?
e. first or last day of the meeting?

16. How will your age, sex, background, regional accent, or training affect your credibility with this audience?

17. Does this audience have biases? Will their sex, age, region, training, or specialty affect how they respond to your message?

18. Is this audience's attendance mandatory or voluntary?

19. Will your examples be familiar to this audience? Are they generalists, specialists, interns, students, nurses?

20. List three challenging questions they might ask.

Visual Aids

21. Will you have any visual aids?
a. slides   b. overheads   c. hand-outs

23. Write a statement of purpose for each visual.

24. Are all visuals for the audience and not just for the presenter? Are you using your slides as a teleprompter?

Topic Research

> *It usually takes more than three weeks to prepare a good impromptu speech.*
>
> Mark Twain

Your research should be designed to match the *subject, purpose, audience,* and *setting* of the presentation. Once you are clear about these, you can begin a literature search to determine what has been studied and what controversies exist. While preparing for a presentation, keep careful notes on data bases, indexes, and book collections you consult.

For many physicians, the first step in preparing a presentation is writing an outline. Others, however, need a little more warming up. For them, preparing a presentation is like putting together a jigsaw puzzle. First you lay all the pieces out on a table. Next you group the pieces with similar colors. Once pieces of the same color are together, you can find pieces that interlock. Some people like to complete putting all one-color pieces together before moving to another color; others work in one color for a while and then in another color for a while. The end result is the same. Slowly, as more pieces begin fitting in their proper places, a clear picture emerges. Or, in the case of the presentation, a clear message emerges.

The following is a step-by-step procedure I often use when working one-to-one with a novice physician–presenter to prepare a typical 30-minute talk.

1. **Gather all your research** and write it up in one long rough draft. The purpose is to get all your ideas and facts laid out, even if they are disjointed. This step is similar to arranging all the pieces of the puzzle face up on the table. At this point there is no obvious picture.

2. **With a red pencil, underline three or four key points** in your rough draft. Keep in mind your audience and purpose, then write the key points, one each, on a separate piece of paper. This step is similar to arranging the puzzle pieces according to the main colors—blues, reds, yellows.

3. **Find statements, facts, statistics, and examples** in your rough draft that support your main points. List them under a key point. With your puzzle pieces arranged by similar color, you can now begin to see where pieces fit together.

4. **Evaluate the examples** you use to illustrate your main points. Do you have too many? Not enough? Your audience's time is precious; don't waste it with inappropriate anecdotes or irrelevant information. If it is irrelevant to the audience and purpose, get rid of it.

5. **Use concrete examples.** Studies show that listeners are more likely to remember facts accompanied by clear, understandable illustrations and examples. Develop colorful, audience-specific imagery, metaphors, or similes to explain difficult concepts. Relate new material to something the audience already knows. For example, if you are explaining a new procedure, compare it to the current standard procedure.

6. **Write a detailed outline.**
   - I. Introduction (approximately 10% of the time)
   - II. Body (approximately 80%)
     - A. Key point
       1. Supporting data or example
       2. Supporting data or example
       3. Significance
     - B. Key point
       1. Supporting data or example
       2. Supporting data or example
       3. Significance
     - C. Key point
       1. Supporting data or example
       2. Supporting data or example
       3. Significance
   - III. Conclusion (approximately 10%)

7. **Check for logical development and explicit transitions.** Be able to write or explain the relationship between one key point or example and another. As you go from one point

to another, make clear to the audience that you are leaving one aspect and moving to another. Let your audience know where you are going and how your new point relates to the preceding one. Use words and phrases such as *likewise, in contrast, additionally, next, finally, as a result, similarly, conversely,* and *therefore.*

8. **Mark on the outline where to use a visual aid.** Keep in mind that a visual aid should be used only when it can explain an idea more clearly or quickly than you can. For example, you could *tell* an audience the facial characteristics of infants born with fetal alcohol syndrome or you could *show* them a photograph. Likewise, you could *list* for your audience numbers and statistics about the incidence of prostate cancer or you could *show* them a simple line graph emphasizing how the incidence of prostate cancer dramatically increases each decade after age 60. Be sure to write the purpose of every visual to justify its use. Be relentless. If you can't explain why the visual is essential, don't use it. (We'll talk more about visual aids in Chapter 9.)

9. **Ask a colleague to review your outline.** Having a mentor or colleague work with you at various stages of the development process can be extremely helpful and can save time. Frequently, he or she can point out problems that you have entirely missed. Have you selected the major points? Are they logically arranged? Is there anything that isn't clear?

10. **Develop an introduction.** The function of your introduction is to clearly state your message and purpose, to outline the argument that supports it, and to prepare listeners for the detailed discussion that will follow. It should take 5–15% of the allowed speaking time. Keep in mind the 60-second hearing test—if you don't grab the audience's attention in 60 seconds, you probably don't grab it at all. The best way I know to keep the audience's attention is to tell them up front what's in it for them. For example, to a group of pulmonology fellows on the topic of antibiotic therapy for chronic bronchitis, you might begin by saying: "Would you like an antibiotic that keeps your patients out of the hospital, is safe, effective, and less expensive than current

therapy?" That introduction is going to make the audience listen. You can also begin your talk with a humorous story, a startling statement, a rhetorical question, a statistic, a reference to a previous speaker, a quotation, or a definition. Be sure to make your "hook," or opening remarks, appropriate and original. Avoid clichés and tired jokes.

11. **Develop a strong conclusion.** Many speakers have dynamite openings and a powerful, interesting message only to drop the ball at the end. You need a strong wrap-up. You've introduced them to what you're going to tell them; you've told them your message, now you need to reinforce what you've told them—and do it with a bang. If your talk is a "do this" talk, end with a call to action, such as, "If you are concerned about the inadequate security in the hospital emergency department, I urge you to sign the petition at the back of the room."

As you are doing your research, you will find more information than you can use. How can you determine what to include and what to discard? Your purpose and your audience will help you to set boundaries on the material. Without those boundaries, your subject can overwhelm you and your audience. Your goal is to be well organized, clear, concise, and to deliver your message in short, easy-to-follow segments. Again, keep in mind if you are giving a 30-minute talk, your audience will only be able to remember about three or four main ideas.

Don't be discouraged by how much information you can't include. You'll be grateful you have the information during the question-and-answer period. If there is information that you cannot include but feel would be useful to your audience for further study, you can always provide handouts with tables, charts, or a bibliography.

The Text

Always prepare a typewritten version of your presentation; a physical model you can work with. When writing your presentation, remember you are writing for the ear. There is a distinct difference between writing for the eye and writing for the ear. Information that we obtain through reading and listening is stored differently in our memories. With printed material, the eye can jump from passage to passage, then circle back and review. With the spoken word, the memory can retain only bits and pieces of information, moving forward in a strict linear fashion without an opportunity to review. As a result, the listener often has trouble recalling what was said a few moments earlier. Thus, in order to make our spoken message as clear as possible we should:

◆ **Repeat.** Tell your audience what you're going to tell them, tell them, then tell them what you told them. Why? Because the average speaker talks at a rate of 100 to 120 words a minute. We can read and think at a rate of about 800 words a minute. We listen at a top rate of 400 words a minute. So, as a presenter speaks, a listener's mind can be drifting around, occasionally coming back to the presenter. Even the most exciting speaker won't hold everyone's complete attention. In fact, it is estimated that people listen intently for only three of every ten seconds, and their minds wander for the other seven. To get your message across, you will have to say it more than once and repeat key words.

◆ **Use short sentences, familiar words, active verbs, and parallelism.** Overly long sentences can cause problems for both the listener and the speaker. Listeners get lost; speakers get breathless. Try thinking of your presentation as a talk rather than a speech. You'll sound more natural and less imposing. And again, don't try to sound overly scholarly. It usually ends up sounding pretentious. Keep in mind that the verb is the strength in the English language; use it. Instead of saying "Implementation of the plan was done on the managerial level," say "Managers implemented the plan." Finally, try parallelism: "I came. I saw. I conquered." It's extremely effective, which is why it was a favorite speaking technique of two memorable speakers, President John F. Kennedy, Jr., and the Reverend Martin Luther King, Jr.

◆ **Use signposts.** Help your reader through your talk. Use words and phrases to tell them where you are going. "There are three steps in this procedure: first . . . second . . . third . . ."

"This concludes step one. Next we will consider . . ." "Now that we have concluded the discussion on the signs of dependence on benzodiazepines, we can move on to withdrawal from benzodiazepines." Use transition words such as *in addition*, *as a result*, or *finally*.

◆ **Avoid obscure or difficult-to-pronounce words.** Don't use words or phrases with which you are not comfortable. You don't want to take the chance of bumbling and stumbling through passages, or worse, confusing or antagonizing your audience with unclear abbreviations, foreign expressions, or esoteric and confusing terms.

◆ **Use contractions.** When we speak to each other in conversation, we are always using contractions. Our ears are used to hearing them. Use them in your presentation. They will make you sound conversational, relaxed, and not so robotic.

◆ **Replace dull, abstract, or general words with exact words.** Remember that audiences will understand better and retain longer words and ideas that they can visualize. Speakers who overuse abstract or general words tend to make drab, lifeless presentations. Replace vague terms like *around 50%* or *almost half* with exact terms. And replace tired terms like *good* and *nice*, with fresher, more accurate terms. Two good word sources are *The Synonym Finder* by Rodale and *Roget's Thesaurus*. Keep in mind that you're not looking for the biggest or most impressive word, but the most precise and expressive.

Getting Ready for the Delivery

Nothing destroys a well-organized talk faster than its delivery in a mumbled monotone by a speaker who obviously wishes he or she were anywhere except on the platform. Deadly delivery, unintentional punctuation with *ah*s and *er*s, and nervous mannerisms evoke an audience reaction ranging from boredom to sympathy or embarrassment. All are obstacles that keep the audience from getting the message. Preparation and practice are the solution.

◆ **Don't memorize your talk,** unless you have a fail-safe memory. With memorization, you run the risk of forgetting a segment and staring dazedly at a roomful of confused people. There is a happy medium between reading an entire talk and memorizing it. Practicing your whole talk four or five times should make you comfortable with the material.

◆ **Use storyboards** with text on the left and commentary on the right (see Figure 5.2). On the commentary side, you can make notations like "Pause." "Smile." "Look at audience." Try to use numbered notecards instead of 8½-by-11-inch paper. Notecards are easier to handle and don't rustle when moved. Use a highlighter to mark sections you want to emphasize. Some people only need one-word cues. Recently, I attended a presentation by a physician on pleural biopsy. The audience was captivated, not because the topic is so thrilling but because the speaker was enthusiastic, knowledgeable, and entertaining. After the talk, which was twenty-five minutes long, I asked the speaker if he had used notes. He showed me one 3-by-5-inch notecard. On it was written, "Indications," "Complications," "Technique." Clearly, not all of us could, or should, go into a presentation with just one 3-by-5-inch card. But it is something to aim for.

◆ **Practice your talk** in small segments. Once you have a thorough grasp of the whole talk, practice segments separately and randomly.

◆ **Use a conversational tone.** Think of your presentation as a chat. You'll be more likely to smile, use hand gestures, and facial expressions.

◆ **Practice with a tape recorder.** Listen for fillers like *ers* or *uhs*. Listen carefully for enunciation and articulation.

◆ **Practice your presentation in the situation** you will actually be in, such as a classroom, a lecture hall, or a hotel ballroom. Practice using a lectern. One physician I know told me how he had his prepared text, left his seat for the stage, put on the microphone, placed his text on the lectern, and suddenly realized he couldn't see the words. He'd forgotten his glasses. Practice with a microphone. Hearing your voice amplified for the first time can be startling.

Figure 5.2 Example of a Storyboard

PLACE NOTES.
ATTACH MIKE.

Transplantation   SMILE BEFORE BEGINNING.

Rarely, since the first successful
kidney transplant more than
twenty-five years ago, has there
been as much anticipated ex-   EYE CONTACT.
pansion of transplant surgery's
role in treating end stage organ
failure as exists today. Projected
survival rates are improved, and   PAUSE AND LOOK
transplantation of organs other   AT AUDIENCE.
than kidneys, for example liver
and heart, is accepted as of
proven value. This expanded
role is attributed to several fac-   SHOW 1ST SLIDE.
tors: new, more selective im-
munosuppressants; improved
histocompatibility typing and
surgical technique, better pa-   PAUSE AFTER EACH SLIDE.
tient selection, earlier operative
intervention, earlier and more
accurate detection of rejection
episodes, and a better under-   MAKE EYE CONTACT.
standing of the immune rejection
mechanism.

◆ **Ask a friend to videotape you** practicing your presentation, then study the tape carefully. I don't recommend first-time speakers videotape themselves. It's too distressing and they may never get up again. However, I do suggest to speakers who have had some success in presenting that they videotape themselves. It is a great way to see how you use your hands, facial expressions, and eye contact. You can also catch distracting mannerisms that you weren't previously aware of. Recently we were videotaping a pharmacist giving a presentation. When he saw the tape he said, "I pushed my glasses up eleven times. I never knew I was doing that."

◆ **Practice. Practice. Practice.**

Helping the Natives Understand You

Many physicians in North America know English as a second language. Communication can be a problem for them, in part because many native English speakers feel awkward mentioning to someone with an accent that they don't understand what the person said. Instead, they will just smile and nod occasionally, hoping to bluff their way through a conversation or lecture. If English isn't your native language, have someone with whom you feel comfortable listen to you practice your presentation. Ask the person to jot down words or phrases that he or she has trouble understanding. Ask the person

Frequently, nonnative physicians in our speaking seminar will ask if I think attending classes in English as a Second Language at the local college would help them to be better understood. My answer is generally, "No." I have found most physicians know English. They can read it and understand spoken English. The main problems most nonnative physicians have are pronunciation and articulation. If you find that your accent and pronunciation are problems, seek the help of a speech therapist. They are trained to correct pronunciation and articulation problems. Nonnative physicians who have taken this advice have reported remarkable improvement in their ability to be understood by audiences. The following are other hints to make yourself better understood.

- ◆ Slow down. Speaking slowly allows audiences time to absorb your message.
- ◆ Repeat and rephrase.
- ◆ Tell listeners to interrupt you if they are uncertain what you said. It would not be inappropriate to say, "Occasionally people have a hard time with my accent. Please feel free to stop me and ask me to repeat or clarify."
- ◆ Ask listeners periodically "Are you able to understand me?"
- ◆ Give certain friends and associates permission to correct you. Tell them that you would appreciate their help in improving your pronunciation. One-to-one dialogue is much more beneficial than practicing with an audiotape.

One final tip comes from a physician from Ireland. Although English is her native language, she feels that when she speaks at large meetings or lectures her accent distracts audiences from listening to her message. To help them stay focused on her words and not her accent, after introducing herself and saying, "Good morning," she shows them a slide with a picture of Ireland and says, "For those of you who were wondering about my accent, I am originally from Ireland." She briefly describes the photo and then begins her talk.

Essay

◆

Effective Speaking

Howard Spiro, M.D.

To be an effective speaker, you must be confident that you know more than your audience and, at the same time, you must be careful not to talk down to your listeners. In the academic clinical circles that I frequent, it is vitally important to be up-to-date on "the literature," for there will always be one earnest young resident or practitioner who has read the latest *Lancet* or *Hospital Practice*. Inevitably, he or she will ask your opinion of some relatively recondite but recent subject. If you are quick enough, you can twist your answer to fit a question which your questioner did not ask and the audience will be none the wiser. Still, to earn the esteem of your audience, you must know your topic.

You must also focus what you want to say. Sharpen your goals. Too many medical speakers are so loaded with information and so anxious to impart everything they know that they very quickly lose the audience in a mass of detail. Decide ahead of time what three or four points you are going to make; summarize them on a slide; tell your audience at the beginning that these are your topics; and then, at the end of your talk, remind them of what you have said. In the middle of your speech you can be funny, witty, discursive, or dull, but always finish with a summary, for that is what they will remember.

Keep eye contact with some members of the audience to see whether you have their attention. If your eye meets the gaze of several members of the audience, they will fear to fall asleep. I find it useful to focus on three or four people in the first rows and talk to them, but I also try to look at people all over the auditorium. Watch an experienced

Howard Spiro, M.D., is Professor of Medicine and Director of the Program for Humanities in Medicine, Yale University School of Medicine, New Haven, Connecticut.

public speaker like a politician to see how he or she first turns to one side and then to the other. Even if they do not maintain eye contact, on television at least, they give that impression.

Be careful not to talk just to the chairperson of the group. It is disconcerting to find how many speakers direct their remarks to the head of the department. Not only does this suggest undue deference, but it impolitely prevents the head from wool-gathering! Do not direct your gaze solely at the most important person in the audience. Your talk is for everyone. You are the expert; talk to everyone in the confidence that you know your topic. The topic, by the way, ought to fill you with enthusiasm.

A good speaker has confidence that what he or she is saying is important, useful, and worth remembering. Even if you have given the same talk twenty times, it may well be new to your audience. You should show the same energy and enthusiasm as if you were giving the talk for the first time. Or at least the second. Don't be pompous, but believe in what you are saying. Don't be sententious, but recognize the importance of your words. The best teachers I have known could have recited the telephone book to an audience with such gusto that both they and the audience might think they were hearing it for the first time.

Tell the audience something old and something new. Physicians cannot remember as much as you might give them credit for and, in any case, a certain amount of repetition is the best way to teach. If you can work several new observations or studies into your talk, so much the better. Best of all, if you have some new way of looking at an old topic or some ordered way for people to remember the important points, you will be an even more effective speaker. Don't just string out a whole series of facts that could be related, but assemble your main topics and, under them, arrange the subsidiary ones, going from the big topic to the smaller ones. People remember—and appreciate—relationships in a hierarchy better than a string of unrelated points. Spending time on such lists *before* your talk is time well spent. Ask yourself why the order is the way you present it: could it be better, more logically ordered? A few important points are better than a lot of little ones.

Don't get bogged down in detail, unless you are talking to a group of experts as vitally interested in what you have to say as you are. Too often you will be talking at the end of the day to a group of weary doctors who have had a lot of stimuli during the day and are often anxious for the libations or victuals that will follow your speech. If your talk is in the morning, on the other hand, they are bright-eyed and bushy-tailed, but may be anxious to go to their work. They are usually ready to move on, especially if they have attended for compulsory CME credit or for other credentials.

Never go over fifty minutes if your talk is scheduled for an hour. No speaker who spends less time on a speech than was scheduled has ever been listed as a failure. However, you should not end what has been scheduled as a one-hour talk in thirty minutes because your audience will feel slighted and may believe that you have not prepared enough or, worse, that you have nothing to say. But allowing ten to fifteen minutes for questions, particularly if you have been contentious, is always a good idea. If you are really enthusiastic about your topic, you will probably do more teaching in the first half-hour than in the last ten or fifteen minutes of informal responses to questions.

Slides are a staple of medical talks, for uncertain reasons, but they are used to remind the audience of your main points. Do not ignore your slides but, on the other hand, do not stay glued to them. Good speakers do not read their slides, but simply point to the topics with an electric pointer that they flick off rather than wave it like a magic marker across the screen and along the wall. Learn how to suppress the pointer. Otherwise, the audience will follow it like the Pied Piper.

Do not put too much material on a slide and do not have too many slides. As I have already warned, some speakers allow their enthusiasm for a topic make them provide more information than the listener wants. Your topic may be very important to you, but light humor, repetition, and so forth are always important.

Do not underestimate your audience, but on the other hand do not overestimate them either. Everyone likes to hear a clear exposition of a difficult topic, but few will be as well-read on the topic as you are. Treat your audience like peers, but deftly give them information as if they already knew it.

You should know your topic well enough not to have to rely on a manuscript. It is all right to have one in front of you, but it should be a guide and nothing more. A good way to begin is to write out key sentences and let your tongue and mind work out the rest. But that requires practice, practice, and more practice.

Different speakers have different styles. A very good way of learning to be a fine speaker is to watch others, analyzing what they do, how they speak, and how their slides look. Don't stand behind a podium if you can possibly help it, but if you are nervous, that's okay. Be yourself; talk to people and not to the microphone and you will do fine.

I find humor essential for a speech, as essential as for life. I don't have a collection of cartoons, and I dislike the ritual joke at the beginning of a talk. But if something arch or funny occurs to me while I'm talking, I usually share it with my audience. That's not to say that I don't have some standard "one-liners," but they all come to me spontaneously during my talks. Of course, I never know how to accept the comment afterward; "That was very entertaining!"

Chapter Six

◆

Delivery

To Read or Not to Read

There will be occasions when you will have to read your talk—when you are responding to a lawsuit, when you are talking to the media on a delicate topic, or when time or the situation does not allow for advanced preparation and rehearsal. If you must read your talk, remember that reading aloud is a skill. Here are some tips on how to read more effectively:

- **Tape record yourself reading your text.** Listen carefully to how you sound. Do you sound like you're reading? If so, practice reading with more emphasis, pauses, voice modulation and inflection. Mark passages on the storyboard where you want emphasis or where you need to enunciate better.
- **Study newscasters** like Connie Chung, Tom Brokaw, Diane Sawyer, and Peter Jennings. They're all professional readers. Notice how they use inflections, pauses, modulations, facial gestures, and eye contact to show emphasis.
- **Read the text as if you are chatting** with one person instead of 30, 300, or 3000. Allow yourself to use your body for emphasis. Don't forget to smile.
- **Maintain eye contact with your audience.** When you look up from your text, don't just look straight ahead; make eye contact. The more you practice, the more you will know what the text says and you will be able to look up at the audience more frequently. Making eye contact helps relieve speaker anxiety and helps the audience stay focused on your message.

- **Write the text on the top third of the page.** That way you can keep your eyes and head up. Or use 5-by-7-inch cards. They don't rustle when moved.
- **Practice. Practice. Practice.**

The Power of Nonverbal Communication

When people leave after your presentation, they don't walk out with just information. They walk out with an *impression*. In fact, 60% of our communication is nonverbal, social anthropologists say. That means when we stand before an audience, our posture, facial expressions, voices, hand gestures, our whole body dynamics communicate more than our actual spoken words.

Voice

A person's vocal quality can be high, low, smooth, scratchy, breathy, resonant, nasal, or guttural. These vocal characteristics are based mostly on physical characteristics, but they can be changed more than most of us realize. One bright and articulate physician I know has a naturally high voice. "All through college," she said, "I rarely spoke in class. My voice was so squeaky I sounded like a whiny, little girl. Although I was an A student, who could take me seriously?" In her senior year, she began working with a voice coach. Using breathing and other exercises she was able to modify and lower the pitch of her voice. Today, she is not only a respected professor of medicine but also a much sought-after speaker. If you don't have a naturally pleasing voice, work with a voice coach, who can often be found in the music department of colleges and universities.

When you are practicing with a tape recorder, listen to your voice. Inflection, pauses, tone, and pace are important nonverbal communicators and help avoid the dreaded monotone. Here are some other tips to help make the most of your voice.

- Drink a small amount of warm water before a presentation. It will relax your vocal cords. Avoid carbonated drinks.

- ◆ Lower the tone of your voice and speak slowly to emphasize important information.
- ◆ Use pauses to let your audience absorb important information.
- ◆ Be sure to pause after a rhetorical question. It gives the audience time to formulate its own answers.
- ◆ Avoid long, rambling sentences. They tend to lose the listener and leave the speaker breathless. Use shorter sentences and don't forget to breathe.
- ◆ Avoid the common habit of letting the last words of your sentences drop. It suggests a lack of confidence or conviction. Practice emphasizing the last two or three words in a sentence.
- ◆ Avoid speeding up at the end of your presentation. The end of your talk should be the strongest part.
- ◆ Talk to your audience, not your visuals. Stand near the screen to minimize travel.
- ◆ Pause after presenting a new visual to give your audience time to react to visual information.

Finally, nervousness can alter our voices, making them higher, breathy, and quaky. Voice consultants offer easy ways to relax and keep your voice in control.

- ◆ Slow down. Nervousness tends to make us want to talk faster. Consciously slow down and enunciate each word. If you use notecards, put in one corner of the card, SLOW DOWN.
- ◆ Practice lowering the pitch of your voice. Women in particular find that nervousness makes their voices go higher and get shakier.
- ◆ Take a deep breath. Short breaths reduce voice quality.
- ◆ Relax your upper body. Shrug your shoulders; shake your arms; rotate your head.

Eyes

One book on public speaking said that to alleviate nervousness a speaker should look at the tops of audience members' heads. I can't imagine worse advice. Eye contact is good for the audience to keep them interested, but it is also important for the speaker. Think about one-to-one conversations you have. Are you nervous? Do your palms sweat? Does your heart pound? Does your mouth go dry? Probably not. Why then when you get up in front of thirty people do you become nervous? Having talked to hundreds of speakers and having sat through hundreds of presentations, I have found a speaker's failure to make eye contact with the audience is one of the main contributors to audience boredom and speaker nervousness.

When we talk one-to-one with someone, we watch our listener's gestures, eyes, and face for clues. Frowns tell us they may be confused. Raised eyebrows tell us they are shocked or surprised. Crossed arms tell us they may be skeptical. Smiles tell us we're doing okay, and nods tell us we are being understood. With these clues, we can determine whether to slow down, speed up, emphasize a point, or skip an example. Watching the audience keeps the speaker tuned into their needs. Without these critical audience clues, we might as well be free-falling. Experienced speakers, as well as inexperienced speakers, will tell you one of the most disconcerting experiences is to be standing at a lectern in front of hundreds of people when the house lights go off and the spotlight goes on. It is terrifying to suddenly lose contact with your audience. That's why, even when I'm using slides, I keep some of the house lights on so I can see my audience. You will find, paradoxically, audiences without faces are far more frightening than audiences with faces.

Eye contact has another benefit. It's a long-held belief that the honest person has a tendency to look you straight in the eye when speaking. Recent research suggests some scientific basis for this belief. Speakers who were rated as "sincere" looked at their audiences an average of three times longer than speakers who were rated as "insincere." Studies have also shown that people are inclined to avoid eye contact when they are uncomfortable or feel threatened. Keep this in mind during the question-and-answer session. Should you be asked a difficult or hostile question, make every effort to maintain eye contact with the audience. Also be aware of whether you tend to look more to one side (are a "right-looker" or a "left-looker"), and be sure to look occasionally at the other side of the audience.

Body

Posture, gestures, and facial expressions all effect the outcome of your presentation. First impressions do count. However, if you are well prepared and enthusiastic about your topic, body gestures will come automatically and naturally. Once you have given several successful presentations, have someone videotape you. You will quickly see distracting gestures or mannerisms that you want to get rid of. Here is a list of distracting behaviors to watch for on the videotape.

- ◆ Aimless walking about like a caged animal
- ◆ Slouching or hanging on to the lectern
- ◆ Fiddling with your glasses
- ◆ Playing with a pencil, pen, or paper clip
- ◆ Jingling the change or keys in your pocket
- ◆ Rocking, either back and forth or side to side
- ◆ Avoiding eye contact by looking at the floor or looking at the ceiling
- ◆ Twisting or clenching your hands
- ◆ Giggling or laughing nervously
- ◆ Mad-moth syndrome caused by waving the laser pointer

Certain gestures or mannerisms that you have can occasionally become distracting if they are frequently repeated, for example, clearing your throat, saying *er* or *um*, patting or twirling your hair, or opening and closing your jacket.

Clothes

The audience will equate a neat appearance with a well-prepared presentation. It is a good idea to always wear well-fitted, comfortable clothes. You don't want to be worrying about a skirt that's too short or a jacket that's too tight when you're giving your presentation. A good motto is to dress comfortably and appropriately, adapting your clothes to the people you are addressing. If most of the audience will be in a suit, wear a suit. Likewise, if your audience will be dressed in casual clothes, follow that lead.

Podium, Lectern, Microphone, and Laser Pointer

Before we discuss equipment frequently used by speakers, let's make clear the distinction between a *lectern* and a *podium*. They are not the same. The word *lectern* means the reading desk and comes from the Latin word *legere*, which means "to read." *Podium*, on the other hand, means a dais or raised platform in a hall or large room. Hence, a speaker stands on the podium and rests his or her notes on the lectern.

The podium, lectern, microphone, and laser pointer are all devices to help our audiences better see and hear what we have to say. In order to make them work for you, check them all out *before* you begin your talk. Nothing is more annoying to an audience than a speaker who spends precious audience time trying to figure out how to work the microphone or laser pointer.

Approaching the Podium

Because of anxiety, many speakers approach the podium as if they were walking to the gallows. Keep in mind that, even before your talk begins, you will be sending a message to your audience by the way you stand and walk up onto the podium. Try to appear confident and enthusiastic. If you are introduced, remember to smile at your introducer. When you reach the lectern, don't rush. Take a moment to collect your thoughts, lay out your notes, and adjust the microphone.

Lectern

You've gotten from your seat to the lectern. Now what? Well, the lectern can either work for you or against you, depending on how you use it. The following are some tips to make the most of the lectern.

- ◆ Avoid clutching the lectern like someone going down for the third time. The lectern is there to hold the microphone and your notes, not you. It's fine to rest your arms lightly on the lectern but avoid the white-knuckle treatment.
- ◆ Avoid using the lectern as a shield. A lectern can be a physical barrier between you and the audience and, as such, it can interfere with communication. Why? If you stand behind a lectern during your entire talk, the audience only sees part of you—your head. Behind the lectern, you forfeit valuable

communication tools—your body and hands. Watch experienced speakers who have the ability to capture their audiences' attention. They get out from behind the lectern. They use it only as a place to set their notes or gently rest their hands.

◆ Place your notes as high on the lectern as possible. In this way, you won't need to lower your head far, and you can maintain eye contact with your audience.

◆ Check the height of the lectern ahead of time. Because I am relatively short, I find that when I stand behind some lecterns, all that the audience can see is a pair of eyes or a talking head. When I am checking the equipment ahead of time, if I find the lectern is too tall, I request a small table in place of the lectern. If I need a microphone, I either hold it or use a lavaliere. Avoid standing on a box or crate; it's too risky.

◆ Check ahead of time that you can see your notes on the lectern. If you wear glasses, particularly bifocals, make sure that your notes are legible from where you will be standing.

Microphone

The microphone, like the lectern, can work for you or against you. It's best to find out in advance what type of microphone you will be using and, if possible, test it before you are to speak. Audiences are weary of the time-worn question, "Can you hear me back there?" Here are the different types of microphones and the pros and cons of each.

◆ **Stationary.** This microphone is usually fixed to the lectern and adjustable in height. The drawback to this type is your movements are restricted. Usually you can turn your head back and forth but not move more than a foot away. When adjusting it, try to adjust it gently to avoid the grating or squealing sound that often happens when speakers fiddle around with the microphone. The best position is about chin level.

◆ **Lavaliere.** This microphone hangs around your neck, leaving your hands free, which is particularly nice if in one hand you're holding the slide remote control and in the other hand you have a laser pointer. Another advantage of the lavaliere is that you can move around. Just be alert not to get tangled up in the cord as you move.

◆ **Clip-on.** This microphone usually clips on to the lapel of a jacket and has the same advantages as the lavaliere. Women, particularly, will want to know in advance if they will be using a clip-on mike, so they can wear something with a collar or lapel.

◆ **Hand-held.** Frequently, the microphone attached to the lectern can be removed. If you like to get out from behind the lectern, holding the mike might be an option. Again, though, watch you don't get tangled up in the cord. And keep in mind that if you are holding a remote control and a laser pointer, you won't have an extra hand for the microphone.

◆ **Wireless remote control.** This is a miniature microphone that clips to the tie, blouse, or coat lapel with a wire leading to a portable power pack that clips to the waist. Speakers like this type of microphone best because it frees the hands, but doesn't require a cord to get tripped up on.

With all microphones, remember they pick up all sounds, including the rustling of papers, clinking of jewelry and pens, and anything hitting the mike. They can also pick up comments you make under your breath, either to yourself or to someone else on the podium. Using a mike, you won't need to speak loudly; a normal conversational tone is fine. You will, though, want to be conscious of the *p*, *b*, and *s* sounds. Microphones are particularly sensitive to these sounds, so you may want to speak them a bit more softly.

Laser Pointers

These are great for pointing out small sections of slides, particularly a slide of a radiograph or electrograph. They can throw light a distance of 50 to 100 feet. Here are a few words of caution about the laser pointer:

◆ Use the laser pointer sparingly and never with word slides. Avoid the "sing-a-long with the bouncing ball" effect.

- ◆ Rest the pointer on your opposite forearm if you want to avoid the dancing ball caused by a nervous, shaky hand.
- ◆ Be sure to turn the laser pointer off when you aren't using it. Otherwise, you might look out and see only chins as the audience follows the bouncing ball on the ceiling.

The Question-and-Answer Period

The question-and-answer period following a presentation is similar to the "letters to the editor" section in medical journals. Audience members can comment on similar research or findings, pose intriguing questions about current research, and offer thoughtful suggestions for future research. They can also challenge, object, denounce, provoke, dispute, and badger. Maybe that's why nothing puts fear in the hearts of young physicians like the challenging questioner.

How can you prepare for postpresentation questions? Knowing your audience, subject, and purpose will give you a good idea of the kind of questions you might get. Here are some other useful tips for the question-and-answer session:

- ◆ **Tell the audience before you speak that there will be time for questions at the end of your talk.** Before you begin the Q-and-A session, put a time limit on it. "I have about ten minutes left if there are any questions." Then stick with it.
- ◆ **Beware of the two most common mistakes** presenters make during the question-and-answer session: (1) Answering the question too quickly. Give the questioner a chance to ask the entire question before jumping in with an answer. (2) Answering too much. Be brief and to the point, emphasizing again your main points.
- ◆ **Rephrase the question.** Restating the question allows you time to gather your thoughts. It also allows you to repeat the question for those who didn't initially hear it.
- ◆ **Use the question to reinforce your message.** Keep your purpose in mind and use every appropriate opportunity to support it. For example, your purpose is to raise money for the new arthritis clinic in the hospital. Someone asks you,

"Why aren't you raising money for AIDS research?" You can state that, like arthritis research, AIDS research is important. Then restate why you are proposing a new arthritis clinic, repeating statistics and examples.

◆ **Be honest if you don't have an answer.** Don't try to bluff your way out of a question. Tell the questioner that you honestly don't have the answer, but that you will find out and get back to him or her. Then do it.

◆ **Find an expert in the audience.** If you anticipate a question outside your expertise, see if you can find someone who is an expert on the topic and ask him or her to be in the audience. Then, should such a question come up, you can defer to the expert. Being prepared relieves you of worry about questions you can't answer, gives the audience a good impression of you as a well-prepared speaker, and allows the expert to momentarily be in the spotlight.

◆ **Be prepared to ask yourself a question.** How do you handle the situation if, after you have said you will now take questions, there is silence? The best approach is to have a question ready. You can then say, "One question that I frequently get is . . ." This technique often gets the ball rolling with a reticent group.

◆ **Don't let one person monopolize the Q-and-A session.** The question may be the questioner's, but the response belongs to the entire audience. To avoid allowing one person to monopolize, use your eyes. When the questioner asks you the question, look directly at him or her. Then, when you answer, look at the questioner momentarily before making eye contact with others in the audience. This breaks that one-to-one conversation and discourages the questioner from interrupting, disrupting, or jumping in with another question.

◆ **Be a leader and keep it moving.** Keep the questions on track. If a question is irrelevant say, "That question really deals with another subject. After the meeting I'll be happy to talk to you about it. Next question?" At other times you may get a questioner who wants to take the time to deliver his or her own message. You will need to interrupt the questioner and say, "I'm afraid we'll have to move on to another question." Then quickly turn to another questioner.

◆ **Don't lose your temper.** If someone badgers you with hostile questions, don't respond with a hostile or sarcastic remark. Be diplomatic. Try to use the question to reinforce your message. The more out-of-control the questioner gets, the calmer you will want to appear.

◆ **Take questions from all parts of the room.** Frequently, young physicians focus only on the chief or chair of their departments. When you are giving a presentation, remember the rest of your audience and give others an opportunity to ask questions.

◆ **Always end on time.** This can't be emphasized enough. Nothing upsets an audience of other speakers more than the speaker who ignores the clock. Just make sure to leave yourself enough time to offer a brief summary to wrap everything up: "In summary . . ."

◆ **End on a positive note, thank your audience, and smile.**

Performance Anxiety

> *The one important thing I have learned over the years is the difference between taking one's work seriously and taking one's self seriously. The first is imperative and the second is disastrous.*
> Margot Fonteyn (*Women's Wit & Wisdom*, 25)

Rapid pulse. Sweaty palms. Pounding heart. Quivering voice. Trembling hands. Jumping stomach. Trembling knees. Sound familiar? They're the all-too-common symptoms of performance anxiety. And all the knowledge in the world won't guarantee a successful presentation if you're so nervous that your symptoms overshadow your words. Indeed, nervousness and apprehension are what speakers fear most about public speaking. There are countless suggestions for overcoming performance anxiety. These include deep breathing, meditation, medication, visualization, biofeedback, and prayer. But, having watched and spoken to hundreds of speakers, I have found that there are really only four ways to prevent performance anxiety:

- Prepare
- Be enthusiastic
- Practice
- Have realistic expectations

Preparation

Before you get up to speak, know your subject, audience, and purpose. The last thing a presenter needs is surprises. Speakers tell me that one of their most common fears is being asked a question they can't answer. If you have thoroughly researched your subject, you should have the answers to most questions you are asked. And if you don't have the answer, you won't be panicked at the prospect of saying, "I don't know the answer to that question, but I'll find the answer and get back to you." Knowing who will be in the audience will help you anticipate some of the possible questions. Spend time putting yourself in the minds of some audience members. Write down three tough questions you might ask if you were in the audience. Knowing exactly what your purpose is will help to keep you on track both as you are delivering your message and answering questions. In short, thoroughly knowing your subject, audience, and purpose breeds confidence and excitement at the prospect of delivering your message. The following are some further preparation hints.

- Ask to be the first speaker at a meeting where there are several speakers. Your audience will be more attentive, and you will have less time to become nervous.
- Practice pronouncing the name of the person who will introduce you, so when you get up to speak you can say, "Thank you, Dr. So-and-So" without stumbling over his or her name.
- Hand-carry your slides or overhead transparencies if you fly to the location where you will be speaking. Otherwise, you can guarantee if you fly to Denver, your slides will fly to Dallas.
- Carry a spare lightbulb if you are going to use a slide projector or overhead.
- Carry a handkerchief.
- Get explicit directions to the location of the talk. If you are giving a talk in a different location or town, make sure you

know exactly where you are going and how long it will take you to get there. Once I was told a meeting where I was speaking was at the Westin Hotel. I asked directions to the Westin at the hotel where I was staying. I got to the Westin to find there was no such meeting taking place. I quickly called the person who had invited me to speak and found out that the meeting was at the Airport Westin, not the Downtown Westin. Although I got there on time, I felt, and probably looked, frazzled.

Enthusiasm

Why is enthusiasm so important in calming the fear demons? Think of presenters who have the knack of capturing their audience's attention. What do they all have in common? Enthusiasm, energy, and an adamant belief in what they are saying. What names immediately come to mind? Maya Angelou, Mario Cuomo, Gloria Steinem, Ross Perot. These men and women have zeal they have learned to translate to their audiences. Bottom line: If you don't believe in your subject, you'll have a hard time convincing anyone else to believe in it.

Practice

Confidence comes from practice. The more you speak in public, the better you will become at it. Speakers who seem to have the knack for keeping their audiences riveted to every word will tell you that the secret to their success is practice. Many of the qualities that make a person a dynamite speaker you can practice everyday. For instance, practice making eye contact with people; practice modulating your voice; practice reading aloud; practice standing up straight; practice smiling.

Realistic Expectations

Nervousness frequently comes from the speaker's unrealistic goals. Perfection should *not* be your goal; improvement and development should. Be willing to forgive yourself. All of us do dumb things at one time or another. In fact, I often tell my audiences some of the dumb things I've done while giving a presentation. Usually we all have a good laugh, and my audience seems to relate better to me since I'm willing to be a real human being with them. Don't take yourself too seriously. Prepare, believe in your topic, and practice; then if you make an error, learn from it and quickly move forward.

The following facts should help take the edge off the nervousness.

- **Nervousness before a presentation is natural.** In fact, a certain amount of anxiety is good. It will keep you on your toes. After two thousand performances of *Othello*, Sir Laurence Olivier forgot his lines. He said it was God's way of keeping him anxious. Every talk, no matter how often you give it, should be fresh.
- **If you suffer performance anxiety, you're in good company.** Cicero, the brilliant Roman orator, wrote: "I turn pale at the outset of a speech and quake in my every limb and soul." Other sufferers of performance anxiety include Willard Scott, Barbra Streisand, and Lily Tomlin.
- **Most anxiety doesn't show.** At a recent medical meeting, we conducted an informal study of anxiety and public speaking. Presenters were asked to rate their anxiety levels from 1 (no anxiety) to 5 (overwhelming anxiety) during a talk in front of a small group. The majority of speakers rated them-selves as 3 or 4. But when asked to rate the level of anxiety of the same speakers, the audience usually rated the speakers 1 or 2.
- **Eye contact with the audience can reduce a speaker's anxiety.** As I mentioned earlier, lack of eye contact between speaker and audience not only increases audience boredom, but also increases speaker anxiety. When you are delivering a talk to a group of people, they look at you and they expect you to look at them. That doesn't mean you just scan faces. It means you look directly at someone and hold that contact until you complete a thought, usually for about five seconds. This direct eye contact can help you concentrate on your message and stay focused. Scanning overloads your brain because the faster the eyes scan, the more extraneous information the brain receives. The result of this sensory overload

is that you'll talk faster, lose your focus, and perhaps stumble off track. Because most people avoid eye contact when they are uncomfortable, when you are giving a presentation, you need to concentrate on maintaining eye contact with your audience.

◆ **Interaction with the audience reduces anxiety.** Make your presentation as interactive as possible. Ask questions of the audience early in the presentation or invite questions from the audience as you go along. Audiences that have the opportunity to participate are inclined to be more attentive.

◆ **Exercise before a presentation helps calm the jitters.** Try doing a real physical workout—running, swimming, racquetball—a couple of hours before your presentation to get your body loosened up.

◆ **Yawning relieves nervousness.** Have you ever noticed that when someone is nervous or frightened, he or she yawns? It's the body's way of getting more oxygen, much like deep breathing. If deep breathing seems too unnatural, try yawning a few times before a presentation.

◆ **Alcohol should be left for the postpresentation celebration.** Alcohol can deceive you. It will only make you *think* you're doing a better job. And what about the beta blockers? Frequently, in the speaking seminars I get that question. Since I'm not a physician or a pharmacist, I really can't make any therapeutic comments about using beta blockers before a presentation. Therefore, I turn the question back to the audience. In general, I ask, what is an audience's number one complaint about presentations? Is it that the speaker is too nervous? Usually not. The number one complaint is that speakers are dull. Now, do we want to take a drug that's going to dull us even more?

◆ **Arrive early to the place you will be giving a talk.** You can greet people as they come in. I find having met a few people ahead of time seems to reduce my anxiety once I get up to talk.

◆ **Beware the lone skeptic.** In almost every group you will find at least one person whose body language indicates that he or she is skeptical, suspicious, disbelieving, unimpressed, or downright hostile. Your first reaction may be to focus on that person to try to win him or her over. Don't bother. Frequently the signals you are receiving are not related to you. Concentrate on the rest of the group who is sending more positive feedback.

- ◆ **Humor can break the ice.** Humor in presentations, like humor in life, makes it all a little more bearable. When used effectively, humor can establish rapport and good will and can relax both the speaker and the listeners. Just beware of jokes that might offend any audience members. I've heard speakers start a joke by saying, "I apologize to the ladies in the audience . . ." or "I hope there aren't any psychiatrists in the group." They then go on to tell a joke at someone's expense. At the cost of sounding priggish, I'd have to say I think any speaker who needs to apologize for his or her humor is treading in dangerous waters—no matter how powerful the speaker feels.

- ◆ **Although a speaker's main complaint is nervousness, the audience's main complaint is boredom.** Think of your last presentation. During which part were you most nervous? If you're like most people, it was during the first sixty to ninety seconds. And, too, if you're like most people, to control that nervousness, you did what we call "dampening down." That means you stood more rigidly. You avoided eye contact. You talked too fast, with no modulation or inflection in your voice. In fact, in an attempt to keep your nervousness in check, you were doing many of the things we know bore an audience. And to make it worse, you were doing them in that crucial first sixty seconds, the time during which the audience is deciding whether to give you their attention. What's the solution? Translate that initial nervousness into energy and enthusiasm. Practice what professional athletes do. Pump yourself up before the presentation, so that by the time you reach the lectern you will be eager to go.

Occasionally, I meet a physician for whom speaking in public is more than just discomforting; it's sheer terror. If you find even the thought of speaking to a group causes heart palpitations and light-headedness, there is help. Individuals who want to improve their speaking skills can hire a speaking consultant. Unfortunately, a speaking consultant can charge as much as $3,500 a day. Other less expensive options are college courses on public speaking, a Dale Carnegie training course, or Toastmasters, a nonprofit organization dedicated to helping people improve their speaking skills. Toastmasters advertises "learn-by-doing workshops where men and women can improve their speaking skills in an atmosphere of fellowship and enjoyment." Members, I am told, give impromptu talks, prepared speeches, develop listening skills, learn to conduct meetings, and learn parliamentary procedures. Toastmasters groups can be found in most cities. Check your telephone book.

Chapter Seven

◆

Common Speaking Situations

Physicians are called upon to speak in a variety of situations. The general guidelines for speaking that we have already discussed—know your subject, audience, and purpose, be well organized, clear, and concise—apply to each of the following special speaking situations. However, each of these may also present unique opportunities and problems to a speaker.

Lectures

The purpose of a lecture is to prompt enthusiasm and stimulate thought, yet most lecturers merely announce facts. Memorable teachers stimulate questions and, in the process, learning. No doubt, Socrates was one of the great teachers in history. His method entailed the use of carefully selected questions that led students to think and, in time, arrive at new understanding about the subject being discussed. J. Willis Hurst, M.D., Professor of Medicine at Emory University School of Medicine, defined a teaching–learning equation: "First the learner must have the factual information, use that information in a new thought process, then use the thought process in day-to-day work" (1992, p. 26).

If you are giving a lecture, your goal is to stimulate thought and learning. Students can get the facts in books, articles, and handouts. Your job is to put practical meaning to the facts. You can do this by selecting a problem, defining it, and giving memorable examples that are relevant to the audience. In addition to offering appropriate examples, visual aids, and occasional humor, you can stimulate interest in the following ways.

- **Present a problem.** Include your audience in the discovery process. One of the most interesting lectures I attended was given by a pediatric cardiothoracic surgeon to residents on the topic of transposition of the great arteries. He wanted to convey three main points. As opposed to merely stating each point, however, he formatted three questions, which, if answered correctly, would state his main points. As the lecture progressed, I could feel the excitement in the room.

- **Provoke your listeners.** Another way to stimulate learning is through provocation. Several years ago, I attended a meeting of general surgeons. One surgeon, who had written extensively on procedure X, got to the lectern and stated that in his opinion procedure X was no longer the most effective treatment for disease Y. The rest of his talk qualified his statement, but his opening remarks grabbed the audience's attention and certainly stimulated interest and curiosity.

- **Encourage interaction and interruptions.** This technique is useful only if the audience is small. If the audience is large, you run the risk of losing those in the audience who do not share the questioner's interests or concerns. In general, the experienced speaker knows when opening a lecture up to the audience is a wise idea.

- **Be creative with visual aids.** One physician, who volunteers in a family-planning clinic, gives a lecture once a month about birth control to teenage mothers. The physician didn't feel she was getting through to her audience, although she knew her subject and purpose. One day, instead of showing the young mothers pictures of different birth control devices, she decided to bring a sample of each into the lecture and pass them around. Once the young women could see and touch the devices, they had a host of questions and comments previous audiences had never had.

- **Debate instead of lecturing.** Debates can be exciting. They clearly show that there are two sides to a question. When two experts argue skillfully it automatically stimulates the audience. I have seen the debate format work particularly well in a Medical Ethics class.

◆ **Arrange a panel discussion.** For example, if the topic is Current Approaches in the Treatment of Parkinson's Disease, you might have a panel that includes a neurologist, a social worker, a pharmacist, a patient, and a family member. In this way, the audience can see and hear the problem from all perspectives. Panel discussion is a useful way to help young specialists stay alert to the whole patient.

Finally, if you are a teacher, ask your students for suggestions on new formats.

Grand Rounds

Grand rounds have long been one of the principal educational activities in teaching hospitals. The major objective of grand rounds is to provide updates in diagnosis, treatment, and research. Case presentations are often included, although patients are rarely present for examination or interview, which supports the observation by many physicians that grand rounds has been transformed from a patient-centered activity into a one-hour, one-topic conference.

In 1990, Peter J. McLeod, M.D., from the department of medicine at McGill University, sent a questionnaire to the chairpersons of the departments of medicine at fifty-three Canadian teaching hospitals. The following are suggestions from respondents for improving grand rounds.

◆ Patient-related problems should be the focus of grand rounds. Select clinical cases with attention to their value in illustrating important, relevant problems and advances in understanding the fundamental abnormalities of functions. Formal discussion should be intimately related to the case presented.
◆ Select speakers not necessarily for their expertise in the subject matter but, rather, for their ability to hold the audience's attention. Solicit local speakers who are known to be skilled lecturers more often than visiting guests, whose skills may not be known.

- Regular audience evaluations of speakers can improve the overall quality of the presentations.
- Basic science topics should be appropriately interwoven into the case discussion.
- Because learning is augmented through direct visual experience, consider a return to the practice of having patients present in the lecture hall.
- Because active participation enhances learning, reserve at least fifteen minutes at the end of a forty-five-minute talk for questions and discussion. A successful question-and-discussion period requires a chairperson who can adeptly promote controversy and discussion and involve audience members without intimidation or embarrassment.
- The department chair must continue to insist on punctual and regular attendance ("Medical Grand Rounds: Alive and Well and Living in Canada." Reprinted from, by permission of the publisher, *CMAJ*, 1990; 142(10): 1053–1056).

Keep in mind that grand rounds is primarily a teaching tool. As you prepare your grand rounds lecture, focus on the three steps in the process of learning: (1) identification of the facts, (2) incorporation of the facts into a new thought process, and (3) use of the thought process in day-to-day work. Focus on "solving a patient's problem." Select a patient or a topic of interest, focus on one aspect of the problem, and relate it to your audience's everyday practice. For example, if the topic is Rheumatoid Arthritis, make the topic manageable and useful by narrowing the topic, for instance, Chicken Bone Cartilage in the Management of Rheumatoid Arthritis. Finally, for each main point you make, use one or two clear, relevant examples to support that point.

The Ten-Minute Talk

Most medical meetings today require presentations to be in the form of ten-minute talks, followed by a three- to five-minute question-and-answer period. In many ways, these large meetings with ten-minute talks going on simultaneously in several rooms, from morning to night, have become what one physician calls an "information circus." Nevertheless, in spite of the circus quality of the meetings, ten-minute talks are probably here to stay. Here are some suggestions to consider when planning one.

- ◆ **Prepare your abstract.** Before you can give a ten-minute talk, you will need to submit an abstract to the selection committee. If the selection committee is reviewing 200 abstracts, the ones that are clear, concise, well organized, and describe well-designed, original work will be selected before those lacking such qualities. (See Chapter 2 on writing abstracts for meetings.)
- ◆ **Design your talk.** Once your abstract has been selected, begin putting together your talk. Focus on scientific reliability as you describe objectives, methods, results, and conclusions. Because your time is strictly limited, you will be able to include only a fraction of what you might include in a written article. Choose only the most important aspects of each section. Make your selection based on what the audience might want or need to know, not on what you want them to know *you* know.
- ◆ **Select your visual aids.** Choose only visual aids that are absolutely necessary and that can explain better and more quickly what you would say. For a ten-minute presentation, use no more than six slides. (See Chapter 9 on visual aids.)
- ◆ **Decide whether to read your text or use notes.** Some meetings discourage reading texts at the lectern. Others expect it. Know ahead of time if there are restrictions on reading your talk. If you must read, use a tape recorder to practice.
- ◆ **Avoid being rude** about other speakers, using inappropriate humor, and reacting in kind to critical comments, snide remarks, or hostile questions.
- ◆ **Adhere to the time limit.** It is only fair to your audience and to other speakers. At most meetings there is a red light on the lectern. When that light goes on, conclude immediately; otherwise, they'll send out the proverbial hook.
- ◆ **Don't be intimidated by experts in the audience.** Focus on the most important points and present them clearly and concisely.

Talks at International Meetings

The reason for presenting your work at international meetings is the same as for presenting material at a national meeting: to exchange scientific information. The following are some suggestions if you are asked to speak at an international meeting.

- **Be aware of language differences** and choose your words carefully. Avoid abbreviations, colloquialisms, slang, acronyms, and jargon. Concentrate on speaking slowly, pronouncing each word clearly, and pausing frequently.
- **Ask ahead of time about the equipment** you will be using, for example, a slide projector or carousels. Your slides will not fit into the standard equipment in some countries.
- **Use bilingual slides** with English on the left side and the language of the foreign country on the right side. If possible, use a dual projector, so each slide won't be crowded with bilingual text.
- **Meet with the translator,** if you will be having one, in advance. Give him or her a copy of your talk. Ask if there is anything you can do to make the process successful. If possible, rehearse with the translator so that you become comfortable with each other. Remember to speak to the audience, not to the translator.
- **Carry a duplicate set of slides.** If anything should happen to your slides, it could be very difficult to locate them or to duplicate them in a foreign country.
- **Respect the protocol of the host country.** Inquire in advance about local courtesies or customs, such as recognizing important audience members.

Administrative Meetings

In addition to medical meetings, physicians are frequently asked to attend or chair other types of meetings, including Clinical Pathology Conferences (CPCs), Morbidity and Mortality conferences, faculty and staff meetings, and Quality Assurance meetings. What's the most common complaint about meetings? Too many of them! Other complaints are (1) too long, (2) too many people, (3) wrong people, (4) poorly planned, (5) poor leadership, (6) attenders are unprepared, and (7) conclude with no resolutions.

Everyone agrees poorly planned and conducted meetings are a waste of time and money. On the other hand, well-managed meetings are an effective communication tool within an organization. Important decisions are made, ideas are generated, and information is shared. The following suggestions may make your next meeting more productive.

- ◆ **Confirm the need.** Hold only meetings that are absolutely necessary. Meetings are ideal when you need to solve problems that are complex or affect many people, exchange technical information, or explain a complex policy, procedure, or situation.
- ◆ **State the purpose.** Every meeting must have specific, stated objectives and goals. Before calling a meeting, ask yourself, "What exactly do I hope to accomplish in this meeting?" You should be able to state this clearly and concisely, and it should be on the agenda that you send to attenders ahead of time.
- ◆ **Publish the agenda.** Having an agenda is the most critical element of effective meeting management. Agendas not only help attenders come prepared, but also force the leader to be organized and prepared. Make the agenda realistic; don't include more topics than possibly can be discussed.
- ◆ **Specify participants.** Invite only people who have reason to attend. All meeting participants should (1) know and understand the subject matter, (2) be able and willing to make a contribution, (3) have the power to make decisions, and (4) represent a group that will be affected by decisions made at the meeting.
- ◆ **Limit number of participants** according to your purpose. A problem with many meetings is that too many people attend. Meetings tend to be more productive when the number of participants is low. Analyze your agenda to see if everyone needs to be present for each item. It might be possible to divide the agenda so that some people need attend only the first half of the meeting, and others can arrive for the second. A good rule of thumb is to limit the audience to ten for a

meeting to identify a problem. Problem-solving meetings are best accomplished with five to seven people; training sessions should be kept to fifteen to twenty, fewer if hands-on instruction is part of the agenda.

- **Choose a good meeting place and time.** The room should offer proper ventilation, comfort, accessibility, and the necessary equipment. It should also be free from distractions and interruptions. Schedule meetings when people are apt to be at their best. Avoid holding meetings on Monday mornings, Friday afternoons, and the hour after lunch.

- **Start and end on time.** This sends a message to participants that their time is respected. Because physicians are often late, you might consider beginning the meeting with less urgent business. Out of fairness to those who arrive on time, avoid recapping for latecomers.

- **Start the discussion** by introducing the topic and the meeting participants and their departments.

- **Stick to the agenda and stay task-oriented.** Although you want to encourage participation, avoid getting sidetracked. Direct the discussion by seeing that the group moves steadily to a solution or conclusion. If an important topic that is not on the agenda comes up, poll attenders for an agreement to address it at the current meeting. The agenda should serve as a contract with the attenders and it should not be changed without a consensus.

- **Be a leader.** Many meetings have been disasters because the meeting organizer didn't take charge. Encourage participation and support members in expressing their opinions, even on controversial or volatile issues, but discourage arguments. You will need all your tact and diplomacy to resolve conflicts. Don't let one person dominate the meeting.

- **Provide transitions and summaries** as you go along to help participants see what has been accomplished and what remains to be done. At the conclusion of the meeting, recap the decisions and actions planned as a result of the meeting to make sure that everyone is in accord about who is to do what and when.

- **Analyze the meeting** immediately after it concludes. Jot down what worked, people who made the contributions, suggestions, and ways you might improve the next meeting.

◆ **Send out minutes.** Within two days of the meeting, distribute minutes to all attenders, highlighting what was accomplished, projects to be done and by whom, and announce the time and date of the next meeting. In your minutes, ask for suggestions on how to improve meetings.

Responding to the Media

If you are asked to appear on television, preparation will be important. Impromptu interviews are often a disaster. Paul Casella, poet and communications expert, found this out the hard way. One morning he received a call from a TV station, asking him for an interview. Flattered by the request, he agreed to the interview. He was told the crew would be there in thirty minutes. For the next thirty minutes, Paul ran around his apartment throwing clothes under the bed, tossing dirty dishes in the cupboard, frantically dusting and vacuuming. "When the doorbell rang," he recalls, "it suddenly dawned on me, I didn't have the vaguest idea what I would say, or more important, what I *wanted* to say. I was totally unprepared and later, when the clip was shown, it was obvious. The apartment had never looked better, but I'd never looked worse."

Remember that videotape is a flat, two-dimensional medium. The following suggestions will help you look your best when appearing on TV.

◆ **Establish ground rules in advance.** Ask about general areas to be covered. Indicate topics you will not discuss. Don't be intimidated. Ask about the opportunity to retape or otherwise correct misstatements. Ask about the length of the interview.
◆ **Think of possible questions you might be asked ahead of time.** Include in your list antagonistic as well as supportive questions.
◆ **Select a couple of main points** you would like to make and emphasize these at each opportunity.
◆ **Concentrate on what you want to say.** Let someone else worry about the technical aspects. Your job is to make your message accurate, clear, well-organized, and concise. The job

of the studio technicians is to assist you to communicate effectively.

- **Don't let the interviewer or reporter bully you** into speaking before you are ready. Take your time and answer as clearly as possible. If you get off track, stop talking. Ask to start again.
- **Avoid the temptation to look at the camera.** Look at the interviewer. If there is no interviewer and you are just speaking, look above the lens and you will be less distracted than if you looked directly at it.
- **Avoid jargon or technical terms** if the audience members are not physicians.
- **Correct the interviewer immediately** if he or she says something that is incorrect.
- **Follow the rules for reading a speech** (Chapter 6) if you are going to be using a teleprompter. With a teleprompter, there is the tendency to lapse into reading instead of speaking.
- **Limit your movements.** The camera tends to exaggerate them.
- **Don't assume that the media are your enemy**. Most people in the news media want to work with you to get the correct information to the public.
- **Do not wear a pin-striped shirt.** As you move, the stripes will cause a wavy rainbow effect across the screen.
- **Be enthusiastic and smile.**

Chapter Eight

◆

Speaking Is Good Public Relations

Neil Baum, M.D.

The human brain starts working the moment you are born and never stops until you stand up to speak in public.

Anonymous

There is no better way to ethically escalate your reputation than through the medium of public speaking. Unfortunately, our medical training does not provide us the skills necessary to become good public speakers.

When you stand in front of an audience, you have a position of authority. Combine that authority with your medical background, your information, and a dynamic presentation and the result will be that the audience will follow your recommendations and suggestions. When people follow you and listen to your suggestions and perhaps become your patients, that translates to more success. There is nothing as exciting and psychologically rewarding as making a presentation to the public and having someone in the audience write on the patient's demographic sheet that he or she became a patient

Neil Baum, M.D., is Clinical Assistant Professor of Urology at Tulane Medical Center and Louisiana State University of Medicine, New Orleans, Louisiana.

after listening to you speak. By following a few simple guidelines (see Figure 8.1), you will learn to generate patients from your public speaking.

Preparation

The best speeches are those that are prepared well in advance. Giving a speech is not a situation in which you can "wing it." You cannot take a carousel of slides that you use for a presentation to physicians at grand rounds and use the same material for a lay audience. You will only bore and confuse your audience, and it is unlikely they will leave your presentation and call for an appointment. Your fellow physicians may tolerate and even expect a talk punctuated by technical charts, graphs, anatomic drawings, photos of surgical specimens, and medical jargon. Lay audiences expect straightforward explanations of complicated subjects, direct information, and suggestions for improving their health and well-being. Good presentations are crisp, clear, and concise.

Getting on the Program

First of all, you need an audience. Where do you look? Today the public is very interested in health and wellness. It is easy to find audiences willing to listen to you talk about health-related topics. Social, civic, and professional associations frequently offer speakers and presentations in programs that accompany their regular meetings. Some of the most common organizations (to some of which you may already belong) are the local Chamber of Commerce, the Kiwanis, the League of Women Voters, the local PTA, and church groups. Your local chamber of commerce can furnish you a complete list of organizations in your community.

It is a good idea to select an organization with members you would like to target for your practice. Obviously, if you are a pediatrician, you will not want to speak to the local chapter of the American Association of Retired People. But, the local Parent-Teachers Association would probably welcome a talk about children's health.

Figure 8.1 A Checklist for Public Speaking

_____ Select organizations with memberships likely to be interested in your subject areas.

_____ Contact an organization and ask for the program chairperson's name.

_____ Write a letter to the program chairperson outlining your subject areas, your credentials in medicine and in specialty areas, and why the organization's membership would be interested in your talk. Include your CV.

_____ Follow up with a phone call to the program chairperson two to three weeks after sending the letter.

_____ Mark the speaking engagement on your calendar.

_____ Get information on your audience from the program chairperson (the number of people expected, the age range, etc.).

_____ Prepare your speech. Create a circular presentation, so the beginning and end emphasize the same points. For the middle, use case histories, slides, and so on, to illustrate your points.

_____ Write your introduction. It should be one or two minutes long.

_____ Practice your speech several times until you are comfortable with your delivery. For feedback, tape it or have someone listen to your presentation. Be sure to time it.

_____ List items to take with you to the engagement (hand-outs, brochures, slides, slide carousel, etc.).

_____ Arrive early. Survey the "playing field." Do audio checks, projector checks, and so on.

_____ Give your speech.

_____ Conduct a question-and-answer period. Bring questions on 3-by-5-inch cards to "seed" the audience and get the process started. Think about likely questions and what answers you would give.

_____ After your talk, meet audience members and distribute hand-outs and brochures.

_____ Write a thank-you letter to the organization. Ask for a copy of its membership mailing list.

_____ Capitalize on the mailing list. Send notices to members when you begin offering a new procedure or service.

_____ Turn your speech into an article for the local newspaper.

In this era of managed care, there is no better way to attract potential patients in a health plan than to contact the employer or the company's nurse and offer a "brown bag" presentation on some health-related topic.

In contacting most civic, social, and professional organizations, there are correct channels to follow. If you would like a speaking engagement at a selected organization, call and find out the name of the program chairperson. Let the organization know that you're available. Many programs are scheduled six to twelve months in advance. Take this into consideration when you contact an organization.

Before you contact the organization, decide on several presentation topics. Then send a letter to the program chairperson offering to talk on these topics (see Figure 8.2). Notice that the letter mentions (1) my qualifications to talk on the subject, (2) the length of time I will talk, (3) the content of the presentation, and (4) the intention to call in a few weeks. In your letter, discuss the potential benefits to the group, why members would be interested in the topics, and why you are the one to make the presentation. Spend a few moments on the potential benefits to the audience. Not only will this get the attention of the program chairperson, but it will also form the basis of your presentation. Try to picture yourself as a member of the audience. Each member of the audience will be listening with only one thing in mind—What's in it for me? When you answer that question, you will have captured the attention of the meeting planner and, ultimately, your audience. The letter should also include your curriculum vitae, the names of organizations for which you have spoken, and other materials that emphasize your expertise. Make a follow-up phone call two to three weeks after you send your introductory letter.

Know Your Audience

The more you know about your audience, the better you can tailor your presentation to its needs and the more likely it is that some members of the audience will become your patients. Before preparing your speech, ask the program chairperson for background information about your audience. It is important to know the purpose of

Figure 8.2 Letter of Introduction to an Organization

(Date)

(Meeting Planner)
(Organization)
(Address of Organization)

RE: Presentation on prostate cancer

Dear (Meeting Planner):

In 1990, nearly 20,000 men (nearly half the capacity of the Super-dome) died from cancer of the prostate gland. Many of them could be alive today if they had had an annual prostate examination, because with early detection prostate cancer can be successfully treated.

I am a urologist in private practice at Touro Infirmary. I have prepared an educational talk for men and their partners on cancer of the pros-tate gland. My talk is a slide presentation 20-25 minutes long followed by 5-10 minutes of questions and answers. During the presentation I will (1) describe the anatomy and function of the prostate gland, (2) describe the methods of early diagnosis of prostate cancer, and (3) briefly men-tion the treatments for management of prostate cancer. I will provide everyone in the audience a hand-out that summarizes the presentation.

I am enclosing several articles I have written on prostate cancer, includ-ing a recent article from the *Times Picayune*. I am also including a few letters of recommendation from previous talks that I have given in the community.

I will give you a call in two weeks to discuss the possibility of talking with (name of organization).

Sincerely,

Neil Baum

Neil Baum, M.D.

the organization, how many people are expected to attend, how much the audience already knows about the topic, who have been the previous speakers, what were their topics, the age range of the audience, the educational background, and possible areas of challenge or resistance if your topic is controversial. For example, a talk on male health problems would be prepared differently for women at a Junior League meeting, for a male service club such as Knights of Columbus, or for a senior citizens' organization.

Sending a survey is the best way to learn about your audience and the goals and objectives of the meeting planner (see Figure 8.3). I do this, especially if I am being paid to make the presentation, because I want to be sure that I truly understand the needs and wants of the audience. For example, if I am speaking on behalf of a pharmaceutical company, I will give the meeting planner, often the pharmaceutical representative, the survey and ask him or her to complete it and return it to me or to call me on the phone and answer the questions. It has been my experience that you avoid embarrassing yourself or the pharmaceutical representative when you go over the questions in the survey before your presentation. I have also found that the meeting planners appreciate this courtesy.

Preparing Your Speech

"Tell the audience what you are going to tell them, then tell them, and finally tell them what you told them." This old adage about public speaking still holds true. All successful presentations have a circular structure; the end comes back to reinforce the beginning.

I suggest that you focus on what you want the audience to do as a result of listening to your speech. State this goal or objective in the introduction and again emphatically at the conclusion. If, for example, I am talking to middle-aged men during Prostate Cancer Week, I might have as my objective that all men over fifty years of age should have an annual rectal examination. I might start my talk with the number of new cases and the number of deaths from prostate cancer per year, then state that early detection by a digital rectal examination and a PSA test is essential in diagnosing and curing the disease. I also try to paint a word picture by referring to the fact that the number of deaths from prostate cancer in the United States will be more than half the capacity of the Superdome, a well-known landmark in my community. I might end my presentation by saying, "Some of you here in the audience may be sitting on a curable prostate cancer. Call your physician or your urologist and get a rectal examination so that you can enjoy the rest of your life!"

Essentially your point of view in a presentation should be fired like a rifle bullet hitting the center of the target. A speech that does not have a single point of view ends up like a shotgun with buckshot everywhere around the target. However, a crystal-clear point of view is like the bullet of a rifleman hitting the bull's-eye of your audience. It is the one thing that you want them to leave with at the end of your presentation. When you can accomplish this, you are indeed an effective public speaker.

Another example is from a talk on erectile dysfunction. I tell them that I will discuss the causes of impotence, the means of evaluation, and the treatment options for this common medical problem. I conclude by returning to the beginning: "You have all taken the first important step and that is coming here this evening to get information. Now take the second step and call a urologist and find the cause of your problem—statistically you have one—and get the appropriate treatment. No one, in 1996, needs to suffer the 'tragedy of the bedroom.'"

Once you have the beginning and the conclusion, you can fill in the middle and have a memorable speech that will motivate your audience to take positive action.

In the middle portion of your speech, present two or three main points using illustrations, examples, stories, case histories, or visual aids whenever possible. For example, when I talk about urinary incontinence, I use a balloon to illustrate the bladder and my fingers compressing the neck of the balloon serve as the urinary sphincter. When I release my fingers from the neck of the balloon it makes a sound that produces a predictable giggle in the audience. I then remark, "When it is a balloon leaking air, that is funny. But when it is your bladder losing urine, that is no laughing matter." This visual aid clearly explains the functional anatomy of the bladder and the urethra better than any drawing from *Gray's Anatomy of the Human Body*.

Figure 8.3 Prepresentation Survey

Meeting planner:

Organization:

Date of presentation?

Title?

The Audience

How many do you anticipate will attend the presentation?

What percentage of the audience will be primary-care doctors and what percentage will be specialists?

Are the physicians just beginning their careers? Mid-career? Or nearing retirement?

Will the audience be made up of physicians only or staff and physicians?

What are the health-care trends in your community?

What are the objectives of the audience?

Are there topics that you would specifically like me to include in my presentation?

Are there subjects or topics that I should avoid?

Are there physicians or members of the hospital staff that you would like me to mention or include in my presentation? Please provide their names.

Are there unique historical aspects of the community, the hospital, or the medical staff that I might include in my presentation? Please provide specific information.

The Program

What is the result you would like to have after my presentation?

What speakers have you had in the past year who addressed benign enlargement of the prostate gland (or whatever topic you plan to cover)? How were their talks perceived or accepted?

Will I be speaking before or after a meal? Will alcohol be served?

How long would you like me to speak?

Would you like me to include a Q-and-A session? Would you like me to be available afterward to answer questions from the physicians?

Who will introduce me?

Can I provide an introduction?

Can I include audience participation?

Can I make my presentation interactive with the audience? (Please provide a hands-free microphone, and a long cord for the slide advancer. I would also like name tags for the audience written with a wide felt pen or magic marker so that I can read the names.)

Will you make copies of the hand-out for the audience?

Will you agree to pass out the hand-out *after* the presentation?

Meeting Planner

What are you hoping to accomplish by having me speak to your medical staff?

Would you like me to provide a letter to your physicians describing the presentation and include several copies of articles I have written on medical marketing?

You are welcome to make an audio- and/or videotape of my presentation. I only request a copy of the tape.

If you support each main point with a variety of materials, make sure every piece of material refers to the main objective of your presentation. If possible, include a personal story about yourself, a friend, or a family member. This adds a human touch. Always remember, however, to protect confidentiality by omitting names and identifying details unless you have the person's explicit permission to tell the story and to reveal his or her identity.

Another suggestion is to mention celebrities or historical figures who have suffered from the medical problem you are talking about. For example, when discussing nonsurgical management of urinary stones, I tell the story of Ben Franklin, who had bladder calculus that caused intermittent urinary retention. Franklin was able to relieve his urinary retention by standing on his head and allowing the bladder calculus to fall away from the bladder opening. "So," I tell my audience, "Ben Franklin was not only one of the founders of our country but also the founder of nonsurgical management of urinary tract obstruction." There are hundreds of such stories about the health problems of historical figures, such as John F. Kennedy's famous bad back and Addison's disease or Abraham Lincoln's Marfan syndrome. One good source of medical anecdotes is *The Illustrated Treasury of Medical Curiosa* by Art Newman.

If your talk centers on a new procedure or test, you might introduce a patient who has successfully undergone the procedure or test. This is very effective and adds credibility. For instance, if I talk about impotence, I ask one of my patients to come and discuss how his life improved following treatment of the problem.

There are several caveats about using patients in your presentations. First, select "Mr. Average," rather than a patient who is too sophisticated, because many members of the audience won't be able to relate to him or her. I usually ask a potential patient–speaker to attend one of my presentations without the pressure to speak or to watch a video of a presentation where I have used a patient–speaker before, so that they know what to expect. I then explain what I want to cover. If it is a surgical procedure, I suggest he or she tell the audience what the symptoms were before the surgery, how the surgery helped resolve the complaints, and what the postoperative recovery period was like. I find that these are the concerns most people in the audience have and they want to hear from someone who has actually experienced the surgery. If the patient takes questions from the audience, I stand beside the patient and protect him or her from embarrassing questions or questions that they can't possibly answer. I also ask permission to tape (audio or video) a patient–speaker and use the tape when I don't have access to a patient–speaker such as when I am speaking at a great distance from my community. Finally, I send the patient a thank-you note or a small gift afterward in appreciation for giving the time and having the courage to get up and tell his or her story to a group of strangers.

Finally, focus on the benefits by recommending that those in the audience follow your advice or suggestions. For example, if you talk about prostate cancer, wrap up the presentation by urging the audience to get an annual rectal examination. By emphasizing the personal benefits to the members of the audience, you can hold their attention and motivate them to action. Don't ever forget that your audience buys benefits. When you have answered their question, "What's in it for me?" you will move them from the audience to the appointment book.

An effective presentation helps the audience listen, remember, and act on what you say. You become an effective speaker when you are the right person presenting the right message to the right audience at the right time in the right manner.

Getting the Audience's Attention

An excellent talk needs an attention-grabbing title. A narrative or descriptive title seldom generates excitement or enthusiasm for your presentation, but a catchy title creates advance interest in your presentation. You can get ideas from best-selling book titles or famous movie titles. The following are some of my own presentation titles. Instead of "The Evaluation and Treatment of Impotence," I now use the title "Impotence: The Tragedy of the Bedroom Can Be Conquered." Instead of "Vasectomy: An Alternative to Contraception," I use "Vasectomy: No Way Baby!" Instead of "Marketing Your Practice Using Techniques from Industry and Business," I use "If Domino's Can Deliver Pizza, We Can Deliver Quality Health Care."

An attention-getting title does not require the talent of Madison Avenue geniuses. Any catchy title creates interest and will encourage people to attend a talk. One "do not" on catchy titles: do not use them for presentations to medical colleagues unless the setting is informal, such as a luncheon or dinner presentation.

Practice Makes Perfect

You now have your presentation and you are on the program. What next? Like any activity that you don't perform regularly, you need to practice until you are comfortable with the job at hand. Reduce nervousness and build confidence by rehearsing. If you don't rehearse, then don't present! One of the easiest ways to practice is to tape-record your practice sessions. Then replay the recordings to check your delivery and serve as your own coach or critic. You can use the recording right before the presentation to remind you of the fine points and the details of your material. You might also want to rehearse in front of your spouse and get his or her feedback as well.

Polishing Your Presentation with Slides

Have you ever attended a meeting where the speaker used slides with graphs and tables from *The New England Journal of Medicine* and the *Journal of Clinical Investigation*? Odds are that most of you have. And a good percentage of audiences for those talks were probably bored or confused by the materials. Typically, illustrations from medical journals and texts contain so much information and so many lines and numbers that the audience "gives up" and fails to follow the rest of the presentation mentally.

Whether you give a talk to your colleagues or to a lay audience, you don't want them to fall asleep. So you need to employ an armory of public-speaking techniques. If your presentation has good content and is delivered with style and enthusiasm, slides will reinforce, enhance, and support your material.

In general, an effective slide is one that can be understood in four seconds or less. Think of your slides as billboards: If you can't read the message as you pass it at 60 MPH, then it's a waste of the advertiser's money. The same holds true with your slides. If the point can't be understood in just a few seconds you are not only wasting your audience's time, but you will also lose its ability to concentrate on your presentation.

The four elements to consider when creating effective slides are content, style, color, and space. Whether you create your own slides or pay someone to do it, you need to recognize the importance of these elements and to use them to maintain interest.

Slides should not be inserted haphazardly into your talk. They should act as signposts to your audience, pointing them in the direction you want their attention to go. As you review your presentation, figure out where the best places to insert slides would be (ideally at thirty- to forty-second intervals). Your slides should emphasize pertinent points in your speech at logical transitions.

Dr. Robert Zollinger, a professor of surgery at The Ohio State University in Columbus, is considered by his surgical colleagues to be one of the best medical speakers. His talks to colleagues on medical subjects (and to lay audiences on his beloved rose gardens) are fascinating, humorous, and, most important, memorable. It is no accident that Dr. Zollinger's slides match the high quality of his verbal presentations. He has made a science out of a well-placed slide show.

In his class on general surgery, which I attended as a medical student at Ohio State, Dr. Zollinger stressed that a good slide contains only two colors, has fewer than twenty words, and the graphs have no more than two lines. Material reproduced from medical journals, where the reader has unlimited time to study it, is not appropriate for a slide presentation.

The best slide presentations use a consistent color combination. A variety of color combinations and graphic styles tends to confuse the audience rather than grab its attention. If you use consistent color combinations, consistent graphic techniques, and a consistent writing style, your slides will continuously build one upon the other along with your presentation. Change color combinations only for a purpose, such as to differentiate sections within your talk or distinguish subjects within a longer talk.

Making Preparations

Prepare a checklist of everything that must be brought to your presentation, including slides, hand-outs, brochures, calling cards, and so on. Hotels, hospitals, and lodge facilities frequently have sophisticated audiovisual equipment. If this is the case, you can request hands-free microphones, remote-control slide projectors, double screens, laser pointers, or additional lighting. If you need or would like additional audiovisual equipment, such as a VCR to show a tape of your patient, then submit your request in writing to the meeting planner.

A good speaker, like a good athlete, arrives early to inspect the "playing field." Larry Bird, the basketball great from the Boston Celtics, reportedly dribbled the ball for hours on a basketball court so he could identify the dead spots on the floor and avoid them during the game. Is it any wonder that he was a member of the Dream Team and an All-Pro player for several years? You should be familiar with the room, the microphone system, the slide projector, and the audiovisual equipment before you start to speak. Ask the program chairperson whether technical-support personnel can show you where everything is located in advance. Nothing is more distracting at the beginning of a presentation than to test the microphone by saying "Can you hear me?" or to ask "Would someone adjust the focus on the slide projector?" It has been said, "You don't get a second chance to make a good first impression." You will have missed out on the opportunity of the first few seconds when nearly everyone in the audience is paying attention to you. Arriving early and completing a checklist are details that should be attended to before the presentation begins.

"Let Me Introduce Myself"

Don't take chances with your introduction. This key element of public speaking is often overlooked or left in the hands of the meeting planner. Because it sets the stage for your presentation, treat it as *your* responsibility.

An introduction should create excitement and enthusiasm for the speaker. This cannot be accomplished by sending your CV to the meeting planner and having him or her read where you went to medical school and where you did your residency. Therefore, prepare your own introduction, making it about two to three paragraphs, double spaced, so it will be easy for the introducer to read. An ideal introduction is forty-five seconds long. Send one copy to

Figure 8.4 The Introduction of the Presenter

NEW ORLEANS INTRODUCTION

Dr. Neil Baum is a board-certified urologist at Touro Infirmary and Southern Baptist Hospital. He is a clinical assistant professor of urology at Tulane Medical School. His areas of interest and expertise include impotence, diseases of the prostate gland, and infertility. He has written articles on these subjects that have been published in numerous medical journals and textbooks. Dr. Baum has written several books and writes articles for the *Times Picayune*, *Gambit*, and *New Orleans Magazine*. He writes the monthly column entitled "Man to Man" in *New Orleans Health and Home*.

Dr. Baum's talk today is entitled "The Unique Health Problems of Men." I believe you are in for a very informative and entertaining presentation. Please help me welcome Dr. Neil Baum.

---

the program chairperson and bring an extra copy with you in case the original gets lost or the introducer has changed.

The introduction should include three essentials: (1) something interesting about you and the reason you were selected to speak; (2) the topic and its importance to the audience; and (3) one or two relevant facts about you. Mention the title of the presentation at the end. The final words of the introduction should be your name (see Figure 8.4). A good introduction is like an American Express Card: "Don't leave home without it!"

Don't Run Out the Door

You have delivered an informative, well-planned presentation. Don't be in a hurry to pick up your slides and leave. You should now be ready for the question-and-answer session. One way to get the ball rolling is to "seed" the audience with a few questions that you would like to have asked. I usually have one or two prepared questions on 3-by-5-inch cards that I give to a couple of audience members before I speak. I ask them, "If there are no questions, would you mind asking this one or one of your own?" Handing out questions beforehand is another reason to arrive early. In the event that there are no questions coming from the audience members, I will start the Q-and-A session by saying, "One of the most common questions that I am asked is . . ." and then proceed to answer the question. If these methods do not stimulate audience questions, ask a member of the audience a question such as, "Have you heard about the free prostate cancer screening program available at my hospital?"

It is also a good idea to anticipate some of the frequently asked questions regarding your subject. If you give the presentation often, you will hear certain questions repeated and should have answers to these questions ready. If your topic is controversial, you must be prepared to field questions or comments from audience members with an opposite point of view. This is seldom a problem for most educational or informative medical talks. In the event that you can't answer a question, say so honestly. Then take the audience member's name and address afterward and offer to locate the answer.

After you entertain questions, have a thirty-second windup that again states your purpose, the benefits, and the "call to action."

Whenever my talks are part of a seminar for office staff or other personnel, I furnish evaluation forms and invite the audience to fill them out. These evaluation forms are one page long and have room for rating the talk and blanks for additional suggestions. They provide invaluable feedback on presentation skills (see Figure 8.5).

After your presentation, audience members may come to the front to congratulate you and offer compliments on your presentation. Many will also come to ask how to get in touch with you. Make sure you have enough hand-outs for everyone in the audience. The hand-outs can be sheets prepared by you or members of your staff that briefly review your topic and give audience members information about you and your practice. It has been my experience that it is better to distribute these after the presentation because you want the audience members focused on you, not reading your hand-out, during the presentation. I have been amazed at how long people will hold on to my hand-outs—sometimes 6–12 months—before they call to make an appointment with my office. If you don't have a prepared hand-out, you can give those who ask a copy of your office brochure or business card.

Figure 8.5 Seminar Evaluation

TOPIC: Motivating your staff to market your practice

SPEAKER: Dr. Neil Baum
           New Orleans, Louisiana

DATE: February 6, 1996

PLACE: Lafayette, Louisiana

Please rate the following on a scale of one (1) to five (5). Let five represent excellent and one be poor or substandard.

	poor	satisfactory	average	very good	excellent
	1	2	3	4	5
Presenter's knowledge of the topic	___	___	___	___	___
Usefulness of hand-outs	___	___	___	___	___
Relevance of the topic	___	___	___	___	___
Overall rating of the seminar	___	___	___	___	___

What are one or two ideas you received that you could use in your practice?

_____

_____

_____

_____

What other topics would you like to have presented in seminars?

_____

_____

_____

_____

Do you have other suggestions or comments?

_____

_____

_____

_____

When the presentation is over and you have left the site, you still aren't finished. Send a thank-you letter to the head of the organization that invited you. It is also helpful to ask for a letter of recommendation to use as a testimonial regarding your speaking skills. In addition, you should request a mailing list of the membership to add to your data base. For example, I have given talks to senior citizens on "Intimacy and the Senior Years." When I started performing balloon dilatations of the prostate gland, I sent all of the male members of those audiences a copy of the newsletter from my office discussing the technique. This generated several new patients.

Many organizations will ask to audio- or videotape your presentation. I gave a lunchtime presentation on "The Unique Healthcare Problems of Men" to a group of executive men at one of the oil companies in New Orleans. They asked to videotape the talk and had copies distributed to the oil rigs in the Gulf of Mexico. The men who remain on the oil rigs for fourteen consecutive days often watch videos from the rig's library. I have received dozens of referrals from men who watched the tape and never were in the audience of the presentation. I always give permission for taping and request the first copy, which is usually the best quality. I use it to critique my presentation, and sometimes send it as an example of my talk to potential meeting planners.

Finally, you have spent many hours working on and delivering your presentation. The material is current and informative. Consider stretching the mileage of your presentation by turning the speech into an article for a local magazine or newspaper. This usually requires minimal effort, because most of the material is in the text of your speech and only has to be converted from a conversational to a more formal style. Your hospital public relations and marketing departments can be helpful in this area.

Opportunities to speak are everywhere. All of us make our living as communicators. Try communicating as a public speaker. It is one of the most effective methods of marketing and promoting your medical practice.

Chapter Nine

◆

Visuals and Equipment

Excellence in graphics consists of complex ideas communicated with clarity, precision, and efficiency.

Edward R. Tufte (1990, 15)

Do you remember the slides of Martin Luther King? Abraham Lincoln? Mark Twain? Winston Churchill? Of course not. They never used slides. And these men were four of the most memorable speakers in history. They didn't need slides because they were their own visual aids. That is, they were speakers who used all their communication tools—facial expressions, posture, body language, hand gestures, voice, clothes, eyes—in order to communicate.

Today, there are still some excellent speakers, and listening to them is as much a visual experience as it is an auditory one. Think of teachers or speakers who held your attention. Did they need a lot of slides or overheads to make their point? Probably not. Many physician–speakers don't want to hear it, but the truth is, when people come to see your presentation, they come to see you—not your visual aids. In other words, if you are unprepared, unrehearsed, poorly organized, unclear, inaccurate, rambling, or worse yet, really have nothing of value to say, no visual aid, no matter how magnificent, is going to save you. I'm not suggesting you go immediately to your slide carousel and throw out all your slides; what I am suggesting is that you reevaluate just exactly why each slide is there.

What Good Are Visual Aids?

The effectiveness of visual aids is well known. Research shows that most of the information stored in the brain is received visually. We also know that information seen has a much greater chance of being remembered than information heard. Studies by the Wharton School of Applied Research Center concluded that oral presentations using visual aids are deemed 43% more persuasive than presentations without visual aids, and that speakers who use visual aids are perceived as better prepared, more credible, and more interesting than speakers without visual support (Peoples, p. 4).

Given the data, it's understandable why almost every physician–speaker out there has a carousel full of slides or a briefcase full of overhead transparencies. When done well and appropriately, visual aids can boost your credibility with, and impression on, your audience. The question remains, then, if everyone has all these visual aids, why are so many presentations bad? Remember the seven deadly sins of speaking listed in the Introduction to Part II? One of them was *unnecessary or poorly designed visual aids*.

Fallacies about Visual Aids

The most common audience complaint I hear about visual aids is "Too many." Having sat through hundreds of medical talks, I think it's safe to say that the majority of physician–speakers are addicted to slides and overheads. I think the addiction is based on several fallacies.

- **If one is good, ten is better.** We are a culture that often values quantity over quality. We determine success by who has the most. Many people believe, mistakenly, the more slides the presentation has, the better. Not true. Too many visual aids can overwhelm and bore the audience. The result: the audience tunes out.
- **Visual aids are good teleprompters.** If you are unprepared, disorganized, and unrehearsed, no visual aid, no matter how well done, can save you. There is nothing more boring than

having a speaker read his or her slides or overheads to us. The result: The audience is annoyed because time is valuable. Why, they think, didn't this speaker just send us copies of the visual aids and save us the time of coming to a presentation?

◆ **Anyone can make good slides and overheads.** Although there is plenty of high-tech equipment available, using expensive equipment doesn't guarantee well-designed visuals. Developing effective slides takes preparation, organization, and a knowledge of basic design principles.

◆ **Physicians are not graphic designers.** Indeed, physicians are scientists, not graphic designers, but that doesn't mean they can afford to ignore basic design principles. When using visual aids in a presentation of data, the data will only be as good as the design.

◆ **Medical audiences have learned to live with bad visuals.** I'm often told, "You'll never change the way physicians give presentations. The old ways are too ingrained." Nowhere are bad habits more perpetuated among physicians than in their writing and speaking skills. These skills come to most physicians by watching their superiors. It's time to break the pattern. Your time and the time of every person in your audience is too precious to waste on poor presentation of data.

Qualities of Good Visual Aids

The visual aids used by physicians in meetings, talks, and lectures don't have to be bad. Making a good slide is as easy as making a bad slide. Before looking at each type of visual aid separately, let's put your current visual aids to the test. Are they:

◆ **Purposeful?** Can you define the purpose of every visual? Each should serve a specific purpose for the audience, *not* for the presenter. Are you constructing slides or overhead transparencies to help you read your way through the presentation? If so, you are well on your way to boring your audience.

- **Accurate?** The value of any visual depends on the integrity and care with which the data was collected and analyzed. No table, graph, or chart, however carefully designed or colored, can rescue inaccurate data.
- **Selective?** Avoid the temptation to overwhelm your audience with visuals loaded with detail. The audience members can only remember so much and will tune out you and your message if they are feeling bewildered or dazed.
- **Concise?** Data should be presented only once. The same data should not be presented in both a table and a graph, or in both a table and a map. Your time is limited, so you need to choose and design visuals that quickly and accurately convey your message.
- **Consistent?** Similar data should be displayed in similar form. Visuals for a talk should be prepared in the same size so that all words, lines, colors, styles, and other elements are consistent. Avoid alternating between graphs, maps, and tables merely for variety; it can be distracting and confusing.
- **Focused?** A table, graph, or map should make a point. The point should be apparent from the design of the visual and, whenever possible, should be stated in the title.
- **Clear and Simple?** Abbreviations, awkward phrases, and confusing details make a visual difficult to grasp. Similarly, in graphs and maps, careless choice and arrangement of design elements such as labels and legends causes visual distraction. The more complex the science, the more simply and clearly it must be communicated.
- **Effective?** Graphs, illustrations, charts, photographs, and maps are visual media. In order for them to be effective, keep words to a minimum. Your visuals should be immediately understandable and all words should be easy to read.
- **Convincing?** Make sure the message you are trying to give is made quickly and clearly. For example, if the point of a bar graph is to show a comparison of treatment response between placebo and clomipramine in Obsessive-Compulsive Disorder, the difference should be readily apparent.
- **Independent?** A visual should, as the saying goes, speak a thousand words. If after you have made your visual, it takes

a thousand words to explain it, you need to go back to the drawing board. A table, along with its title and footnotes, and a graph, illustration, or map, together with its legend, should be understandable without extensive explanation.

Choosing the Best Medium

The medium you choose for your presentation depends on a number of factors, including what the subject, purpose, audience, and setting are, how large your audience is, what equipment you have, and how long you have to prepare. Each medium has its advantages and disadvantages.

The Chalkboard and Flip Chart

Chalkboards and flip charts are two of the oldest, simplest, easiest, most accessible visual communication devices. Chalkboards and flip charts bring a certain spontaneity to a presentation. In a problem-solving meeting or teaching situation, the chalkboard or flip chart may be the best method but, in other speaking situations, it has its limitations:

- ◆ Presenters must turn their backs to the audience to write.
- ◆ Writing takes up precious audience time.
- ◆ Writing interrupts the flow of ideas.
- ◆ Printing legibly and quickly is difficult.
- ◆ Chalk or markers can break or screech and are often messy.
- ◆ Visibility limits you to a small group.

Chart Presentations

These large artboards can be elaborately finished or may just be rough finals—both work well. Today most people use overhead transparencies or 35-mm slides.

Overhead Transparencies

In overhead projections, a transparency is placed on the surface of the projector and the image is projected to a white matte screen mounted on a wall or stand. Overhead transparencies are most appropriate for small to medium-sized audiences (no more than fifty people). Because of the advantages, overhead transparencies are widely used by physicians.

Advantages of Overhead Transparencies

- The presentation can be made in a fully lighted room.
- The presenter faces the audience, allowing better eye contact and audience interaction.
- The projector is placed at the front of the room beside the speaker, who has complete control and can operate it without assistance.
- They are inexpensive and the equipment is easy to use.
- They can be made quickly on a laser printer or photocopier.
- Color is an easy option using markers, color transparencies, color tapes, press-on letters, or a color printer or photocopier.
- Additions can be made directly on the film with a marker or overlay sheets.
- Revisions can be done easily and quickly.
- Equipment is relatively portable.

Disadvantages of Overhead Transparencies

- Transparencies are often difficult to handle during a presentation. They are slippery, and a nervous presenter may have a hard time holding on to them.
- Transparencies are more difficult than slides to store and carry. A carousel of eighty slides is less cumbersome than eighty overheads with cardboard frames.
- If the presenter gets too close to the lighted area, his or her face will take on a ghoulish appearance.
- Projectors can be noisy.

If possible, produce your text for transparencies on a laser printer. It will be easy to read and look very professional. Keep in mind that big and bold is important. You should be able to read your copy (unprojected) from 10 feet away. Mount transparencies in frames, then label and number each in case they should reshuffle themselves on an unplanned trip to the floor. Have a secure place to put transparencies after you have used them. Place a piece of cardboard between each one to prevent the transparencies from sticking together.

Positioning Yourself to Use Overheads

Where you place yourself in a room during a presentation is a form of nonverbal communication. The way you handle the equipment and move around it says something about your professionalism and confidence. Don't let the projector get in the audience's way of seeing you. Place the screen and projector on your left as you face the audience. Audiences are accustomed to moving their eyes left to right. The advantage of having the screen on your left is that their eyes begin on you, then move to the screen, and then return to you. When pointing to the screen, use your left hand. Stay close to the screen as you speak. If you walk away from the screen, you divide the audience's attention.

Slides

Presentations consisting of projected 35-mm slides can be informative, colorful, and exciting. That's the good news. The bad news is that they can also be distracting, both for the audience and for the speaker.

Not long ago, I was working with a group of physicians on their presentation skills at a meeting of the American Urology Association. Each physician gave a six-minute, videotaped presentation. Most of these presentations were segments of other talks they had already given or were about to give. Although every presenter used slides, we focused the video camera only on the speaker. After rolling the tape for three minutes, we stopped the tape and asked each speaker to give the remaining three minutes not using any slides. Of course, their first reaction was, "That's not possible." It took some cajoling and persuading, but finally we convinced each of them that he or she knew the material well enough to just talk about it for three minutes. Afterwards we compared the two sections of tapes—a speaker using slides and the same speaker not using slides.

The difference was amazing: Using slides, speakers focused on the slides. They turned their backs to the audience; they talked to the screen; they frequently looked down at, or fiddled with, the remote control; they read the slides; they used more *ers* and *ums*; and they rarely looked at the audience. In contrast, not using slides, the speakers focused on the audience. They had more eye contact; they smiled more; they had more facial expression; and they used more body language. The message to all of us that day was clear: If you let them, slides, or for that matter any audiovisual equipment, can interfere with communication.

Slides have many advantages, and when designed and used appropriately, there is no question they can enhance your presentation. You should also be aware, however, of their disadvantages.

Advantages of Slides

- ◆ Camera equipment and processing services are widely available.
- ◆ Slides show realistic pictures or art work.
- ◆ Slides can be seen by large audiences.
- ◆ Slides can be designed for projection in rooms of various sizes.
- ◆ Equipment allows for multimedia and multi-image capabilities.

Disadvantages of Slides

- ◆ Room lights must be dimmed and controlled.
- ◆ Slides require skill in designing.
- ◆ Making slides requires special equipment.
- ◆ Art work must be specially prepared.
- ◆ A long lead time is necessary.
- ◆ Slides can get out of sequence, upside down or backward.
- ◆ The room may not be adequately set up for slides.
- ◆ Heat from the projector's lamp may burn film.
- ◆ Slides may get stuck to each other and become blurred.

What's Wrong with This Slide?

During the Speaking for Excellence seminar, we present a slide show entitled, "Physicians' Slides: The Good, the Bad, the Ugly." Each slide demonstrates one of several common problems we see in physicians' slides.

- ◆ **Too much data.** This is the most frequent problem I see in physicians' slides. Make all your slides simple and succinct. A slide is usually seen for less than thirty seconds, so the impact has to be immediate. A good slide makes no more than one point that adds to, emphasizes, highlights, or explains the speaker's words. Avoid trying to make one slide do the work of many. The result is visual confusion. For complicated subject matter, it is far better to use two or three simple slides than one complex, cluttered, unclear slide. Use no more than five lines per slide.

- ◆ **Inappropriate design.** In determining the best design for a chart or graph, ask yourself the question, "What am I trying to show—trends, magnitude, rate of change, percentages of the whole, a comparison?" Your answer will determine the type of graph or chart to use. For more information on graphs and charts, see Chapter 3.

- ◆ **Pie charts with too many pieces.** Pie charts show relationships among component parts. Arrange the pieces according to size with the largest piece starting at twelve o'clock and going clockwise. No segment should be smaller than five percent. For the purpose of slides, limit the number of pieces in a pie chart to five. Put the percentages inside the pie and the name of each piece outside. To emphasize one piece you can pull it out from the pie. Never pull out more than one piece of pie. Avoid using legends showing color; the small pieces of color are often hard for audiences to distinguish.

- ◆ **Line charts with too many lines.** Line charts show trends or movement over time. The independent variable—the variable that changes regularly—should be on the horizontal axis, for example, months, years, or hours. The dependent variable— the variable that changes irregularly—should be on the vertical axis. Limit the number of lines in a line graph to three. Differentiate the lines from each other by symbols or colors. Always indicate the zero point of axes. If you use colors to distinguish lines, make sure there is a recognizable contrast between the colored lines. Remember, line charts can only show trends; they do not work well when you are trying to show exact amounts.

- **Illegible tables.** Use tables to show exact amounts. Limit the number of vertical columns to four and horizontal rows to seven. Be sure column heads really indicate what the numbers in the table represent.
- **Graphs with too many columns, bars, or colors.** Limit the number of columns to four, bars to five, and use color discriminately.
- **Flow charts that go on and on.** If you put too much on your slide, the type will be too small to read. Don't try to cram everything on one slide. If you must show a flow chart or algorithm, try using a progressive disclosure; one slide per box or section. You can give the audience a hand-out with the entire chart on it to study in detail after the presentation.
- **Indecipherable images.** Electrocardiograms, echocardiograms, histograms, pathological specimens, and radiographs are hard to project. Use these images only if they can be made clear to everyone in your audience. It is possible to highlight the feature you want to illustrate by marking the feature with an arrow or by cropping the film in a way that accentuates the feature.
- **Trying to translate one medium to another.** Frequently physicians take a photo, table, chart, or illustration from a textbook or journal and make a slide from it—often not giving credit to the original author. There are two problems with this. First, graphics taken from a book or journal rarely translate well to slides. Most tables and charts in books and journals are meant to be studied, often for a minute or more, and, as a result, have too much data for a slide. It is a cardinal rule: Never be in a position to say, "I know this slide has a lot of data, but I'd like you to just look at line 4, row 8." Make a separate slide of line 4, column 8. The other problem with taking a graph or chart from a textbook or journal is that it's against the law. Although I don't know anyone serving time for breaking copyright laws, I do know physicians who have compromised their ethics and professionalism by not giving credit to the original author. If there is a particularly effective graphic in a book or journal that you would like to use, design

it so that it is appropriate for a slide and list the source at the bottom of the slide.

◆ **Distracting type styles or colors.** Don't overdesign. With the equipment available today, you'll have hundreds of options and choices when it comes to colors and types. Avoid the temptation to use all the type styles and all the colors. Select them to make a point, not for aesthetic purposes. Leave the hype and dazzle to MTV. Your slides should be clear, concise, and consistent. A safe type style is Helvetica Bold. Safe colors are a blue for background, yellow for headlines, and white for text. Stay away from pastel backgrounds; they will appear to be faded slides.

◆ **All capital letters.** We read by recognizing shapes. If all the shapes are similar, as capital letters are, it takes longer to read. In fact, reading all caps takes a reader approximately 13% longer than reading a mix of uppercase and lowercase letters.

Example:

TRANSABDOMINAL RETROPERITONEAL LYMPH NODE DISSECTION USUALLY IS RECOMMENDED FOR TERATO- AND EMBRYONAL CARCINOMA AND ADULT TERATOMA. IRRADIATION MAY BE EFFEC-TIVE IN SEMINOMA, USING 30–50 GY (3000–5000 RADS) TO THE ABDOMINAL AND MEDIASTINAL LYMPHATICS AS WELL AS THE LEFT SUPRACLAVI-CULAR AREA, DEPENDING ON STAGING.

Transabdominal retroperitoneal lymph node dissection usually is recommended for terato- and embryonal carci-noma and adult teratoma. Irradiation may be effective in seminoma, using 30–50 Gy (3000–5000 rads) to the ab-dominal and mediastinal lymphatics as well as the left supraclavicular area, depending on staging.

If you want your type to be bigger, don't use all caps; increase your font size.

◆ **Inappropriate italics.** Italics are hard to read in longer bodies of copy. Italics should be reserved for foreign words, book or journal titles, species and genus names, or virus names.

Example:

Pityriasis Rosea is a self-limited, mild, inflammatory skin disease characterized by scaly lesions, possibly due to an unidentified infectious agent. It may occur at any age but is seen most often in young adults. In temperate climates, incidence is highest during spring and autumn.

Pityriasis Rosea is a self-limited, mild, inflammatory skin disease characterized by scaly lesions, possibly due to an unidentified infectious agent. It may occur at any age but is seen most often in young adults. In temperate climates, incidence is highest during spring and autumn.

◆ **No titles or titles that are too long.** Remember that your audience will be "dropping out" of your presentation every few minutes. When they "drop back in," you want them to get back on track as soon as possible. Descriptive titles that summarize the point of the slide will help.

Example:

Long: Doses of some common sedatives and anxiolytics that have produced physical dependence.

Concise: Sedatives and anxiolytics: Doses that produce dependence.

◆ **Invisible numbers or letters.** One of the slides we show in the seminar is of a table listing numbers. The background is green, the numbers in each column are red. To most people the table looks fine. To those who are color blind, the columns look empty. Remember, approximately eight million people in the United States have red–green confusion.

◆ **Lack of parallelism.** For a parallel structure, keep the grammatical structure of your text the same; balance nouns with nouns, prepositional phrases with prepositional phrases, verbs with verbs, and infinitives with infinitives.

Example: Factors in Giving an Effective Presentation

Not parallel

- ◆ Being prepared
- ◆ Always know your subject

- ◆ Knowing who your audience is
- ◆ Setting
- ◆ Why you should practice

Parallel

- ◆ Prepare
- ◆ Know your subject
- ◆ Know your audience
- ◆ Know your setting
- ◆ Practice

Here is further advice from Lisa Puglia, a communications consultant, on how to make your slides and overheads as memorable and as effective as possible.

- ◆ **Consult a graphics designer** or vendor about style, colors, cost, and time of production—before you design your visual aids. In the long run, it can save you time and money. If you use an audiovisual production house to make your slides, be aware that the fees can be exorbitant. For example, a simple word slide can cost up to $50. A slide with a table, graph, or chart can cost between $75–$125. A slide using camera-ready art is about $25 and a slide that requires original art can be $90–$200. These fees don't include editing or "rush" charges.
- ◆ **Recognize the added costs of a "rush" job.** If you need your slide or overhead quickly, you can incur a "rush" charge that could be an additional 10%–200%, depending on the slide and amount of lead time.
- ◆ **Recognize the added costs of changes and corrections.** Proofread your hard copy *before* you give the go-ahead to the production people to image them into slides. Any changes you make after you receive the slides will be costly. For example, a simple word slide that would cost $50 to create and image will cost you up to $160 if you make changes after the slide has been imaged and you need a "rush." This doesn't include holiday and weekend fees.
- ◆ **Select a 35-mm slide projector with autofocus capability.** Audiences are easily distracted by out-of-focus slides.

- **Use a clean, glass-beaded screen** to make your slides project best.
- **Build progressive visual sequences on slides.** Reveal one line of information at a time to generate visual interest and renew the audience's attention.
- **Follow the 4-by-4 rule.** If you use bullet (·) points in a word slide, use no more than four bullets, no more than four words to a bullet.
- **Face the audience with the screen on your left.** Whether you use overheads or slides, stand next to the screen.
- **Use a remote control for the projection.** "Next slide, please" wears pretty thin after thirty or seventy times. If possible, tape the remote control onto a table or lectern, so your hands will be free except when changing the slide.
- **Rein in the laser pointer.** The laser pointer is helpful in directing the audience's eyes to the exact spot where you want them to focus, "Note at the top of the radiograph . . ." The laser pointer should not be used to "bounce" through words and should be turned off as soon as you make your point.
- **Never plunge the audience into total darkness.** Dim the lights around the screen only. Leave some light on the audience. You want to maintain eye contact with your audience at all times.
- **Pause each time you change slides.** It will give you time to collect your thoughts and the audience time to ingest what they are seeing.
- **Always keep your feet aimed at the audience.** In this way, you'll never be caught talking to your slides.
- **Stop on red.** Avoid using red in large doses; it can be visually assaultive and it tends to bleed when used for numbers and letters. It also has a negative connotation when used in financial graphs.
- **Ask permission, please.** Before using a slide with the photograph of a patient, you must have written permission from that patient.
- **Always provide data points** to the production company or department when asking for graphs. Without this information, the graphic artist can only guess at what you want and it can be time consuming and inaccurate.

◆ **Type the original copy** you send to the production company or department. Handwriting can be difficult to decipher. Also, if you want to indicate changes on the proofs, use a red pen and circle the change.

Dual Projection

Dual projection can be a very effective means of conveying information. Used incorrectly, however, it can be a disaster. In addition to Dr. David Swanson's practical advice in his essay at the end of this chapter, the following suggestions will help make the most of dual projection.

◆ If you want to use dual projections, you should have two projection screens. If only one screen is available, single projection is preferable.
◆ Slides must be complementary. Here are some examples of good pairs:

a list	PAIRED WITH	examples
facts	PAIRED WITH	comment about facts
a table	PAIRED WITH	a correlating graph
X ray before	PAIRED WITH	X ray after
op photo	PAIRED WITH	diagram
path specimen	PAIRED WITH	photomicrograph
foreign language	PAIRED WITH	English

◆ Dual projection is *not* a way to show twice as much material in a given time. Here are some examples of pairs that do not work.

  1. Two unrelated sets of data or ideas
  2. Slides that force the audience to look at one slide while the presenter talks about the other

◆ When you use dual projectors for case presentations, it is effective to show the clinical information on one screen and a clinical photograph on the other.
◆ Information relating to radiographs can be paired. An effective way to present an operating-room (OR) sequence to an

audience is to project the OR photograph on one screen and a simple line drawing on the second screen to orient the viewer. An artist can use the slides as a basis for making the drawings. You may even want to have the artist observe the surgery.

◆ To avoid appearing like a laser light show, advance both carousels at the same time. You want to convey information, not dazzle your audience.

Buy Smart: Selecting Presentation Packages

Although most hospitals have their own audiovisual departments, many physicians don't have this luxury. If you'd like the option of designing your own charts, graphs, illustrations, and tables, you may want to look into setting up your own system. The total cost of establishing a system to produce quality slides is variable. An average cost is approximately $8000, based on the cost of an IBM-compatible personal computer, software packages, and a film recorder. Film recorders cost about $6000. An alternative to buying a film recorder is to use a modem to transmit data to a slide service bureau, where the cost of imaging is only about $10.

Among the better presentation software programs are Harvard Graphics, Aldus Persuasion, Lotus Freelance, DrawPerfect, Microsoft PowerPoint, and Charisma. What's the best one for you? It really depends on your criteria. Criteria to consider before buying are:

◆ **Organization.** First look at how the program organizes the task of creating a presentation. The best packages provide outlines so you can rough out your presentation then automatically build slide titles, bullet charts, and speaker notes from outline entries. Make sure the program maintains a dynamic link between the outliner and the slide views. A spell check and search-and-replace option are also helpful features. Perhaps the most useful organizational time-saver is a global editing feature that lets you apply predefined templates that automatically position graphic elements, format text charts, and color backgrounds.

◆ **Charting.** Any presentation graphics package will automatically take your data and generate it into a column graph, bar graph, line graph, or pie chart. Look for a program that provides variety and meets your specific needs.

◆ **Drawing and text.** If you intend to draw your own art for slides, look for a program with a variety of drawing tools and symbols. Select a program that includes scientific, technical, and medical symbols. If you use mostly word slides, select a program that offers a variety of fonts and allows you to control leading, paragraph spacing, and kerning.

◆ **Production.** All programs provide a built-in communications module for uploading your files to a professional slide-making facility—Autographix, Magicorp, and others—via modems. Check to see if you can convert your files to the slide-making facility you will be using. Conversion by a production company is expensive.

◆ **Service and support.** Even the best programs can leave you confused and floundering for advice. Check the vendors' support policies, such as hours, toll-free help lines, and fax service. Always check maintenance contracts to see the different options.

Slides: Format, Colors, and Typefaces

Today, with sophisticated computer software, almost any physician can design his or her own slides. That's both good and bad. It's good because it saves time and money. It's bad because most physicians aren't trained as designers. And one of the main reasons that slides are distracting is that they are poorly designed.

If you design your own slides, you would be wise to get some advice from a design expert. Ask about type styles and sizes, as well as colors. For those who don't have access to an expert, there are some standard guidelines:

Format:	All type should be from the Helvetica family, preferably Helvetica Regular. To improve readability, there should be no more than *seven words to a line* and no more than *five to seven lines of copy per slide*. Format the slide horizontally, not vertically.
Margins:	5 picas (approximately 1 inch)
Background:	Blue

Title:	Centered; 30 pt Helvetica Bold; all caps; yellow
Subheading:	28 pt Helvetica Regular; aqua
Bullets:	9 pt; yellow
Bulleted text:	26/30 Helvetica Regular; uppercase and lowercase with first letter cap; white
Sub-bulleted:	1 pica long dashes and 6-point dashes; type size and face: 26/30 Helvetica Regular; uppercase and lowercase with first letter cap; white
Source:	Flush left; white
Tab charts:	Horizontal tab heads: 26/30 Helvetica Bold; yellow
	Vertical tab heads: 26/30 Helvetica Bold; yellow

The Ideal Slide in a Nut Shell

- Keep horizontal aspect and 2:3 ratio.
- Limit content to one subject.
- Use a maximum of five to seven lines of text, including title.
- Use no more than seven words per line.
- Choose an optimal typeface such as Helvetica.
- Column charts: Limit to four columns.
- Bar charts: Limit to five to seven bars.
- Pie charts: Limit to five slices in a pie chart; put percentages inside pie, labels outside.
- Line graphs: Limit number of lines to three to four.
- Tables: Limit number of vertical columns to four and horizontal rows to seven.
- Limit the use of capitals and italics.

Hand-outs

It is often a good idea to give the audience printed copies of visuals used in a presentation to add to their meeting notes. One advantage of overhead projection is that copies of overhead transparencies for distribution can be made quickly on a laser printer or plain-paper copier. However, it is better not to hand out copies of your visuals until after the presentation so audience members will pay better attention during the meeting instead of shuffling through the hand-outs. Distribute hand-outs before or during a meeting only if they are needed during the meeting for note taking. Make sure to tell the audience that they will receive a hand-out following the presentation. A good hand-out should include

- ◆ a brief summary of the presentation,
- ◆ an outline of the structure of the presentation, main points and supporting data,
- ◆ charts, graphs, and tables explaining complex data, and
- ◆ a bibliography.

Choosing the Best Medium

Read the following scenarios and decide how you would design appropriate visual aids. First, examine the subject, audience, setting, and probable purpose. Then, decide what type of visual aid would be most appropriate: videos, slides, overheads, hand-outs, or blackboard. Next, decide what type of graphic would be appropriate: table, map, graph, photo, or line drawing.

1. You are giving a ten-minute presentation to a group of hospital nurses. Your topic is HIV-related infections. Your purpose is to show seasonal differences.

   January: 41 cases   July: 17 cases
   February: 39 cases   August: 17 cases
   March: 36 cases   September: 18 cases
   April: 27 cases   October: 22 cases
   May: 19 cases   November: 31 cases
   June: 19 cases   December: 36 cases

   Possible solution: The purpose is to inform. Your objective is to show trends and change over time. The line graph would work well; the seasonal differences would be clear and memorable.

2. A regional meeting of trauma surgeons has been scheduled. They want you to show the most frequently injured organs in abdominal trauma in your regional trauma center. How

would you design a visual to convey the following information?

> Type of trauma and organs injured: **gunshot wounds** (small bowel—28%, mesentery/omentum—10%, liver—18%, colon—26%, diaphragm—18%), **stab wounds** (liver—21%, colon—19%, small bowel—36%, stomach—24%), **blunt trauma** (spleen—41%, liver—15%, retroperitoneal vasculature—12%, kidney—27%, small bowel—5%).

Possible solution: The purpose is to inform. You want to show components of a whole. You will need three slides with one pie chart on each; one for gunshot wounds, one for stab wounds, one for blunt trauma.

3. You have been invited to talk to fourth-year medical students preparing for exams. You want to show the emotional manifestations that are suggestive of child abuse: failure to thrive; inadequate parental stimulation and interaction; passive and overly concerned with pleasing adults; parental reluctance to give a history of injury; history that is incompatible with the developmental capability of the child; an inappropriate response by the parents to the severity of the injury; delay in reporting the injury.

Possible solution: Your purpose is to teach the audience enough about the topic to enable them to answer questions on an exam. In order to encourage learning, interact with the group and stimulate audience participation as much as you can. If the group has fewer than twenty people, you could use a blackboard, eliciting answers from the audience. If more than twenty, the presenter could use progressive slides, adding point to point. You should also include hand-outs with all the information you discuss, as well as a bibliography and a list for further reading.

4. At a luncheon meeting of the Women's Auxiliary, you have been given thirty minutes to raise money for an AIDS clinic. How can you convince this audience that they should support your project with both their money and their time? What, if any, visual aids would work best?

Possible solution: Your purpose is to inform and convince. Avoid overwhelming this group with statistics. Slides with simple line charts or bar charts showing how the incidence of AIDS continues to grow would work well. You would probably want four slides: a chart showing the incidence in drug users, gay men, women, and children. The purpose would be to show that AIDS is no longer a disease only of drug users and gay men. You might also want to show slides with photos of patients, health-care workers, and volunteers at the clinic.

5. You are asked to speak at the Rotary Club monthly meeting. The audience is mostly men, ranging in age from 30 to 78 years. Your topic is prostate cancer. You want to show that adenocarcinoma of the prostate accounts for a significant number of malignancies in men over age 50, and the incidence increases with each decade of life. You also want to discuss symptoms, treatments, and prognosis. What are some possible approaches to the content of the presentation and the visual aids that would best support your main ideas?

   Possible solution: The purpose is to inform and possibly motivate men in the high-risk group to get checked for prostate cancer. This group probably doesn't want to have slides or overheads with lots of statistics and tables or photos of patients. Slides showing simple line drawings of the location of the prostate and digital examination would be appropriate. Additionally, a simple line graph showing the incidence of prostate cancer would make the point quickly and clearly that, after the age of 60, the incidence rises dramatically with each decade of life.

6. You have been requested to give a thirty-minute talk at a dinner meeting of internal medicine physicians. You are being sponsored by a drug company that makes drug X. Your topic is "Effectiveness of Drug X in Reducing Migraine Attacks." Design a visual to compare the average number of headaches in a placebo group and those in the drug X group over a six-month period.

Average Number of Headaches

Month	Placebo Group	Drug X
January	6	5
February	8	3
March	6	2
April	7	2
May	6	1
June	8	1

Possible solution: Your purpose is to inform and convince. A paired-column graph with months on the horizontal axis comparing a placebo with drug X would work well. Note you may need to use two slides if the data appears crowded.

7. You are an orthopedic surgeon talking to college athletes about the most common sports-related injuries and their treatment and prevention.

    Possible solution: Your purpose is to educate, in the hopes of preventing injury. You might want to bring a skeleton to show bone structure. In addition, you could use slides with simple line drawings to show common injuries to muscles and ligaments. You could also bring in other orthopedic devices used in rehabilitation.

8. You have to give two presentations. The topic for both is the same: "Organ Donation." The audiences are different: (1) emergency medicine residents, and (2) high school students. How might the content and visual aids differ in each presentation?

    Possible solutions: Clearly, you would not be able to give the same talk to each group. Why? Because the audiences and purposes are entirely different. The purpose in giving a talk on this topic to emergency medicine physicians might be to inform them of the need for healthy organs for transplantation and to educate them on ways to approach families of people who die in emergency rooms about donating organs. A table or chart comparing and emphasizing the number of people waiting for organs and the number of organs available would work to show the need in a clear and memorable fashion. A hand-out of an actual permission form for donating organs would also be useful to this audience. To make your talk as interesting and informative as possible, you might replace lists of data and statistics with stories about actual cases and how each was handled.

Your purpose in giving a talk on the subject of organ transplants to a group of high school students would be to inform them of the need for organs, to encourage them to consider becoming donors, and to educate them on how to go about becoming an organ donor. You could use the same slide you had used with the emergency medicine residents comparing the number of organs needed and the number available. Stories of actual cases would also be far more interesting to this group than a carousel of slides showing numbers and statistics. Obviously, you will want to talk to high school students on a level they can understand, while avoiding the macabre.

9. You have been asked to talk to a group of medical interns. Your topic is "The Need for Physicians in Rural America." You want to show the geographical distribution of physicians throughout the United States.

   Possible solution: Your purpose is to convince new physicians to consider practicing in rural areas. A distribution map would work well.

10. You will be giving a twenty-minute talk to a group of pediatric nurses. The topic is "Reconstructive Surgery to Correct the Cleft Lip and Palette."

    Possible solution: Your purpose is to educate. In this case a dual projection would work well. You could show the X ray before surgery paired with the X ray following surgery, an operative photo paired with a diagram, a "before" photo paired with an "after" photo.

Essay

◆

Dual-Projection Presentations

David A. Swanson, M.D.

It is virtually impossible to attend a medical meeting today and not see presentations made using dual projection, that is, simultaneous projection of two two-by-two-inch transparencies. However, even though everyone's doing it, everyone's doing it badly. It is likely that you will see this potentially effective technique abused and actually handicapping the presentation. Speakers must remember why slides are used during presentations and understand how bad slides risk breaking the fragile bond with the audience—a risk *more* than doubled by showing two slides at once.

Good slides, used correctly, help focus the audience's attention and highlight portions of the information to be understood and remembered. Slides help emphasize and summarize; we remember best what we can see. However, anything that confuses the audience or breaks its concentration creates a barrier between the speaker and audience. One of the most common distractions occurs when the speaker is talking about one thing, and the slide on display shows something unrelated to what's being said.

Dual projection increases the risk of this happening if there is different information on two slides. In fact, this distraction illustrates the

David A, Swanson, M.D., is Professor of Urology, The University of Texas, M. D. Anderson Cancer Center, Houston, Texas.

The author gratefully acknowledges the editorial assistance of Sunita C. Patterson, Editor in the Department of Scientific Publications at The University of Texas M.D. Anderson Cancer Center.

single most important rule of dual projection: don't use it to show twice as much information. If you discover while practicing that you can project and talk about only some of the slides you would like to show and still stay within your time limit, do *not* switch to dual projection in order to be able to show all of them. I fail to see any advantage to showing two different text slides (with two different ideas) at the same time, talking first about the left one and then the right one while both remain on display. It does not speed up your presentation, and your audience is likely to be looking at one slide as you discuss the other. To be effective, the information on the two slides must be complementary. They should show essentially the same information in different ways. This means that you have to know whether you will use single or dual projection when you plan and make your slides. I'm certainly not a poet, but I feel like I've written a couplet when I create an effective pair of slides that present complementary information.

What slide combinations work well together? A list—particularly with bullets—paired with an example or illustration; similarly, an outline (especially if highlighted) with a fact or example. A fact with a brief comment is a good pair. A table of information with a graph of the same information is a particularly effective combination. Other examples are a drawing, X ray, or pictorial paired with an intraoperative photograph or other clinical example; an X ray taken before treatment and one taken after treatment; a photograph of a gross pathologic specimen and a photomicrograph. In each case, the second slide complements the first without presenting conflicting information.

A few exceptions seem to work even though they do not strictly follow this rule. For example, you might show a chest X ray plus a CT scan of the abdomen of the same patient; or a series of progressive steps during an operation (or clinical response to treatment) in which you are clearly leading the audience through a sequence. You will have to decide whether the pair risks dividing the audience's attention. For example, even if I have multiple conclusions I prefer not to show two conclusions at a time on left and right screens, although I *might* occasionally project the conclusion on the left (one to a slide) and a very short commentary on the right. I think the key to using two text slides effectively is to make them very brief and closely related; the audience must be able to absorb each statement in virtually one glance and should not have to return to that slide for better understanding.

If you cannot find an appropriate slide to make a complementary pair, which is far more likely to happen if you prepared your slides without the intention of making a dual-projection presentation, use a blank slide on the right and show the text or information slide only on the left-hand screen. If you notice that the majority of your slides are paired with blanks, consider carefully whether you should be using single projection instead. In many respects, however, the blank slide is your most important slide: its use prevents showing a divisive pair; its occasional use helps emphasize the slide you are showing, such as your conclusions; and it permits you to always advance both carousels simultaneously.

There are a few more caveats. Always find out in advance whether there will be two projectors and two screens available at your meeting. Sometimes a room will have two projectors but only one screen, and two slides can be shown only by reducing the size of the image in half, which is not acceptable because it drastically compromises legibility. Remember that two projectors and two carousels double (quadruple?) your chance for a projection problem such as a jammed slide or other failure to advance one of the carousels. Having watched many speakers try to get the correct pairs matched up again by jockeying one and then the other carousel back and forth, I like to have a list in my pocket showing the slide sequence in each carousel. If necessary, I can refer to the list, know where I am, and tell the projectionist exactly how to synchronize the two carousels again.

With all of the potential problems, why should you want to use dual projection at all? Many would say you shouldn't, but I don't agree with them. There are probably only a few reasons, but I still find them compelling—in some presentations. First, dual projection definitely offers the potential for a little "pizzazz"; it can make an ordinary presentation a little less so. The visual appeal of your presentation helps hold audience interest. Second, there are some presentations that lend themselves particularly well to dual projection, such as those that have a lot of clinical examples, or those that show many gross pathologic specimens plus photomicrographs, or similar combinations. Third, you may be able to give a clearer presentation by showing the organization on the left (an outline, for example, highlighted as you move through it) and the information on the right, so that the audience always knows where you are in the presentation. Finally, dual projection is a challenge that presents unique problems, most of which can be solved only by advanced planning, and careful planning benefits any presentation. So remember: double your pleasure, double your fun/double your headaches with dual projection!

◆

Useful Resources

Below is a list of some of the better reference books and articles on the topic of writing and speaking. The ◆ indicates particularly good references for physicians.

Dictionaries and Thesauri

American Heritage College Dictionary. 3d ed. Boston: Houghton Mifflin; 1993.
Dorland's Illustrated Medical Dictionary. 27th ed. Philadelphia: WB Saunders; 1988.
Melloni's Illustrated Medical Dictionary. 2d ed. Baltimore, MD: Williams & Wilkins; 1985.
The Random House Dictionary of the English Language: 2d ed., The New Unabridged.
Roget's International Thesaurus. 5th ed. Edited by RL Chapman. New York: HarperCollins Publishers; 1992.
Stedman's Medical Dictionary. 25th ed. Baltimore: Williams & Wilkins; 1990.
◆ *The Synonym Finder.* JI Rodale. New York: Warner Books; 1978.
Taber's Cyclopedic Medical Dictionary. 17th ed. Philadelphia: FA Davis Company; 1993.
Webster's Collegiate Dictionary. 10th ed. Springfield, MA: Merriam-Webster; 1993.

Guides to Grammar and Usage

American Usage and Style: The Consensus. RH Copperud. New York: Van Nostrand Reinhold; 1980.

Dictionary of Modern English Usage. HW Fowler. Revised and edited by E
Gowers. 2d ed. New York: Oxford University Press; 1965.

Handbook of Medical English Usage. S Merne. Oxford: Heinemann Professional Publishing; 1989.

The Handbook of Good English. ED Johnson. New York: Washington Square
Press; 1991.

◆ *Medical English Usage and Abusage*. E Schwager. Phoenix: Onyx Press; 1991.

Modern American Usage: A Guide. W Follett. Edited and completed by J
Barzun. New York: Hill & Wang; 1966.

Webster's Dictionary of English Usage. Springfield, MA: Merriam-Webster;
1993.

Webster's New World Guide to Current American Usage. B Randall. New York:
Simon & Schuster; 1988.

*The Words Between: A Handbook for Scientists Needing English, with Examples
Mainly from Biology and Medicine*. 2d ed. JM Perttunen. Helsinki:
Kustannus Duodecim; 1986.

Style Manuals

◆ *American Medical Association Manual of Style*. 8th ed. C Iverson and others.
Baltimore: Williams & Wilkins; 1988.

The Chicago Manual of Style. 14th ed. Chicago: University of Chicago Press;
1993.

◆ *Council of Biology Editors Style Manual: A Guide for Authors, Editors, and
Publishers in the Biological Sciences*. CBE Style Manual Committee. 5th
ed. Bethesda, MD: Council of Biology Editors, 1983.

*Medical Style and Format: An International Manual for Authors, Editors, and
Publishers*. EJ Huth. Philadelphia: ISI Press; 1987. Distribution by Williams & Wilkins.

◆ *Publication Manual of the American Psychological Association*. 3d ed. Washington, DC: American Psychological Association, 1983.

Washington Post Deskbook on Style. R. Webb. New York: McGraw-Hill; 1990.

Words Into Type. 3d ed. Englewood Cliffs, NJ: Prentice-Hall; 1974.

Guides to Writing

*Communicating in Science: Writing a Scientific Paper and Speaking at Scien-
tific Meetings*. 2d ed. V Booth. Cambridge, England: Cambridge University Press; 1993.

◆ *The Elements of Style*. 3d ed. W Strunk, Jr, and EB White. New York: The Macmillan Company, 1979.

◆ *Essentials of Writing Biomedical Research Papers*. M Zeiger. New York: McGraw-Hill, Health Professions Division; 1991.

Get to the Point: How to Say What You Mean and Get What You Want. K Berg and A Gilman, with EP Stevenson. New York: Bantam; 1989.

How to Write a Paper. GM Hall. London: British Medical Journal Publishing Group; 1994.

◆ *How to Write and Publish Papers in the Medical Sciences*. 2d ed. EJ Huth. Baltimore: Williams & Wilkins; 1994.

Medical Writing: A Prescription for Clarity. N Goodman and M Edwards. Cambridge: Cambridge University Press, 1991.

The New Writer: Techniques for Writing Well with a Computer. JP Mitchell. Redmond, WA: Microsoft Press; 1987.

◆ *On Writing Well*. W Zinsser. New York: Harper & Row; 1980.

Problem-Solving Strategies for Writing. 4th ed. L Flower. New York: Harcourt Brace Jovanovich; 1993.

Revising Prose. 3d ed. RA Lanham. New York: Maxwell MacMillan; 1992.

Scientific Writing for Graduate Students. P Woodford. Bethesda, MD: Council of Biology Editors; 1986.

Science and Technical Writing. P Rubens. New York: Henry Holt; 1992.

Speaking and Writing for the Physician. LT Staheli. New York: Raven Press; 1986.

Simple & Direct: A Rhetoric for Writers. J Barzun. New York: Harper & Row; 1985.

◆ *Style: Ten Lessons in Clarity and Grace*. 4th ed. JM Williams. New York: HarperCollins; 1994.

Technical Writing. R Bly and G Blake. New York: McGraw-Hill; 1982.

Thinking on Paper. JH Barton and VA Howard. New York: Morrow; 1986.

Write to the Point and Feel Better About Your Writing. B Stott. New York: Columbia University Press; 1991.

◆ *Writing to Learn*. W Zinsser. New York: Harper & Row; 1988.

Writing with Precision: Learning How to Write Like a Pro So That You Cannot Possibly Be Misunderstood. 6th ed. JD Bates. Washington, DC: Acropolis Books; 1993.

Writing with Style. JR Trimble. Englewood Cliffs, NJ: Prentice-Hall; 1975.

Statistics

Clinical Epidemiology: A Basic Science for Clinical Medicine. 2d ed. DL Sackett, MD, MSc; RB Haynes, MD, PhD; GH Guyatt, MD, MSc; and P Tugwell, MD, MSc. Boston: Little, Brown; 1991.

How Many Subjects? Statistical Power Analysis in Research. HC Kraemer and
    S Thiemann. Newbury Park, CA: Sage Publications; 1987.
Medical Uses of Statistics. 2d ed. JC Bailer and F Mosteller. Waltham, MA:
    NEJM Books; 1992.
PDQ Statistics. GR Norman and DL Streinder. St. Louis: Mosby; 1986.
◆ *Primer of Biostatistics.* 3d ed. SA Glantz. New York: McGraw-Hill; 1992.
Statistical First Aid: Interpretation of Health Research Data. RP Hirsch and RK
    Reigelman. Boston: Blackwell Scientific Publications; 1992.
Statistics for Health Professionals. S Shott. Philadelphia: WB Saunders; 1990.
Statistics in Medicine. T Colton. Boston: Little, Brown; 1982.

Graphics

Charts and Graphs. D Simmonds. London: MTP; 1980.
*Charts & Graphs: Guidelines for the Visual Presentation of Statistical Data in
    the Life Sciences.* D Simmonds, Ed. Baltimore: MTP Press; 1981.
"Combatting Poster Fatigue." JD Woolsey, Department of Illustration,
    Moore College of Art and Design. *Journal of Neuroscience*; 1988.
Communications Graphics. MP Murgio, New York: Reinhold Book Corpo-
    ration: 1969.
Diagrams, Charts, Graphs. S Bojko. Rhode Island School of Design. Zurich:
    Zurich Graphis Press; 1985.
The Elements of Graphing Data. WS Cleveland. Monterey, CA: Wadsworth; 1985.
◆ *Envisioning Information.* 3d printing with revisions. ER Tufte. Cheshire, CT:
    Graphics Press; 1992.
*Graphics Simplified: How to Plan and Prepare Effective Charts, Graphs, Illus-
    trations, and Other Visual Aids.* AJ MacGregor. Toronto: University of
    Toronto Press; 1979.
Handbook of Graphic Presentation. 2d ed. CF Schmid and SE Schmid. New
    York: John S. Wiley; 1979.
How to Draw Charts and Diagrams. B. Robertson. Cincinnati, OH: North Light
    Books; 1988.
"Illustrative Material: What Editors and Readers Expect from Authors." BP
    Squires. *Canadian Medical Association Journal,* 1990; 142:447–49.
Illustrating Science: Standards for Publication. Scientific Illustration Commit-
    tee. Bethesda, MD: Council of Biology Editors; 1988.
The Presentation Design Book. MY Rabb. Chapel Hill, NC: Ventana Press; 1993.
◆ *The Visual Display of Quantitative Information.* 3d printing with revisions.
    ER Tufte. Cheshire, CT: Graphics Press; 1992.
A Researcher's Guide to Scientific and Medical Illustrations. MH Briscoe. New
    York: Springer-Verlag; 1990.

Guides to Research and Grants

A Basic Guide to Online Information Systems for Health Care Professionals. RG
 Albright. Arlington, VA: Information Resource Press; 1988.
◆ *The Bench and Me: Teaching and Learning Medicine.* JW Hurst, MD. New York:
 Igaku-Shoin; 1992.
Databases: A Primer for Retrieving Information by Computer. SM Humphrey and
 BJ Melloni. Englewood Cliffs, NJ: Prentice-Hall; 1986.
Encyclopedia of Health Information Sources. 2d ed. P Wasserman, Ed. Detroit:
 Gale; 1993.
◆ *From Residency to Reality.* P Hoffmeir and J Bohner. New York: McGraw-
 Hill; 1988.
An Insider's Guide for Medical Authors and Editors. P Morgan, MD. Philadel-
 phia: ISI Press, 1986.
Interpreting the Medical Literature. 3d ed. SH Gehlbach. New York: McGraw-
 Hill; 1993.
An Introduction to Clinical Research. C DeAngelis. New York: Oxford Uni-
 versity Press; 1990.
Online Databases in the Medical and Life Sciences. New York: Cuadra/Elsevier;
 1987.
Peer Review in Scientific Publishing. Chicago: Council of Biology Editors; 1991.
◆ *Principles and Practice of Research: Strategies for Surgical Investigators.* 2d Ed.
 H Troidl. New York: Springer-Verlag; 1991.
Research: How to Plan, Speak and Write About It. C Hawkins and M Sorgi. Berlin:
 Springer-Verlag; 1985.
Research in Medicine: A Guide to Writing a Thesis in the Medical Sciences.
 G Murell, C Huang, and H Ellis. Cambridge: Cambridge University
 Press; 1990.
Research Proposals: A Guide to Success. T Ogden. New York: Raven Press, 1991.
Studying a Study and Testing a Test: How to Read the Medical Literature. 2d ed.
 R Riegelman, MD, PhD, and R Hirsch, PhD. Boston: Little, Brown;
 1989.
Writing a Successful Grant Application. 2d ed. L. Reif-Lehrer. Boston: Jones
 & Bartlett; 1989.

Guides to Speaking Skills

Do's and Taboos of Public Speaking. RE Axtell. New York: John Wiley & Sons;
 1992.
How to Run Better Business Meetings. Revised ed. The 3M Meeting Management Team. New York: McGraw-Hill, 1987.

How to Run Seminars and Workshops. RL Jolles. New York: John Wiley & Sons; 1993.

◆ *PowerSpeak.* D Leeds. New York: Berkeley Books; 1988.

Presentations Plus. DA Peoples. New York: John Wiley & Sons; 1992.

Smart Speaking. L Schloff and M Yudkin. New York: Penguin; 1991.

Speaking with a Purpose. A Koch. Englewood Cliffs, NJ: Prentice-Hall; 1988.

Toastmasters. PO Box 9052, Mission Viejo, CA 92690-7052; (714) 858- 8255.

References Cited

Ailes, Roger, with Jon Krausharo. 1988. *You Are the Message (Secrets of the Master Communicators)*. Homewood, IL: Dow Jones-Irwin.

American Medical Writers Association, 9650 Rockville Pike, Bethesda, MD 20814, USA; (301) 493-0003.

Asher, Richard. 1986. *Talking Sense*. Edinburgh: Churchill Livingstone.

Auden, W. H. 1981. *The Viking Book of Aphorisms*. London: Dorset Press.

Bjork, Robert. 1983. Writing courses in American medical schools. *Journal of Medical Education* 58(2): 112–6.

Charlton, James. 1992. *The Writer's Quotation Book*. New York: Penguin Books.

Council of Biology Editors. 11 S. La Salle St., Suite 1400, Chicago, IL 60603-1210.

Cuca, Janet. 1987. Why clinical research grant applications fare poorly in review and how to recover. *Cancer Investigation*. 5(1): 55–8.

Cushing, Harvey. 1940. *The Life of Sir William Osler*. London: Oxford University Press.

Flesch, Rudolpf. 1957. *The Book of Unusual Quotations*. New York: Harper & Row.

Grateful Med. Medlars Management System, National Library of Medicine, 8600 Rockville Pike, Bethesda, MD, 20209.

Gray, H; Goss, 1973. *Gray's Anatomy of the Human Body*. 29th ed. Philadelphia: Lea Febiger.

Hoffmeir, P., and Bohner, J. 1988. *From Residency to Reality*. New York: McGraw Hill.

Hurst, J. Willis. 1992. *The Bench and Me: Teaching and Learning Medicine*. New York: Igaku-shoin.

Index Medicus. National Library of Medicine; 8600 Rockville Pike, Bethesda, MD, 20209.

International Committee of Medical Journal Editors. Uniform requirements for manuscripts submitted to biomedical journals. *Annals of Internal Medicine*. 1982; 96:766–771.

Jolles, R. 1993. *How to Run Seminars and Workshops*. New York: John Wiley & Sons.

McLeod, PJ. 1990. Medical grand rounds: Alive and well and living in Canada. *Canadian Medical Association Journal*. 142(10): 1053–56.

Medical Edition Correct Grammar. 1992. Baltimore, MD: Williams & Wilkins, Software Division.

Medline. National Library of Medicine, 8600 Rockville Pike, Bethesda, MD, 20209.

Merriam Webster's Collegiate Dictionary, 10th ed. 1993. Springfield, MA: Merriam-Webster, Inc.

Newman, Art. 1988. *The Illustrated Treasury of Medical Curiosa*. New York: McGraw Hill.

Peoples, David. *Presentations Plus*. New York: John Wiley & Sons.

Preparing a Research Grant. 1992. Bethesda, MD. National Institutes of Health, Division of Research Grants.

Safire, William. 1992. *Good Advice on Writing*. New York: Simon & Schuster.

Spodick, David, and Goldberg, 1991. The editor's correspondence: Analysis of patterns appearing in selected specialty and general journals. *Chest*, 4, 1290.

Staheli, Lynn. 1986. *Speaking and Writing for the Physician*. New York: Raven Press.

Stead, E. A., Jr. 1978. *What This Patient Needs Is a Doctor*. Durham, NC: Carolina Academic Press.

Toastmasters. P.O. Box 9052 Mission Viejo, CA 92690-7052 or call (714) 858-8255.

Trimble, John. 1975. *Writing with Style*. Englewood Cliffs, NJ: Prentice-Hall.

Tufte, E. R. 1990. *The Visual Display of Quantitative Information*, 3d printing with revisions. Cheshire, CT: Graphics Press.

Walker, Annette. Teaching the illiterate patient. *Journal of Enterostomal Therapy*. 1987; 2: 83–88.

Webb, Robert. 1990. *Washington Post Deskbook on Style*. New York: McGraw-Hill.

West, William. 1966. *On Writing By Writers*. Lexington, MA: Ginn.

Williams, P. L., and R. Warwick. 1980. *Gray's Anatomy*, 36th ed. Philadelphia: W. B. Saunders.

Winokur, Jon. 1990. *W.O.W. Writers on Writing*. Philadelphia: Running Press.

Women's Wit and Wisdom. 1991. Philadelphia: Running Press.

Woodford, Peter. 1986. *Scientific Writing for Graduate Students*. Bethesda, MD: Council of Biology Editors.

Zeiger, Mimi. 1993. Toward clearer writing. *Europeon Respiratory Journal*, 6, 457–60.

Zinsser, William. 1980. *On Writing Well*. New York: Harper & Row.

———. 1988. *Writing to Learn*. New York: Harper & Row.

◆

Index